Tourism Development

TOURISM DEVELOPMENT

Saurabh K. Dixit
(B.H.M.& C.T., M.T.M. & JRF-NET)

Reference Press

4831/24, Ansari Road
Darya Ganj
New Delhi-110 002
Phone: 51563444
Fax: 51563334
E-mail: info@essessreference.com
url: http://www.essessreference.com

First Published 2005

ISBN: 81-88583-88-X

Rs.700/-

Published by:
Reference Press
4831/24, Ansari Road, Darya Ganj,
New Delhi-110 002.
Phone: 51563444
Fax: 51563334
E-mail: info@essessreference.com
url: http://www.essessreference.com

Printed in India at:
Mehra Offset Press, New Delhi

Contents

Preface

Tourism in India, in recent past, has registered a phenomenal growth. In view of its increasing incessant importance, tourism compelled the government to establish it as a large income generating source. Though, a lot is still to be done in this sphere to lead it to its zenith, but its stride towards progress is continued and has achieved satisfactorily the predetermined objectives in its long past journey.

The people who are indulged in this field, lack basic pros and cons and substantiality. The present book, 'Tourism Development' will certainly help them to go through its intense observation. The detail in terms of various famous sites, government's intentions, vital steps taken, its increasing significance, basic facilities, hindrances and their deletion and many more factual propositions can be easily availed from this book.

Here is a little effort to endow those with abundant knowledge, who are lacking in this sphere and particularly to those, who are about to decide to venture in the field for business purports.

The suggestions of any sort would certainly boost-up our morale.

Author

1

Basic Elements

Leadership is one of the essential functions that must be performed by all the managers. The success of all the managers largely depends on the capacity to lead their subordinates. However, it is not easier to master the art of leadership.

Leadership has different meanings to different persons. But in terms of managing, leadership is the art of leading others towards a goal. More specifically, leadership is the process of influencing others to work enthusiastically to achieve predetermined goals.

According to Keith Davis, "Leadership is the ability to persuade others to seek defined objectives enthusiastically. It is the human factor which binds a group together and motivates it towards goals."

According to Stoner *et al.*, "Managerial leadership is the process of directing and influencing the task-related activities of group of members."

In the words of Keys and Case, "Leadership is the process of influencing and supporting others to work enthusiastically towards achieving objectives."

In the opinion of Weihrich and Koontz, "Leadership is the art or process of influencing people so that they will strive willingly and enthusiastically towards the achievement of group goals."

Thus, leadership is the process and the art influencing the behaviour, attitudes, activities of people to work willingly and enthusiastically towards the accomplishment of group goals.

Following characteristics highlight the nature of leadership :

> Leadership is a personal quality of a person. It is a behavioural quality and ability to influence others towards accomplishing a goal. Barnard has very rightly stated that "Leadership is the quality of behaviour of individuals whereby they guide people or their activities."

Leadership is a kind of personal quality. But effectiveness of leadership depends on its application or on performance. Peter Drucker has very aptly remarked, "Leadership has little to do with leadership qualities and even less to do with 'charisma'. It is mundane, unromantic and boring. It is work. Its essence is performance."

Leadership presupposes existence of followers. There cannot be leadership without followers. In the words of Koontz and O'Donnell, "The essence of a leadership is followership. It is the willingness of people to follow that makes a person a leader." Thus, effective leader makes his followers to act willingly to achieve the goal.

Leadership is a process of influencing and inspiring others to work towards objectives. Influencing means regulating and changing behaviour, attitudes and feelings of others. The means of influencing others include reward, coercion, expertise, reference and tradition. Leaders can also influence with rational faith, participation and persuation.

Leadership is a continuous process. A leader continuously makes efforts to influence behaviour of his group members. He carries on this process by maintaining free flow of two-way communication with the entire group of his followers.

Leadership involves interpersonal relations between the leader and his group members. A leader influences his group members and at the same time group members also influence the leader. Thus, a leader does not dominate the will of others but tries to relate the wills of many people to get them work as a team.

Leadership is the ability of influencing behaviour of people to work willingly to achieve some common goal. Terry and Franklin state that "It is the activity of influencing people to strive willingly for mutual objectives." Thus, leadership involves of community of interests between the leader and his followers.

Leadership is a shared function. A good leader shares everything with his followers. He shares ideas, opinions, experience, credits, blames and so on with his followers.

Leading is the function that pervades all the levels and functions of management. Planning, organising, motivating and controlling cannot be performed effectively without effective leadership.

Leadership is a dynamic art. No particular style of leadership is effective in all situations. The effectiveness of leadership depends heavily on the situational variables. Therefore, art of leadership is exercised and applied in accordance with the demands of the situations.

Leadership is based on power. A person holding power over others is a leader. By virtue of power, a person is in a position to influence the behaviour of his group members. A leader may derive power from :

(i) superior knowledge, information experience or performance,

(ii) formal authority,

(iii) charisma, and

(iv) distinct personality characteristics.

Leadership may be formal and informal.

Managing and leadership are not one an the same. But it is not always possible to distinguish between them in practice.

Leadership may be positive or negative.

Significant Role

Although some people treat leadership and management as synonymous but the two should be distinguished. The major points of distinction between the two are outlined as follows :

Basis of Distinction	Leadership	Management
Meaning	Leadership is the process or art of influencing people to work willingly for achieving a goal.	Management is the process of getting things done through others.
Formal and informal organisation	Leadership exists in both formal and informal organisations.	Management operates only in formal organisations.
Power and Authority	Leadership is based on power. The power may be derived from formal authority or from any other source.	Management is based on authority which is delegated to a managerial position by a person in superior position.
Scope	The scope of leadership is narrower than that of the management. It is only a function of management.	The scope of management is wider than leadership. Management is the process of certain functions including the leading or leadership.
Relationship	There need not be a formal relationship between the leader and his followers.	There is a formal relationship between a manager and his subordinates.
Structures	Leadership structures are more flexible, open, informal and dynamic than management.	Management is bound by organised formal structures.
Achievement of goal	Leaders achieve goals by influencing and inspiring others.	Managers achieve goals by directing and controlling activities of others.
Guidance	A leader guides his followers through a special kind of behaviour.	Manager guides his subordinates through policies, plans, rules, procedures etc.
Education and Training	There is almost negligible arrangement for formal education and training for leadership.	There are many programmes for formal education and training of management.
Dependence	Leadership does not depend on managership. Hence, all leaders need not be good managers.	Managership includes leadership. Hence, all managers need to be good leaders.
Accountable	Leaders are not accountable for the actions and behaviour of their followers.	Managers are accountable for the actions and behaviour of their subordinates as well as for their own behaviour.

Contd...

Basis of Distinction	*Leadership*	*Management*
Following	People follow the leader willingly.	Subordinates follow the manager by the force of authority, rules and regulations.
Organisational environment	Leaders try to influence and change the organisational environment.	Managers try to adapt itself according to the organisational
Existence of position	Existence of a leader's position depends on the pleasure of his followers.	Existence of manager's position is independent of the will of his subordinates. It depends on the terms and conditions of his service.

The Techniques

Leadership is a dynamic and constructive force in any organisation. It plays a crucial role in the success and survival of an organisation. It is the crucial factor that helps individuals to identify their goals. Newstorm and Keith Davis have very rightly stated, "Without leadership, an organisation would be only a confusion of people and machines, just as an orchestra without a conductor would be only musicians and instruments. The orchestra and all other organisations require leaders to develop their precious assets to the fullest." Briefly the importance and functions of leadership are as follows:

> A leader plays a crucial role in laying down goals and policies of his group or the institution. He acts as a guide in setting organisational goals and policies.

According to Terry and Franklin, "leaders trigger a person's 'will to do', show the way and guide group members towards group accomplishment." Thus, an effective leader guides and inspires or motivates his group members to work willingly for achieving the goals. He makes every effort to direct and channelise all energies of his followers to the goal-oriented behaviour. He creates enthusiasm for higher performance among his followers.

Morale refers to the attitude of employees towards organisation and management and will to offer voluntary cooperation to the organisation. Morale is an internal feeling of a person. A good leader can arouse will to cooperate among the employees. According to Terry, "Leadership triggers a person's 'will to do' and transforms lukewarm desires for achievements into burning passions for successful accomplishments."

A good leader creates confidence among his group members. He does so by providing guidance, help and support in their day-to day work. He even provides psychological support and infuse the spirit of enthusiasm among them.

A good leader constantly tries to develop team-spirit among his group members/followers. He inculcates a sense of community of interests. He provides a satisfying work climate by harmonising individual and group goals. Thus, a leader reconciles conflicting goals and creates team-spirit among his followers.

It has been rightly said, where there is no vision, people perish. Leader give vision to their followers which, in turn, create initiative and enthusiasm among them. The followers use this vision and initiative to take up challenging tasks.

According to Newstorm and Keith Davis, "Leadership is the catalyst that transforms potential into reality." In fact, effective leadership can transform potential or dream into reality. Leaders can identify, develop, channelise and enrich the potentials existing in an organisation and its people.

A leader represents his group members. He is the connecting link between his group members and the top-management. He carries the views and problems of his group members to the concerned authorities and tries to convince them. Thus, he is in real sense an ambassador and guardian of his group feelings and interests. He also protects the interests of his group members against any outside challenge and threat.

> An effective leader can develop and utilise human resource in a most effective way. A leader can influence the activities and behaviour of his followers to contribute their best. In fact, leadership can lift man's vision to higher sights, raise man's standard to higher performance and build man's personality beyond his normal limitations. *[Peter F. Drucker]*

According to Gordon, "In a world of change and uncertainty, business leader becomes a vital element in the very process of change itself." Thus, leaders can induce and introduce change. They are the instrumental in conceiving and managing change. They introduce change by convincing their followers about the positive effects of the change.

According to McFarland, "Administrative leadership is vital to the survival and effectiveness of organisation." No doubt that leadership plays a vital role in the survival and success of an enterprise. The quality of leadership goes a long way in the success and survival of an enterprise. Without effective leadership, many well established enterprises have miserably failed. Glover has also stated that "most failure of business concerns are attributable to poor leadership than to any other cause."

> Leadership is an essential and integral part of management. Effectiveness and efficiency of management largely depends on its leadership qualities. A strong leader can transform a lack lustre organisation into a successful one. Without leadership an organisation is but a muddle of men or machines .... Management activities such as planning, organising etc. are dormant cocoons until leader triggers the power of motivation in people and guides them towards goals. *[Keith Davis]*

Effective leadership can create work environment in which group members can work with pleasure. For this, the leader creates and maintains interpersonal relations of trust and confidence among the group members. Albanese has stated that "leadership is necessary in organisations in order to create work environments that are productive and satisfying for human beings."

An effective leader has qualities to maintain order and discipline in the organisation. He lays down standards of behaviour and sees that his followers follow the same in their behaviour. He shows exemplary behaviour and maintains self-disciple in order to maintain discipline among his followers.

Leaders play crucial role in resolving the conflicts arising in the group. He does it by harmonising the diverse intense interests of group members and the organisation.

It has been widely accepted that a leader should have certain special qualities or traits. A large number of experts have opined about the qualities of an effective leader.

According to Ordway Tead, a leader should have the following qualities :

(i) physical and nervous energy,
(ii) enthusiasm,
(iii) sense of purpose and direction,
(iv) technical mastery,
(v) integrity,
(vi) technical skills,
(vii) friendliness and affection,
(viii) decisiveness,
(ix) intelligence, and
(x) faith.

Terry and Franklin have identified the following qualities necessary for a leader :

(i) energy,
(ii) emotional stability,
(iii) knowledge of human relations,
(iv) personal motivation,
(v) communication skills,
(vi) teaching ability,
(vii) social skills, and
(viii) technical competence.

Prof. Robert L. Katz has found that managerial leaders need three kinds of skills :

(i) technical skills,
(ii) human skills, and
(iii) conceptual skills.

Prof. Ivancevich *et al.* have suggested the following skills as important for managerial leader :

(i) technical skills,

(ii) analytical skills,
(iii) decision-making skills,
(iv) computer skills,
(v) human relations skills.

The skills or qualities of a managerial leader suggested by Katz and Ivancevich *et al.* have already been discussed. A general description of qualities of successful leader is given under the following sub-heads :

> It is rightly said that sound mind resides in sound body. Hence, a leader should have sound health and good stamina to work hard. He should be handsome with charming personality. Such a leader has a lasting impact on the minds of his followers.

A leader should be intelligent. He should have above average level of intelligence. He should be capable of thinking scientifically.

A leader should have self-confidence. He should be fully confident of his actions and decisions.

A leader is, required to have sharp vision and foresight. He should be able to foresee the future trend of events. This quality prepares him for future challenges.

An effective leader is one who has ability to inspire. Hence, he should be capable of influencing people by his ideas, actions and behaviour.

A leader should have ability to communicate effectively. He should be efficient in verbal, written, gestural communication skills.

> A leader should be sincere and honest. His integrity should be above doubts. Sincerity and integrity makes a man truthful, high minded and gives him aspirations and high ideals. *[F. W. Taylor]*

It has been rightly said "without courage there are no virtues." No faith, hope, aspiration etc. can be transformed into realities without courage and will power. Hence, a leader should be courageous.

A leader should be with flexible and dynamic mind-set. He should be capable of adapting ideas and views in accordance with the needs of the changing situations.

A leader should be capable of keeping his emotions under control. Emotional stability and cool temperament are necessary for a matured leader. Hence, he should remain cool, patient and undisturbed by the happening of unusual and unanticipated events.

A leader should have sound judgement power. He should be a shrewd judge of behaviour, actions and events. He should be able to judge the things judiciously.

A leader should be tactful in dealing with people and situations. He should have a sense of humour. These qualities help a leader to get the things done pleasantly without stress and strain.

A leader should have proper education and knowledge. Particularly, the business leaders should have education at least in the field of accountancy, management, economics. It would be better if he has specialised knowledge in the field of management. Moreover, he should have up to-date knowledge of economic laws, policies and events.

A leader should have and acquire conceptual skills. Conceptual skill is the ability to see the organisation as a whole and the relationships among its sub-units. It also includes the ability to visualise how the organisation fits into its external environment. Such ability helps a leader to understand problems and identify opportunities of the organisation and plan accordingly.

A manager-leader essentially needs to have administrative skills. He should be able to implement the plans and policies, to organise and to mobilise resources of the organisation in a pragmatic manner.

A leader should possess and develop analytical skills. These include the abilities to understand the things, situations, and problems in a systematic manner. Such skills are needed in evaluating performance, making decisions and handling complex situations.

A leader should have human relations skills. Human relations skills refer to the ability to work well with others. It includes the ability to understand people and their problems and feelings.

A leader should also possess technical skills. Technical skills relate to job knowledge and expertise. These include the ability to apply methods and techniques in performing the job and the ability to provide guidance and instructions to the followers.

Different Kinds

Leadership style is the general way or pattern of behaviour of a leader towards his followers in order to influence their behaviour to attain a goal. Every leader usually develops his own style of leadership. Hence, style of every leader differs from the other. However, a particular leadership style is affected by the degree of delegation of authority, types of power employed, degree of concern for human relations etc. Thus, there exists different leadership styles. The main styles of leadership are as follows : 1. Autocratic or authoritarian style, 2. Participative or democratic style, 3. Free-rein or *laissez-faire* style, 4. Patternalistic style.

An autocratic leader is one who centralises power and makes all the decisions himself. He tells his followers what to do and expects to be obeyed without question. Thus, such a leader imposes his will on his followers. This style is typically of a person who accepts McGregor's Theory X assumptions. The characteristics features of such a leader are as follows:

(i) He centralises power.

(ii) He makes all the decisions himself.

(iii) He structures the work of his group members, as far as possible.

(iv) He exercises close supervision and control over his group members.

(v) He expects to be obeyed by his subordinates without question.

(vi) He gets the things done through fear or threats of punishment, penalties and so on.

(vii) He motivates his subordinates by satisfying their basic needs, through threats of punishment and penalties.

(viii) He believes in maintaining one-way communication *i.e.* from him to the subordinates.

Autocratic leaders may be of two types :

(i) Pure autocrat or negative leader-He is a dictator and

makes all decisions himself. He superimposes his decisions on his subordinates. He carries out his decision by coercive or negative power. He uses fear of punishment or penalty to carry out his decisions. Thus, it is a negative leadership.

(ii) Benevolent autocrat or positive leader-When an autocrat leader avoids negative coercive power and uses reward power to influence his subordinates, he is called a benevolent autocrat leader. Such a leader shows active concern for the feelings and welfare of his subordinates. He may even encourage their participation in planning but he retains his power to make and execute decisions.

Autocratic leadership has the following advantages :

(i) It provides strong motivation and reward for the leader.

(ii) It permits quick decisions.

(iii) It provides structured work for employees.

(iv) It allows managers to hire less competent subordinates because their principal job is to carry out orders.

(v) It ensures compliance and execution of orders with certainty.

(vi) It permits close supervision and control of subordinates.

(vii) It helps manages to get things done with certainty.

But this style of leadership suffers from the following drawbacks/ disadvantages :

(i) It overburdens managers because of centralisation of authority.

(ii) It creates fear and frustration among subordinates.

(iii) It hampers creativity of subordinates.

(iv) It blocks the free flow of two-way communication.

(v) In the absence of consultation and feedback from subordinates, decisions may cost heavily.

(vi) It is disliked by the subordinates specially when it is negative.

In spite of these limitations, autocratic leadership is suitable in the following situations:

(i) Where subordinates are not educated or untrained or incompetent.

(ii) Where subordinates are submissive and do not want to take responsibility.

(iii) Where leaders do not want to delegate authority.

(iv) When the organisation endorses fear and punishment as accepted disciplinary techniques.

(v) When achievement of target of performance is urgently required in time.

It is just opposite to autocratic leadership. Participative leaders decentralise authority. Such leaders involve subordinates in decision-making process. Thus, decisions are not unilateral. The leaders and their group members work at a social unit. They freely exchange their views and express opinions and suggestions. Such leaders exercise control through forces within the group. The main features of democratic leadership are as follows :

(i) Leader decentralises authority.

(ii) He involves subordinates in decision-making process. Hence, decisions are not unilateral.

(iii) He believes in free-flow of two-way communication.

(iv) He leads by mutual consent.

(v) He explains the reasons for his actions.

(vi) He and his, group members work as a social unit.

(vii) He motivates his subordinates through positive means *i.e.* rewards.

Participative leadership offers the following advantages :

(i) It helps avoid hasty decisions. Hence, it improves quality of decisions.

(ii) It encourages cooperation between the leader and his subordinates.

(iii) It motivates subordinates to perform better.

(iv) It contributes to higher productivity of resources.

(v) It tends to reduce employee grievances, dissatisfaction and turnover.

(vi) It facilitates introduction of change.

(vii) It helps create congenial work environment.

(viii) It helps develop future leaders and, thus, promotes organisational stability.

Participative leadership also suffers from the following disadvantages/limitations :

(i) It tends to slow the decision-making process.

(ii) It tends to dilute responsibility for decisions. It may develop a tendency of buck-passing.

(iii) It tends to reduce the role of the leader at the top.

In spite of these limitations/disadvantages, this leadership style is suitable in the following cases:

(i) Where the organisational goals are well set and understood by the subordinates.

(ii) Where leaders really intend to consider the views and opinions of the subordinates.

(iii) Where the workers are reasonably well educated and trained.

(iv) Where the leaders really desire active involvement of subordinates in decision-making process,.

(v) Where sufficient time is available for attaining the objectives.

Free-rein leadership style is one under which leader uses his power very little. The leader gives high degree of freedom to his subordinates in their operations. He depends largely on his subordinates to set their own goals and make their decision regarding their jobs. Thus, such a leader completely delegates his authority to his subordinates and allows them to make their own plans, procedures and decisions. He simply aids his subordinates in performing their job. He exists as a Contact person with the subordinates' external environment.

Free-rein leadership style is permissive and leader least intervenes his subordinates. The leader remains passive observer but intervenes only during the crisis.

Free-rein leadership is suitable where subordinates are highly competent and duty-conscious. It is successful where subordinates are able to train and motivate themselves. However, chaotic conditions may prevail all over the organisation under such leadership.

Free-rein leadership helps subordinates train and develop themselves independently.

A paternalistic leadership is authoritarian by nature. It is heavily work-centered but has consideration for subordinates. Such a leader tends to look after his subordinates the way farther looks after his children. Such a leader helps, guides and encourages his subordinates to work together as members of a family.

This is a personalised leadership. The leader exercises his authority personally. He maintains direct personal contacts with his subordinates. He treats affectionately them like elderly member of a family. The subordinates, in turn, tend to remain submissive and faithful.

Under paternalistic leadership style, subordinates feel force to meet their leader. They also feel job security. Their problems and grievances are sympathetically considered and solved. The issues affecting subordinates' interests are sympathetically addressed. But this leadership style is usually resented and resisted in modern times.

Selection of Style

These are the four basic leadership styles identified by the experts. But, in practice, no particular leader's style strictly falls under any of these categories. Moreover, no expert can suggest one best leadership style because leadership style is influenced by several forces/factors. A leader should, therefore, consider the following factors/ forces while choosing a leadership style :

> The forces operating in leader include the (leader's personality) characteristics, qualities and job skills, value system, interaction skills, self- confidence, confidence in subordinates, feeling of security 'and so on.

There are the forces that operate in the group which affect leadership. These include perceptions and attitude of group members towards the leader, toward their tasks and towards organisational goals, characteristics, skills, knowledge, needs and expectations of group members, size and nature of the group and so on.

These are the other impersonal forces in the work environment of leader and his group members. Nature of the job and its technology, organisation structure and authority-relationships, organisational goals, policies, control system, trade unions and their influence, political, economic, cultural and ethical conditions of society.

One leadership theory was developed by Robert Tannenbaum and Warren H. Schmidt in 1958. They modified and refined it in 1973.

Tannenbaum and Schmidt developed a leadership continuum. This continuum depicts a range of leader behaviours. It can be seen from the continuum that they identified, variety of leadership styles (seven styles shown) ranging from highly boss centered to highly subordinate centered.

On the extreme left of the continuum, leader behaviour is characterised by exercise of high degree of authority over subordinates. Such leadership style is regarded as boss-centered or authoritarian style. On the extreme right side of the continuum, leadership is subordinate-centered or democratic style. There are many other styles in between these two extremes. These styles vary with the degree of freedom a leader grants to his subordinates.

Tannenbaum and Schmidt instead of suggesting a choice between the authoritarian and democratic styles of leadership offered a range of styles. They emphasised that no one particular style is always right or no other is always wrong.

The two extreme ends of the continuum have been referred as manager power influence and non-manager power influence. In moving from left to right, less and less authority is used by the leader (manager) and more and more freedom is allowed to subordinates in decision-making. In between the two extremes, five more leadership styles have been shown. All the seven styles of leader behaviour are as follows :

> It is the extreme form of autocratic leadership where by the leader/manager is able to take decisions and subordinates are bound to accept and implement the decisions without any modification.

In this kind of leadership, the leader (manager) takes decisions and persuades the subordinates to accept them.

Under this style, the leader/manager arrives at the decision and asks his subordinates to express their views on it. The leader responds to the questions of his subordinates.

In this case leader (manager) takes a tentative decision and review it in the light of the suggestions/views expressed by subordinates.

In this kind of leadership, leader (manager) presents problems and takes decision after hearing the views/suggestions from the subordinates. Under this style, the decision is taken by the group subject to the limits set by the boss.

In this kind of leadership, leader/manager and subordinates jointly make decisions within the limits defined by superior.

Tannenbaum and Schmidt believed that there is one best style of leadership for all situations. Hence, selection of leadership style depends on the demands or forces of the situation. These forces include the following :

(i) The forces operating in the Leader's/Manager's personality, such as his education, knowledge, experience, value system, confidence in subordinates etc.

(ii) The forces in subordinates such as their background, education, experience, values, willingness to assume responsibility.

(iii) The forces in the situation such as size, complexity, goals, structure, climate, values, traditions of the organisation, nature of work, technology used.

Tannenbaum and Schmidt revised the model in 1973 and emphasised that organisational environment and societal environment greatly influence the leadership style. According to them trade union movement, consumer civil rights movement etc. are the important organisational and societal forces which influence leadership style. These forces challenge the rights of managers/ leaders to make decisions or deal with their subordinates. They cannot make effective decisions without considering the interests of the groups outside the organisation.

Main Systems : Prof. Rensis Likert and his associates at the University of Michigan have studied the patterns or styles of leaders. In the course of this research, Likert has developed four systems/styles of leadership that exemplify different behavioural aspects of leaders. They are as follows : System 1 : Exploitative-authoritative leadership System 2 : Benevolent- authoritative leadership System 3 : Consultative leadership System 4 : Participative group leadership.

System 1 : Exploitative-authoritative-System leadership is described as "exploitative-autocratic or authoritative." In this kind of leadership system, leaders/ managers are highly autocratic. They have little confidence and trust in subordinates. They motivate subordinates mainly through fear and punishment. They rarely or occasionally reward them. They make all decisions. They mostly use downward communication and have little interaction with subordinates. Likert found that productivity under this system is mediocre.

System 2 : Benevolent-authoritative-Under this system style of leadership, leaders have patronising confidence and trust in subordinates. Leaders take a very paternalistic attitude. Managers make decisions but subordinates have some degree of freedom in doing their job. Leaders motivate subordinates with rewards and also through some fear and punishment. They permit some upward communication and solicit some suggestions and ideas from subordinates. Under this system, productivity ranges from fair to good.

System 3 : Consultative leadership-In this style of leadership, leaders/managers have substantial but not complete confidence and trust in subordinates. Leaders consult their subordinate managers before setting goals and making policy decisions. However, operating decisions are made at lower levels in the organisation. Subordinates have considerable degree of freedom in making decisions about their job. Leaders usually try to make use of subordinates ideas and suggestions. They tend to use rewards for motivation with occasional punishments. Leaders usually tend to rely on two-way communication.

System 4 : Participative group leadership-Participative group leadership style is the Likert's recommended style of leadership/management. Likert considered it as the optimal style of leadership in our educated and dynamic society.

In this style of leadership, leaders/managers have complete trust and confidence in subordinates. They extensively interact with subordinates. They always try to get and use ideas and suggestions from subordinates.

Thus under this leadership style, the whole group participates in the process of establishing goals and making job related decisions. Leaders tend to give economic rewards on the basis of group participation in goal-setting and decision-making and evaluation of performance on jobs. They tend to engage in free flow of downward, up-ward and horizontal communication. They encourage decision-making across the organisation. Likert's 4 system management leadership is shown in the table given here.

Likert found that managers who applied the system 4 style to their operations had the greatest success as leaders. Likert, therefore, stressed that all leaders should strive towards a system 4 style if they want to maximise the quantity and quality of performance from subordinates.

Theories and Practices : Several theories of leadership have been developed by management theoreticians. These theories may be classified into three categories :

I. Personality theories

II. Behavioural theories

III. Situational or contingency theories

Personality theories are theories that focus on the personal qualities or traits of leaders. Such theories include the following : (A) Great man theory, and (B) Trait theory

(A) Great man theory of leadership-Great man theory of leadership claims that "leaders are born, not made". This theory asserts that great leaders are born with necessary qualities.

Leadership qualities are inherited or carried in genes. Leadership qualities cannot be acquired or developed through formal education and training. Supports of this theory usually prove its validity by drawing examples from the great leader such as Mahatma Gandhi, Pt. Nehru, Abraham Lincoln, Napoleon and others. They were born as leaders, it is asserted. Thus, the great man theory emphasises and implies the following things :

(i) Leaders are born and not made. Leaders are gifts of God to mankind.

(ii) Hence, every person cannot aspire to become a leader.

(iii) Qualities of leadership are inherited or carried in genes from generation to generation.

(iv) The inborn leadership qualities alone are necessary and sufficient for an effective leader.

(v) Leadership qualities cannot be acquired or developed through formal education and training.

(vi) Leadership qualities and effectiveness are independent factors. Hence, situational factors like the nature of followers, demands of the job, and the environmental factors have little or no effect on leaders effectiveness.

The theory has some credibility to the extent that leaders have certain mystic and their followers can realise them. Hence, qualities and actions of such leaders influence and inspire their followers at least to a limited extent. But this theory has been criticized and rejected by many experts for the following reasons :

(i) This theory does not have scientific basis and has no empirical validity. It does not provide a logical explanation of why, how and when an effective leader is born. It is more of a matter of chance that some great leaders were born with leadership qualities.

(ii) This theory does not prescribe the set of essential qualities of a great leader.

(iii) There is nothing inborn leadership qualities. Inborn leaders are imaginary characters.

(iv) This theory is also based on absurd belief that leadership is not affected by the situational/ environmental variables.

(v) Leadership qualities can now be acquired and developed through education and training.

(vi) Leadership qualities alone are not necessary to become a successful leader. Competence to deal with situational variables is considered a most essential leadership quality.

It is a matter of fact that Great man theory is totally rejected by most of the modern theorists.

(B) Trait theory of leadership-Trait theory of leadership is a modified version of the Great man theory. According to this theory leadership is largely a function of certain traits or qualities. This theory states that there are certain unique traits or qualities essentials for a successful leader. Any person who wants to be a successful leader must possess those traits. This theory also emphasises that these traits need not necessarily be inborn but may be acquired through education, training and practice.

The trait theorists have identified a long list of traits related to leadership qualities. Stogdill found the following traits :

1. Five physical traits such as energy appearance and height.
2. Four intelligent and ability traits.
3. Sixteen personality traits such as adaptability, aggressiveness, enthusiasm and self-confidence.
4. Six task related traits such as achievement drive and initiative.
5. Nine social traits such as cooperativeness, interpersonal skills and administrative ability.

Edwin Ghiselli has identified thirteen traits which included eight personality traits and five motivational traits. The personality traits include : (i) intelligence, (ii) initiative (iii) supervisory ability, (iv) self-assurance, (v) affinity for working class, (vi) decisiveness, (vii) masculinity-feminity, and (viii) maturity. The motivational traits include : (i) need for occupational achievement, (ii) self-actualisation, (iii) power, (iv) high financial reward, and (v) job security.

Of these 13 traits, Ghiselli found the following six to be very important leadership traits : (i) supervisory ability, (ii) need for occupational achievement, (iii) intelligent, (iv) decisiveness, (v) self-assurance, and (vi) initiative.

Thus, trait theory is a simple theory. It simply describes the qualities which a person must possess in order to become a successful leader. It, therefore, helps persons to develop such leadership qualities. It is also useful for those who train and develop leaders. But this theory is criticised for its following limitations :

(i) Trait theory is not based on scientific or systematic research. It is only a descriptive theory which states how some persons emerge as leaders. It does not offer any explanation why leaders emerge.

(ii) It offers a painfully long list of traits. Moreover, there is no universally acceptable list of traits for a successful leader.

(iii) It fails to state which set of traits are more important for leaders than others.

(iv) It does not highlight the traits which are necessary for acquiring leadership and which are necessary for nurturing and maintaining leadership.

(v) It fails to highlight the traits which may clearly distinguish leaders from followers.

(vi) This theory does not provide a method of measuring traits in a person.

(vii) It does not consider the whole leadership environment which determines the success of a leader. In other words, it fails to consider situational and environmental factors which determine the success of a leader.

(viii) It does not consider the fact that different roles and positions require different traits. Leaders at higher level more require conceptual skills where as the leaders at lower level more require technical skills. Similarly, leaders at middle level more require human relations skills.

The personality theories focus on who the leaders are (Great man theory) or what the leaders are (Trait theory). Behavioural theory, on the other hand, focuses on what the leaders do *i.e.* on the actual behaviour of the leader.

Thus, behavioural approach of leadership attempts to emphasise actual behaviour or dimensions of behaviour in order to identify leadership. It is based on the premise that effective leadership is the result of effective behaviour of the leader. Hence, success of leadership depends on the behaviour of the leader and not on his traits.

A particular behaviour pattern of a leader (functional behaviour) makes him a successful leader and its opposite (dysfunctional) would reject him as a leader. The functional dimension of leader's behaviour include setting goals, motivating employees towards achievement of goals, making effective communication and interaction, building team-spirit etc. The dysfunctional dimensions of leader's behaviour include inability to accept subordinates' ideas, poor communication and ineffective interaction with employees, poor human relations and so on.

This approach asserts that favourable or functional dimensions of behaviour of leader provides greater satisfaction to his subordinates and hence, they recognise him as their leader. However, this approach recognises the fact that a particular behaviour of a leader may be effective only at a particular point of time and may be ineffective at other times.

Behavioural approach to leadership assumes that a leader uses conceptual, human and technical skills to influence and lead his subordinates.

Several attempts have been made to identify the basic dimensions of leadership behaviour. The most systematic and comprehensive research studies include the studies by Lickert, Blake and Mouton, and studies at Ohio State University and University of Michigan.

Behavioural approach to leadership is an improvement over the personality approach. It identifies the behavioural dimensions of leadership that may contribute to the success of a leader. But this approach does not use scientific tests. It uses questionnaire, observation and interviews to identify dimensions of behaviour. Hence, behaviour dimensions cannot be measured objectively.

Personality theories hold that a leader can be successful if he has certain traits. Behavioural theories, on the other hand, hold that a leader can be successful if he behaves in a particular manner. Thus, both the personality and behaviour theories ignore the effects of situational factors on leadership. The situational approach of leadership emphasises that emergence and success of a leader is largely determined by situational factors apart from the traits and behaviour of the leader himself.

The focus of the situational approach is on the behaviour of a leader in a particular situation and not on the traits or qualities of the leader. This approach stresses that a leadership behaviour which is effective under one particular situation may be ineffective under the other. If a leader behaves in the same manner under all situations, he may fail.

Thus, situational leadership approach states that leadership is strongly affected by the situations under which a leader works. These situations are created by the following forces :

(i) Forces in the leader.

(ii) Forces in the subordinates.

(iii) Forces in the situation.

There are several different situational models of leadership have been developed. Fildler's contingency model, Path-goal model, Blanchard's model etc. are some of the well-known situational leadership models.

Importance of Motivation

William F. Glueck has rightly stated that "motivation is concerned with why people work hard and well or poorly." In fact, motivation is said to be the cause of behaviour. It is the cause what makes people to do things. It is the main spring of action in people. A manager has to find out and understand the cause of particular type of behaviour of his subordinates in order to get the things in the best possible manner.

The term motivation is derived from 'motive'. The term 'motive', implies action to satisfy a need. The need, desire, drive, want, motive are often used interchangeably by the psychologists. Any motive, need, drive, desire or want prompts a person to do something. It is, therefore, said to be the mainspring of action in people. Thus, motivation simply means the need or reason that makes people to do some work or to take some work. For instance, a person needs respect from others. It makes him to do outstanding work. Consequently, he gets praise, recognition, higher pay, promotion and so on. Ultimately he gets respect from others in the family as well as in society.

According to Dale S. Beach, "Motivation can be defined as a willingness to expend energy to achieve a goal or a reward."

In the words of William G. Scott, "Motivation means a process of stimulating people to action to accomplish desired goals."

In the opinion of M.J. Jucius, "Motivation is the act of stimulating some one or oneself to get a desired course of action."

According to McFarland, "Motivation refers to the way in which urges; drives, desires, aspirations, strivings, needs direct control or explain the behaviour of human beings."

According to Terry and Franklin, "Motivation is the need or drive within an individual that drives him or her towards goal-oriented action."

In the words of Mondy *et al.*, "Motivation may be defined as the willingness to put forth effort in the pursuit of organisational goals."

In the words of Mescon *et al.*, "Motivating is the process of moving oneself and others to work towards attainment of individual and organisational objectives."

According to Kreitner, "The term motivation refers to the psychological process that gives behaviour, purpose and direction."

In the words of Robbins and Coulter, "Motivation is the willingness to exert high levels of effort to reach organisational goals, conditioned by the effort's ability to satisfy some individual needs."

In the words of Fred Luthans, "Motivation is a process that starts with a physiological or psychological deficiency or need that activates behaviour or a drive that is aimed at a goal or an incentive."

Thus, motivation is the need or reason that makes people to work or to take action. It includes the processes and forces in an individual that influence or encourage him to act or not to act in particular ways. It arouses or energises the willingness to put in effort in a particular direction.

Following characteristics of motivation highlight the nature of motivation :

> Motivation is internal feeling of an individual. It points out the energising forces within an individual that direct or influence him to behave in a particular way.

Motivation is a continuous or never ending process. It is so because human needs, desires, wants or wishes are endless. All of them can never be satisfied simultaneously. Satisfaction of one need gives size to another need. Therefore, motivation process goes on forever.

Motivation is a dynamic and complex process. It is so because it relates to human behaviour which is never static but dynamic. It keeps on changing continuously.

> The concept of motivation is mainly psychological. It relates to those forces operating within the individual employee which impel him to act or not to act in certain ways. *[McFarland]*

> Motivation refers to the way in which urges, drives, desires, inspirations or needs direct, and explain the behaviour of human beings. *[McFarland]*

It is the psychological process that gives behaviour, purpose and direction.

Motivation is the willingness of an individual to exert effort in the pursuit of organisational goals and to satisfy some individual needs.

Motivation is system-oriented. It is the system that contains three main factors : (a) factors operating within an individual *i.e.* his needs, aspirations, wants, wishes, values etc.; (b) factors operating within the organisation such as organisation structure, technology, physical facilities, work environment etc.; (c) factors operating in the external environment such as customs, norms of society, culture etc. Motivation is the result of interaction among these factors.

> Motivation is a need-satisfying process. An unsatisfied need creates tension that stimulates drives within an individual. These drives, generate a search behaviour to find particular goals that (if attained) will satisfy the need and reduce tension. *[Robbins and Coulter]*

Motivation is the process that energises or encourages individuals to put in effort to achieve organisational goals and to satisfy their needs. Motivation can be positive or negative. Positive-motivation implies use of incentives such as increase in pay, reward, promotion, and so on for better work. Negative motivation, on the other hand, means punishment and penalties such as reprimands, threats of demotion, fear of loss of job etc.

Every individual is an integrated whole in himself. Therefore, whole individual can and should be motivated. A part of the individual cannot be motivated. It is so because motivation is a psychological concept that is concerned with the whole individual.

A frustrated individual cannot be satisfied and motivated. In other words, an individual who is unable to satisfy his basic needs becomes frustrated. Such an individual cannot be motivated until his such needs are satisfied.

It is true that both motivation and morale relate to individual and group psychology. But distinction is made between the two terms. Firstly, motivation is the reason what makes an individual to do work. It consists of forces and procedures that direct or influence an individual's behaviour. On the other hand, morale is individual's or group's attitude and feelings about his work and work situation. It is a resultant state encompassing the willingness to cooperate. Secondly, motivation is an individualistic concept whereas morale is a group concept. Thirdly, motivation is the result of satisfaction of needs, desires, aspirations etc. whereas morale is the result of good motivation.

Motivation is different from job satisfaction. Job satisfaction is the positive emotional attitude of an individual towards his job resulting from his job performance and job situation. It is a psychological contentment which an individual experiences from the factors associated with the job. Motivation, on the other hand, is the result of job satisfaction as well as individual's needs satisfaction.

The Necessities

Motivation is regarded as one of the most important functions of management. Importance of motivation

> can hardly be over-emphasised. Highly motivated people can make things happen in organisations. On the other hand, poorly motivated people can nullify the sounded organisations. *[Allen]*

The importance of motivation is summarised in the following points :

> In the words of Clarence Francis, "You can buy a man's time and physical presence but you cannot buy enthusiasm, initiative and loyalty. You have to earn these things." These can be earned through the process of motivation. Effective motivation system inspires employees to do work or to take action. It prepares them to do their work with full devotion. It creates willingness among the employees to perform their work with great enthusiasm, zeal and loyalty.
>
> Highly motivated employees perform better and higher as compared to the employees with low level of motivation. Motivation is the mainspring of performance. Without motivation, the other contributors to performance become rather irrelevant.
>
> *[Gray and Smeltzer]*

Motivated employees can use their skills and organisational resources more efficiently and effectively. This ultimately results in higher productivity of all the resources of the organisation. David Holt has rightly remarked that "productivity is achieved through excellence and excellence is achieved by having an organisation of highly motivated individuals."

A proper motivation system is key to the effectiveness of all managerial functions. Effectiveness of all managerial functions will go for naught if employees cannot be motivated to fulfill their responsibilities. Planning and organising cannot be successful if the employees are not properly motivated.

Motivation is core of management. Through motivation, managers encourage employees to direct their energies for achieving organisational goals. Thus, motivation helps achieve organisational objectives. Brech has rightly stated that "the problem of motivation is the key to management in action; and in its executive form, it is among the chief tasks of the general manager. We may safely lay it down that the tone of an organisation is a reflection of the motivation from the top."

Motivation help develop human resource in an organisation. Through motivation, employees can be directed to enlarge their job skills. In order to maintain a continual reservoir of well trained and highly motivated employees, a sound motivation system should be in place.

A sound motivation system ensures proper supply of motivated human resource. Such a system in an organisation can also ensure the satisfaction of needs and aspirations of individuals. Thus, it can attract and retain satisfied human resource in the organisation.

Morale refers to the attitude and feelings of employees about their work and work situation. Through motivation, employee attitudes and feelings towards work can be improved. This in turn boosts employee morale.

A proper motivation system promotes close ties between the enterprise and its employees. Employees begin to feel that enterprise belongs to them. Hence, employees become more concerned about the well being of the enterprise. Satisfied employees tend to stay longer and remain regular in the organisation. This, in turn, reduces employee turnover and absenteeism.

It is a research based fact that properly motivated employees are more receptive to new things and ready to accept change. This attitude facilitates introduce change and keep the organisation on the path of progress.

Motivated employees concentrate on finding new and more effective ways of doing a job and utilising resources. Poorly motivated employees usually avoid work and misuse resources. Thus, effective utilisation of resources largely depends on the level of employee motivation.

A good motivation system creates congenial work environment and job satisfaction. Employees tend to work with cooperative spirit and in a disciplined manner. Management also offers them better wages and incentives. Hence, chances of conflict are greatly reduced. All this leads to better industrial relations.

An organisation with motivated staff commands reputation in the business world and the society. Such organisations can easily obtain talented persons whenever the need arises.

Motivated employees can innovate and develop new technology and products for the organisation. There are many organisations where talented employees carry on research regularly and innovate. They develop new technology and products which are essential for the well-being of the organisation and the society as a whole.

There are several theories of motivation. A few important theories are as follows :

I. Maslow's need hierarchy theory.
II. McGregor's theory X and theory Y.
III. Herzberg's two-factor theory.
IV. William Ouchi's theory Z
V. McClelland's achievement theory
VI. Vroom's expectancy theory
VII. Adam's equity theory

First four theories have been described in this chapter.

A.H. Maslow, a noted psychologist, propounded the need hierarchy theory of motivation. It is one of the best known theories of human motivation. According to Maslow, within every human being there is a hierarchy of five needs which are as follows:

1. Physiological needs
2. Safety needs
3. Social needs
4. Esteem needs
5. Self-actualisation needs

Physiological needs are concerned with the basic biological functions of the human body. These needs relate to the essentials for survival. These include the needs for food, water, clothing, shelter, rest, sexual satisfaction, recreation etc. These needs are inherent in the nature of a human body.

Physiological needs are the most powerful motivators as no human being can survive without them. These

> needs are at the lowest level in the hierarchy of needs. Hence, these needs have to be satisfied before higher level needs can be pursued. Therefore, an extremely hungry person can never think for things other than food. He dreams food, remembers food, perceives only about food and wants only food. Freedom, love, and respect are useless since they fail to fill his stomach. *[A.H. Maslow]*

Safety needs are concerned with protecting the person from physical and psychological harm as well as the assurance that physiological needs will continue to be met. These include the needs of job security, economic and social security, *e.g.* pension, insurance etc. There needs can be satisfied by making provisions for pension, group insurance, provident fund, gratuity, safe working conditions, job security and so on. Safety needs begin to doormat when the physiological needs of a person are fairly met.

Social needs relate to the desire to have social interaction, friendship, affiliation belongingness with groups, acceptance, affection, support from others and so on. Such needs become motivators when physiological and safety needs have been fairly satisfied.

Self-esteem needs constitute the fourth level in the hierarchy of needs. These needs arise when physiological, safety and social needs have been fairly satisfied.

According to Maslow these needs are of two types :

(i) Need of self-respect or self-esteem, and

(ii) Needs for esteem from others or public esteem.

Self-respect means the respect in the eyes of oneself. Self respect needs include the needs for self-confidence for competence, for independence and freedom, for achievement, and personal strength. Esteem from other means the respect or image in the eyes of others. The needs of esteem from others includes the needs for prestige, recognition, acceptance, attention status, reputation and appreciation from others.

The four needs described above motivate people by their absence. In other words, when people feel lack of food, clothing, shelter, security, social relationships, self-respect and respect from others, they are motivated to do something or take action. But self-actualisation needs are the needs and aspirations for growth. Such needs motivate people by their presence.

Self-actualisation needs concern the needs for maximising the use one's skills, abilities, potential to become everything that one is capable of becoming. Such needs relate to realisation of one's full potential for development growth arid fulfilment. This category of needs is placed at the apex of the 'need hierarchy' and hence are the highest level of needs.

It is pertinent to note that self-actualisation need is a distinct one. Each person's journey towards self-actualisation is distinct and unique. Therefore, every person finds his own ways for satisfying such needs.

Maslow's need hierarchy theory is based on the following propositions or assumptions:

1. A man is perpetually wanting animal. As soon as one of his wants or needs is satisfied, another appears in its place. This process goes on in every one's life.
2. An unsatisfied or fresh need motivates influences behaviour. Satisfied needs are.........................
3. Needs can be arranged in an order or a hierarchy.

   In this hierarchy, physiological needs are at the lowest and most basic. These needs are followed in ascending order by the safety needs, social needs, esteem needs and self-actualisation needs.
4. There is always a sequence of emergence of needs. Higher level needs do not emerge or motivate unless all lower level needs have been fairly or minimally satisfied.
5. Higher level needs can be satisfied in more than one ways. But the ways to satisfy lower level needs are very limited.
6. Maslow separated the five needs into higher-level needs and lower-level needs. According to him physiological and safely needs are lower-level or lower-order needs whereas social, esteem and self- actualisation needs are higher level needs. Maslow believed that lower-level needs are

mainly satisfied externally whereas the higher-level needs are satisfied internally.

7. The first four needs (physiological, safety, social and esteem needs) motivate people by their absence. In other words, when people feel a lack of food, clothing, sex, security, social relationships, respect etc., they are motivated to work. But self-actualisation needs motivate people by their presence.
8. Maslow believed that no need is ever fully satisfied. Needs can be largely or substantially satisfied.

For motivating someone, a manager should understand that person's level of need in the hierarchy and focus on satisfying needs at or above that level. It is the job of the manager to lift employees from lower-level needs to higher level needs.

Maslow's need-hierarchy theory is best-known theory of motivation. It has received a wide recognition. It has been highly appreciated on the following grounds :

1. It is a logical theory because it recognises that an individual do something to fulfil his diverse needs.
2. It clearly states that satisfied needs are not motivators. Therefore, managers can easily concentrate on unsatisfied needs of their subordinates.
3. It clearly states that a person advances *to* the next level of the need hierarchy only when the lower level need is minimally or fairly satisfied.
4. It offers useful ideas for understanding human needs and ways for satisfying them.
5. It helps to find out the reasons that influence behaviour of a person. Thus, it explains the reasons why people behave differently even in the similar situations.
6. It is a dynamic model because it presents motivation as a constantly changing force. It considers that every individual strives for fulfilment of fresh and higher-level needs.
7. It is a positive theory. It assumes that man is a healthy, good and creative being, capable of working out his own destiny.

8. It is a simple and humanistic theory.
9. It is based on reasonable assumption and has been substantiated by several research studies.

Maslow's theory suffers from the following limitations :

1. It is a simplistic theory and cannot be tested and validated in practice. It lacks empirical testing. It is difficult to interpret and analyse its concepts.
2. Maslow's theory is based on a small sample of subjects. It is a clinically derived theory which may not be accurate in real life.
3. Some criticise on the ground that hierarchy of needs does not exist. Individuals unlikely to behave in such a neat, step-by-step manner while perceiving and satisfying their needs. Moreover, all the needs are present at a given time. For instance, an individual motivated by self- actualisation needs also has the physiological needs. Hence, the need hierarchy is artificial and arbitrary.
4. Need hierarchy may not be the same among all the employees. Generally, socially, culturally and economically advantaged employees have higher-level needs whereas the socially and economically disadvantaged employees have lower-level needs.
5. There are some who argue that there is no evidence that a satisfied need is not a motivator.
6. Similarly, there is no evidence that satisfaction of one need automatically activates the next need in the hierarchy.
7. Human beings are not motivated by their needs alone but also by many other things. Therefore, it is doubtful weather deprivation of a need motivate an individual.

In spite of these limitations, the need hierarchy theory of motivation is important because of its rich and comprehensive view of the needs. The theory is relevant because need hierarchy helps managers to understand the behaviour of people. In the words of Fred Luthans, "The theory does make a significant contribution in terms of making management aware of the diverse needs of humans at work. The number or names of the levels are not important, nor is the hierarchical concept. What is important, is the fact that humans in the work-place have diverse motives."

Theory of Two Factors

During the late 1950s Fredrick Herzberg, a US behavioural scientist (psychologist), and his associates developed two factor theory of motivation. This is also known as the 'Motivation-Hygiene theory'. This theory is based an empirical research on job attitudes of 200 engineers and accountants of a company. The researchers asked two questions from those two hundred employees:

(i) "Can you describe, in detail, when you felt exceptionally good about your job ?"

(ii) "Can you describe, in detail, when you felt exceptionally bad about your job ?"

They were all asked to describe the conditions that had led to those feelings.

Herzberg analysed the responses and revealed that factors which made respondents feel good were totally different from those which made them feel bad. Herzberg grouped those responses in two categories : (i) Hygiene factors or maintenance factors, (ii) Motivators or satisfiers. These are described in the table given below :

Herzberg's Hygiene Factor and Motivators

Hygiene Factors	Motivators
* Company policy and administration	* Achievement
	* Recognition
* Working conditions	* Advancement
* Job security	* Responsibility
* Salary	* Personal growth
* Quality of supervision	* Opportunities
* Interpersonal relations with superiors, co-workers and subordinates.	* Work itself

Hygiene factors or maintenance factors are related to the job environment. There are eight factors : working conditions, job security, salary, quality of supervision, company policy and administration, interpersonal relation and fringe benefits. Presence of these factors in job environment is essential if a reasonable level of satisfaction in employees is to be maintained. The absence or deficiency in these factors can cause dissatisfaction. The presence of these factors is necessary to avoid dissatisfaction and pain in the work environment. These factors do not motivate employees.

According to Herzberg, there are six motivators or motivation factors : achievement, recognition, responsibility, advancement, personal growth and the nature of the job itself. Adequacy of these factors make employees satisfied with their job and consequently motivate them. Their absence, however, rarely dissatisfies or demotivate the employees.

According to Herzbergs job satisfaction and job dissatisfaction are not opposites of each other. Absence of job dissatisfaction does not mean presence of job satisfaction. Satisfaction is achieved through motivators and dissatisfaction results from absence of adequate hygiene factors.

Therefore, managers should maintain adequate amount of hygiene factors in order to avoid dissatisfaction among employees. On the other hand, managers must ensure adequacy of motivating factors in order to motivate employees. However, presence of hygiene factors is essential for creating favourable frame of mind for motivation.

The merits or contributions of Herzberg's theory are summarised as follows :

1. It clearly distinguishes between the factors that motivate employees on the job and the factors that maintain employees on the job. In other words, it clearly states that the presence of hygiene factors is necessary in order to avoid dissatisfaction in employees. On the other hand, the presence of motivation factors is essential to motivate employees. Thus, both the groups of factors have different roles to play.

2. It recommends specific measures (*i.e.* motivators) to improve motivation levels.
3. It helps in understanding the effect of job content on motivation of employees.
4. It explains the significance of job enrichment on the job redesign and motivation.
5. It is a rational approach to motivation.

It clearly explains that the factors which cause job dissatisfaction are different from the factors which cause job satisfaction. In other words, absence of job dissatisfaction is not the presence of job satisfaction. Hence, presence of maintenance of hygiene factors avoid dissatisfaction in employees but does not cause satisfaction. Similarly, presence of motivators cause satisfaction and motivation.

Though Herzberg's theory of motivation has gained wide-spread popularity among managers and management educators, it suffers from the following limitations :

1. It is alleged that research base was very narrow and was not representative enough to make justified generalisations.
2. It is difficult to distinguish job-context factors from the job-content factors. In many cases, job context factors have elements of job-content factors. Moreover, for some individual job content factors, *i.e.,* motivators have no significance because their job-related aspirations are very limited.
3. Sometimes in real life situations, there is no direct cause and effect relationship between satisfaction and performance. Many employees are satisfied with their job but their performance is not high.
4. The methodology used by Herzberg is sometimes questioned. Since raters have to make interpretations, different raters may have interpreted the responses in different ways.
5. It explains the reasons of job satisfaction and dissatisfaction. Thus it is, in fact, not a theory of motivation.

6. Not all the measures of satisfaction have been explored and utilised.
7. It ignores the impact of situational variables on motivation.
8. Herzberg assumes that there is a relationship between satisfaction and high performance. But in his research work he looked only at satisfaction and not at performance or productivity, *[Robbins]*
9. As a matter of fact, two factors are not distinct. Both hygiene factors and motivators may cause satisfaction and dissatisfaction.
10. The theory lays much emphasis on motivators and ignores the impact of hygiene factors on motivation.

Despite these limitations/criticism Herzberg's theory has made significant contribution to the manager's understanding of employee motivation. This is a valuable insight into employee motivation.

A careful study and analysis of these two models would suggest that they are not very much different from each other. Rather there are marked similarities between the two. The similarities between the two are as follows :

1. Both the models are content model. They focus on identifying needs that motivate people to do something.
2. Both the models assume that needs are the driving force that cause a person to do something.
3. Both the models fail to explain individual differences in motivation.
4. Both the models consider the similar needs. Herzberg's hygiene factors correspond to the Maslow's lower-level needs *i.e.* physiological safety and security needs.
5. Both tend to over simplify the motivation process.
6. Both emphasize the same set of relationships.
7. Both deal with the same problem.

Distinction Between Maslow's And Herzberg's Models

In spite of many similarities, the two models differ on the following counts :

	Basis of Distinction	Maslow's Model	Herzberg's Model
	1	2	3
1.	Basis based on hierarchy of needs.	Maslow's model is based on factors that avoid dissatisfaction and pain and the factors that satisfy and motivate employees.	Herzberg's theory
2.	Order of needs in the order they emerge.	Maslow arranged the of needs in this model.	There is no such order
3.	Nature of model	It is descriptive model.	It is prescriptive model.
4.	Essence of th[illegible]ry model is that the unsatisfied needs motiv[illegible] [illegible]dividual to work.	The essence of this gratified or satisfied needs motivate individuals for higher performance.	The essence of model is that the
5.	Effect of [illegible] hygiene factors as motivators of behav[illegible] [illegible]anager offers opportunity to satisfy [illegible] [illegible]hem, employee would exert increased effort.	This model considers factors come into play only when employee perceives them as inadequate.	This model considers that hygiene
6.	Motivators or drive serve as motivator.	Any unsatisfied need serve as motivators.	Only higher order needs
7.	Applicability the human beings working anywhere in the society irrespective of their need level.	It is applicable to all people whose lower-level needs have been satisfied.	It is more applicable to those
8.	Division of needs are divided into primary (lower-level) and secondary (higher-level) and arranged in a hierarchy of five levels.	In this model, needs into hygiene factors and motivators.	In this model needs are divided
9.	Motivators lowest unsatisfied need on the hierarchy motivates employees.	According to this model, correspond roughly to Maslow's higher-level needs, motivate employees or influence their behaviour.	Only motivators, which
10.	Effect of satisfaction of needs	According to this model, once a need is satisfied, must concern it no longer motivates.	According to this model, managers themselves with the satisfaction of employees in order to motivate them.

Prof. Douglas McGregor was a psychologist, management consultant and author. He wrote a book entitled *Human Side of Enterprise.* In this book he described two distinct set of assumptions about people at work. McGregor labelled these set of assumptions as Theory X and Theory Y. He believed that these assumptions influence the thinking and attitude of most managers about the people at work.

Theory X presents a pessimistic or negative view of human nature whereas Theory Y reflects an optimistic or positive view of human behaviour. Both the theories and their assumptions are described in the ensuing paragraphs.

Theory X lists a set of assumptions which presents a pessimistic view of human nature. The assumptions of Theory X are as follows:

1. The average human being inherently dislike work and will avoid work, if possible.
2. Since human beings dislike work, they must be coerced, controlled or threatened with punishment to make efforts to achieve objectives.
3. The average human being prefers *to* be directed.
4. The average human being wishes to avoid responsibility.
5. The average human being has relatively little ambition.
6. The average human being wants security above all other factors associated with the work.
7. The average human being is inherently self-centered and indifferent to organisational objectives.
8. The average human being by nature, resists change.
9. The average human being is gullible, not very bright. He may be duped by charlatans.

Theory Y views human beings in optimistic or positive terms. The assumptions of this theory are as follows :

1. The average human being does not inherently dislike work. Employees find that work is as natural as play or rest if organisational conditions are appropriate.
2. Employees will exercise self-direction and self-control if they are committed to objectives. External control and the

threat of punishment are not the only means to make employees to work towards objectives.

3. Commitment to objectives, is a function of the rewards associated with their achievement.
4. The average human being can be motivated by higher-level needs *i.e.* esteem and self-actualisation needs.
5. The average human being learns not only to accept but to seek responsibility. Avoidance of responsibility, lack of ambition and emphasis on security are generally not inherent human characteristics.
6. The average human being seeks responsibility because it allows him to satisfy higher-level needs.
7. The capacity to exercise imagination and creativity in the solution of problems is widely spreaded throughout the population. It is not the sole province of the managers.
8. Under the conditions of modern industrial life, the intellectual potentialities of the average human being are only partially utilised.

Theory Y suggests or contributes the following thoughts :

(i) Management is responsible for organising the resources of the enterprise for achieving organisational objectives.

(ii) Employees are not lazy or passive or resistant to organisational objectives.

(iii) Work is natural to employees if managers can release and channelise the employees' potential.

(iv) Employees can exercise self-direction and self-control if they are committed to objectives.

(v) Employees commitment to objectives can be ensured if the rewards are associated with the achievement of objectives.

McGregor believed that a manager's view about the employees affect the behaviour or motivation of the employees. If a manager treats employees lazy and irresponsible, the employees will behave accordingly. Conversely, if a manager treats his employees as mature and responsible, they would respond accordingly. Thus, if employees are treated in a Theory X manner, they will become lazy. If they are treated in accordance with Theory Y, they will be motivated and committed to the organisational objectives.

Theory X assumes that lower-order needs dominate individuals. Theory Y assumes that higher-order needs dominate individuals. McGregor believed that Theory Y assumptions were more valid than Theory X. Therefore, he proposed such ideas as participation in decision-making, responsible and challenging jobs and good group relations for maximising employee job motivation.

Though McGregor's motivation theory has its significance, but it is criticised on the following grounds :

1. It tends to over-generalise or over-simplify behaviour of human beings. It is not easy and possible to classify people in two extreme categories.
2. Almost all the employees do not become good or bad because of the views that a manager has about them.
3. McGregor suggests that the job itself is a motivator but it is not so in all the cases. Jobs alone cannot motivate equally to all the persons.

The distinctions between Theory X and Theory Y are as follows:

Basis of Distinction	*Theory X*	*Theory Y*
1	2	3
1. Views about the human behaviour	It represents a negative or pessimistic view of human behaviour.	It represents a positive or optimistic view of human behaviour.
2. Liking for work	This theory assumes that people dislike work and will try to avoid work, if possible.	This theory assumes that people regard work as natural as play or rest.
3. Direction	It also assumes that people seek direction from superior.	It assumes that people will exercise self-direction and self-control if they are committed to the objectives.
4. Responsibility	It assumes that people avoid responsibility.	It assumes that people seek and accept responsibility.
5. Creativity and change	It assumes that people lack creativity and resist change.	It assumes that people are creative by nature and ready to accept change.

Contd...

Basis of Distinction	*Theory X*	*Theory Y*
1	2	3
6. Focus on needs	It focuses on lower-level needs *i.e.* physiological and safety needs.	It focuses on higher-level needs *i.e.* social esteem and self-actualisation needs.
7. Style of leadership	It represents autocratic leadership.	It represents democratic leadership.
8. Role of incentives	It emphasises the role of financial incentive in motivation.	It emphasises the role of non-financial incentives in motivation.
9. Role of job factors or job	It assumes key role of job factors in motivation.	It assumes key role of job itself in motivation.
10. Nature	It is a traditional theory of motivation.	It is a modern theory of motivation.
11. Applicability	It is more applicable to illiterate or unskilled and lower-level employees.	It is more applicable to skilled employees occupying higher positions.

William Ouchi wrote a book entitled, *"Theory Z : How American Business can Meet the Japanese Challenge"*. In this book, he described management practices in a number of U.S. Companies that are similar to those that successful Japanese companies have been utilising for years. Ouchi identified IBM, Hewlett-Packard, Intel, P & G, Eastman Kodak as Theory Z organisations.

According to Mondy *et al,* "Theory Z is the belief that a high degree of mutual responsibility, loyalty and consideration between companies and their employees will result in higher productivity and improved employee welfare."

According to Weihrich and Koontz, "Theory Z refers to selected Japanese managerial practices adapted to the environment of the United States as suggested by William Ouchi. For example, one of the characteristics of Type Z organisations is the emphasis on interpersonal skills needed for group decision-making."

Theory Z is a hybrid management system which incorporates the strengths of Japanese and American management. It describes characteristics common to certain successful Japanese and

American Companies. The distinguishing features of Theory Z are as follows :

> Theory Z suggests strong bond between organisation and its employees. Ouchi has suggested certain ways for this, including the life-time employment and avoiding retrenchment and lay-off. Moreover, financial and non-financial incentives should be offered to motivate employees. Theory Z also emphasises that as against vertical promotions of employees, more emphasis should be placed on horizontal promotions. Such promotions/movements will reduce stagnation. A career plan for each employee should be prepared so that every one reaches to the right position in the organisation.

Theory Z suggests that employee participation should be ensured in decision-making. Employees should be consulted and their suggestions should be considered while making decisions. However, the decisions affecting employees' interest directly should be made jointly. This will increase their commitment to the implementation of the decisions.

Theory Z suggests no formal organisation structure. There should not be charts, divisions, or any visible structure. It emphasises on perfect team-work with cooperation along with sharing of information, resources and plans. Members of organisation should work as a team and solve all the problems with no formal reporting relationships. There should be minimum of specialisation of positions and of tasks.

Theory Z recommends that managers should develop new skills among the employees. Managers should, therefore, recognise the potentials of their subordinates. They develop their potentials through proper career planning, training and incentives. Managers can also use job enrichment and job enlargement techniques for developing their subordinates.

Theory Z also suggests that managers should pay more attention to informal control procedures. Managers should lay more emphasis on mutual trust and cooperation rather than on formal authority in ensuring control. In other words, managers should control through informal mechanisms.

Theory Z requires that there must be climate of mutual trust and confidence between the employees, the managers and the unions. According to Ouchi, trust, integrity and openness are closely related. All these are the prerequisites of a sound organisation. Trust grows where the openness of minds and relationships exists.

Theory Z suggests that more emphasis should be given to evaluation and training than to promotion. The employees should be evaluated over a fairly long period using both quantitative and qualitative measures. This will increase commitment of employees to the organisation.

Theory Z requires that responsibility should be assigned on an individual basis. Individuals should assume responsibility for decisions. However, employees should be allowed to share or participate in decision-making.

Theory Z suggests that there should be non-specialised career paths. The career paths should involve multiple function experience. For this emphasis should be laid on job rotation and broad-based training. This, in turn, gives an employee a better feel for the entire organisation.

Theory Z suggests that there should be holistic concern for people. Such holistic concern should extend beyond the work-place and reflect genuine concern for the total employee personality including the employee's family, hobbies, personal ambition and so on.

Thus, theory Z provides a new dimension of motivation of employees. It is not merely a motivational technique but it provides a complete theory of management. It calls for mutual trust and cooperation between managers and workers.

Theory Z has been successfully employed by the Japanese companies operating in U.S.A. The process of implementing Theory Z in India has already been started.

Maruti Udyog Ltd., a company with Japanese collaboration, is one such company where theory Z is being applied. For this purpose, work-place has been designed on the Japanese pattern. A common canteen has been provided for all the employees irrespective of their position in the company. Similar uniform has been introduced for all. All this has been done to avoid class or group feelings among the employees and to remove status difference among the employees.

Theory Z is considered a comprehensive theory or philosophy of management. It involves a complex amalgamation of management principles and practices for obtaining cooperation of the employees. It provides a complete transformation of motivational aspect of employees. But it suffers from the following limitations of drawbacks.

The provision for life-time employment seems to be difficult for *two* reasons :

(i) No employer would like to retain an employee who is less productive.

(ii) No employee will hesitate to an organisation if there is a better chance of employment.

Theory Z emphasises on common culture in organisations which is very difficult. People come from different backgrounds and environments and with different religion, habits, languages etc. All these create barriers in developing common culture.

Participation in decision-making process is also very difficult. Some managers dislike the idea because it hurts their ego and freedom. In some cases, employees are also reluctant to participate actively in decision-making process because of the fear of criticism. Sometimes, employees are not capable to participate in decision-making. Consequently, participation of employees in decision-making becomes difficult.

There may be operational problems to managers in implementing theory Z. For instance, theory Z emphasises organisation without formal structure. But it is difficult to run an organisation without a formal structure. In the absence of formal structure, there may chaos in the organisation because no one knows who is accountable to whom.

Theory Z is based on the Japanese management practices which are influenced by the Japanese culture. But each country differs in its culture. Therefore, the same management practices cannot be applied to each country.

This theory does not suggest the total solution to motivational problems. It provides a complete philosophy of management.

In spite of all these criticisms, theory Z is becoming popular among many managers and organisations.

Motivation may be classified in the following categories :

> Positive motivation is the process of influencing others to do work or to behave in accordance with the desire of the leader through the use of reward. Thus, positive motivation is based on reward or gain either monetary or non-monetary.' The methods of positive motivation include pay, fringe benefits, praise, responsibility, participation in decision-making, social recognition and so on. Positive motivation creates congenial and optimistic work environment in the organisation. It inculcates sense of belongingness among the employees.

Negative motivation is the process of controlling negative behaviour/efforts of employees through fear and punishment. Thus, negative motivation is based on fear of force or threats. When employees fail to perform desired work or fail to behave in the desired manner, they are threatened or forced not to do so. Such threats or forces include wage cuts, retrenchment, demotion, transfer, reprimands and so on. Experts are of the opinion that as far as possible, negative motivation techniques should not be used. It is due to the reason that in the long-run, negative motivation may result in lower productivity. It creates frustration and hostility among the employees.

Extrinsic or external motivation is one which arises from external factors. It is related to job environment. It is the incentive or reward that a person receives after finishing his work. It includes higher wages, profit-sharing, fringe benefits and so on.

Intrinsic or internal motivation is that which comes from the satisfaction that arises while performing a job. It is an internal reward *i.e.* satisfaction that comes while a person is performing his job. Thus, it is a motivation that arises out of a job itself. It is an internal stimulus resulting from job content and not from job environment.

Herzberg suggested for job enrichment in order to provide intrinsic motivation. Higher responsibility, opportunity for achievement and individual growth, praise social recognition, are the basic sources of intrinsic motivation.

Intrinsic motivators motivate some people more than extrinsic motivators. But in reality both are necessary. If wages, job security, fringe benefits are inadequate, it would be difficult to recruit and retain good personnel. Turnover, absenteeism and grievances will tend to be higher where management ignores extrinsic motivators. Therefore, a sound motivation system should provide both extrinsic and intrinsic; motivators.

Financial motivation is the pecuniary motivation and occurs from direct or indirect monetary benefits. Wages, fringe benefits etc. are the direct monetary benefits. Bonus, profit-sharing plans, pension plans, health insurance plans etc. are the indirect financial benefits.

Non-financial motivation is one which is not associated with monetary rewards. In fact, non-financial motivation is psychic in nature. It comes from the satisfaction of higher-level needs *i.e.* social, esteem and self-actualisation needs. Work environment, praise, recognition, promotions, more authority and responsibility etc. are the non-financial motivators. Financial and non-financial incentives are being discussed in detail in the ensuing paragraphs.

Managers use variety of techniques for motivating employees. Such techniques may be broadly classified under the following two heads :

I. Financial or monetary techniques.

II. Non-financial or non-monetary techniques.

Financial techniques of motivation are those which involve financial expenditure for an organisation and increase money income of its employees. These include (a) pay, (b) dearness and other allowances, (c) bonus, (d) profit-sharing, and (e) fringe benefits and so on.

Fringe benefits are the benefits over and above regular pay and variable payment related to performance. Fringe benefits is, thus, a wider term includes housing, transport, recreation facilities, lunch, clothing and washing allowance or facilities, payment for holidays and leave-travel benefits, free medical services or mediclaim insurance, disability benefits, retirement benefits including pension and gratuity and so on. Thus, financial techniques are the financial incentives that provide pecuniary or monetary benefits or rewards to employees.

Monetary techniques are, thus, pecuniary benefits or rewards to the employees. These are tangible and visible incentives. These incentives can satisfy the physiological and safety and security needs of employees. These also play crucial role in satisfying the social and esteem needs of the employees. Money recognised a symbol of social status and source of power in the modern times. William F. Whyte has, therefore, very candidly stated that "man has not born loving money. He has *to* learn to love it. This learning takes place in varying degrees in various parts of the world." Thus, financial techniques beyond doubt serve most powerful role in motivating employees.

Non-financial techniques of motivation are those which are not associated with financial rewards. Such techniques are mainly psychic in nature. These are associated with the work and work environment. Such techniques contribute to the satisfaction of higher-level needs such as social, esteem and self-actualisation needs. Some of the non-financial techniques of motivation are as follows:

> Job enlargement is one of the modern techniques of motivation. Job enlargement means enlarging or adding more and different but simple tasks to a specialised job. Thus, it increases the number and variety of tasks a worker should do. Consequently, employees are encouraged to learn new skills or take new responsibility. This presumably reduces monotony and boredom and increases satisfaction and motivation of employees. This technique is also called the horizontal job loading.

Job enrichment is another technique of motivation. It is a technique of vertical job loading. It is a technique which focuses on job depth. Job enrichment refers to the basic changes in the content and level of authority and responsibility of a job so as to provide greater challenge to the employees. It is the process of adding several positive inducement and attractions in a job with a view to make the job more interesting, meaningful and challenging. The job-holder is vested with more authority and autonomy for making decisions on operational matters of his job. Thus, it permits self-direction and self-control which, in turn, motivates employees.

According to Herzberg job enrichment is a process of building motivators into jobs. He believed that motivators lead to job satisfaction which, in turn, leads to higher performance. Therefore, Herzberg strongly advocated job enrichment as the most important technique to improve motivation and performance of employees.

It may be pointed out that both job enlargement and job enrichment are the job redesign techniques. But job enlargement is the horizontal job-loading whereas job enrichment is vertical job-loading. Former technique assigns new and more tasks to employees whereas latter grants additional authority, autonomy and control to the employees.

Job rotation is also regarded as a motivation technique. It is a technique in which employees are provided an opportunity to perform different jobs or functions by rotation. The purpose of job rotation is to broaden the scope of job and to increase the knowledge and skill of the employees about the job. This, in turn, relieves employees from boredom and monotony and improves their motivation level.

Praise appreciation and recognition are the most effective and direct means of motivation. These techniques acknowledge the performances of employees to the society. These satisfy the social and esteem needs of the employees. For instance, a pat on the back of an efficient employee brings more happiness to him than the increase in the pay. Managers, therefore, give away prizes, certificates, plaques, letter of appreciation, etc. to the employees performing the best.

Employee participation in management is yet another technique of motivation. Employee participation means involvement of non-managerial personnel in the organisational and managerial activities, such a practice can ensure commitment of employees towards accomplishment of organisational goals. Consequently, employees feel involved in the organisation and their level of motivation improves. Employee participation may brought about by information sharing, suggestion system, consultation, representation on committees, board of directors and so on.

Competition or contests are means of motivation among employees. People usually like to compete with others and win over them. Therefore, managers may arrange competitions or contests for the employees. Managers fix certain goals or standards of performance for employees and challenge them to achieve them ahead of others. The winners are awarded prizes, given certificates of performance or appreciation letters with or without financial rewards. The winner gains recognition for his performance and social status and prestige. This all satisfies his social and esteem needs.

Promotion to a higher post or increase in the status of a person improves his motivation level. Promotion may not always result in more pay or financial rewards but increases social status of the employees. This satisfies his social and esteem or ego needs. Therefore, managers take various measures to increase status of their subordinates. These include, bigger air conditioned chamber with superior furniture and fixtures, personal assistant, cellular phone, computer, lap-top computer, air travel facility and so on.

Delegation of authority to execute a given task often proves to be a strong motivating force. This enables subordinates to have effective control over the work and its environment. Job enrichment also involves delegation of authority.

Employees are motivated to work better if they have a feeling of accomplishment. This feeling can be inculcated by providing more authority, autonomy, applying the MBO technique, better career planning and development and so on.

Security of job-In the modern age, there are threats of loss of job from technological change. By providing security of job, employees may be motivated to work hard.

Employees may also be motivated by creating congenial social environment. For this, managers can carefully plan and execute induction programmes, provide means to socialise employees through rest pauses and recreation programmes, promote the informal relations among the employees. These measures can go a long way in satisfying social and ego needs of employees.

Opportunity for advancement can serve as a strong motivating force. This helps to develop their personality and talent. Such opportunity satisfies social ego and self-actualisation needs.

A quality circle is a group of employees of a work unit who meet frequently with their superior to identify and solve work related problems of their unit. This circle provides an opportunity to express opinions or suggestions in a frank, free and informal setting about the matters relating to product quality, cost and productivity of resources. Such circles, therefore, serve as a means to satisfy employees needs for interaction and self- expression. Hence, such circles are regarded as a means of motivation to employees.

Work climate refers to the physical environment of the work-place. It is the basis of employee motivation. Creation and maintenance of sound work climate is a prerequisite for sound motivation system. Therefore, the factory layout, surroundings, facilities such toilets, canteen, rest-rooms etc. should be properly planned and maintained in order to motivate employees.

There is not exhaustive list of non-financial techniques of motivation. There are many more techniques. A manager should use any or all the techniques keeping in view the needs of the employees and the prevailing circumstances.

According to Koontz and O'Donnel, "A sound motivation system must be productive, competitive, comprehensive and flexible." In fact, a sound motivation system should have the following essentials:

> A motivation system should be purposive. Therefore, motivation system should clearly state its objectives. It must reflect the objectives and philosophy of the organisation.

A motivation system should aim at increasing productivity of the organisational resources. It should be able to increase efficiency and effectiveness of all employees and other resources as well.

As far as possible, a motivation system should be positive- It should adopt a positive approach towards employees. It must aim influencing behaviour and actions of employees through rewards and satisfaction of needs.

Motivation system should be simple to understand by employees. Moreover, it should be simple to implement for the managers. A complex system can never produce the desired results.

A motivation system should be challenging. It should set challenging but attainable goals before the employees.

A motivation system should be competitive for the employees as well as for the organisation. It should be able to create competitive spirit among the employees. Moreover, it must be able to compete with other organisations. In other words, it should be better and more attractive to the employees than that of the competitive organisations. It must be capable of attracting employees of competitive organisations.

A motivation system should consider all the needs of all the employees in the organisation. It should recognise and consider individual nature, perceptions, values, needs and abilities. It should be capable of motivating efficient as well as inefficient employees.

A motivation system should be flexible and dynamic. It should be capable of being adapted to changing needs of the employees and environmental situations as well.

Motivation system should be reasonably stable and permanent. It should be a permanent feature of an organisation. *Ad hoc* motivation system cannot motivate employees on a continuing basis.

A motivation system should be equitable to all the employees. It Should be free from biases to any individual or group of individuals.

There should be direct and positive linkages between performance and reward in the motivation system. The linkages between the two should be clearly made known to the employees.

A motivation system should always integrate organisational goals with individual goals. It should contribute to the achievement of organisational goals along with the individual goals.

There should be a perfect blending or combination of financial and non-financial incentives. This will help in satisfying the lower-level as well as higher-level needs of the employees.

A sound motivation system should be positive but it must contain a provision for punishment too. It must provide for penalty for persistent unacceptable performance and behaviour of the employees.

There should be adequate and effective mechanism for feedback on the application of motivation system. Employees should be periodically informed about their performance and rewards.

2

Salient Features

In the last century, the first fifty years made tourism a major worldwide industry. The emergence of the middle class in Europe along with the technological, political and social events of the day gave a great thrust to tourism. A large number of people were moving out both for leisure and business purposes. This period saw the mass movement of people annually from their home location to another country for a temporary stay for a few days or a week This mass movement of tourists was, however, predominant between Europe and America as the conditions of travel between the two continents were perfect. A fairly good infrastructure was already in existence. The necessary elements for travel like time, money and motivation were present. In addition to international movements there was also growth in domestic tourism. The invention of the motor car in Europe and USA, as also technological advancements in rail transport together with construction of networks of highways, gave a boost to domestic tourism.

Although the annual migration of people began rather more than a century ago, the present-day exodus especially in relation to international tourists is essentially a post-World War II phenomenon. The period between the two world wars can also be associated with the great movement of people for the purposes of tourism as a result of development of various modes of transport, especially the motor car and the aeroplane. The encouraging trend, however, received a setback as the Second World War intervened.

Tourism is sensitive to world economic and political conditions. It can occur on a large scale where the great majority of people enjoy some prosperity and security. Tourism and holidaymaking, on global as well as national scale, is a manifestation of prosperity and peace. As a great number of people in many countries have higher living standards, they can afford to set aside a proportion of their incomes for holidays and recreation.

Air travel blossomed during the post-World War II period resulting in rapid development of tourism. As the world began to settle down after the years of readjustments immediately after the War in 1945, there had been a rapid increase in both domestic and international tourism. The United Nations reported that in the ten-year period between 1955 and 1965, the number of tourist arrivals in some sixty-five countries increased three times from around 51 million to over 157 million. This, however, was only a beginning.

In the 1960s, USA, Germany, UK, France, Canada, Belgium, Luxembourg, The Netherlands, Italy, Switzerland, Sweden, Denmark and Austria represented the twelve main tourist-generating countries. These twelve countries accounted for some three quarters of all international tourist arrivals in the world. The first two—USA and Germany—accounted for more than one-third of the world tourist arrivals. The reasons for this are very clear. These were the countries which enjoyed prosperity and higher standards of living, the two main factors conducive to growth of tourism. The development in the means of speedy transport and communication was also witnessed in these countries more significantly. This rapid increase in tourism in the above countries was therefore the outcome of such factors as prosperity and higher standards of living leading to increased leisure, improved education and, above all, the rapid strides they made in speedy transport and communication.

The trend in the growth of international tourism continues since the mid-1960s. The growth continues to be determined by the living standards in the developed countries. The widespread introduction of holidays with pay to a large majority of people is yet another important factor responsible for growth of tourist traffic.

In 1976, there were nearly 220 million international tourist arrivals in the world. This is an increase of more than 90 per cent over 1965. During 1965-1976, which was a period of intensive economic development in most industrialized countries, international tourism grew at an average rate of over 7 per cent annually. During this period, most of the developing countries were also able to benefit from the growing trend in the developed countries to consume tourist products. As mentioned elsewhere, tourism and its development are closely related to consumers' purchasing power and, in turn, to any domestic or international economic fluctuations. In the year 1974, the world economy was seriously affected by the energy crisis which occurred at the end of 1973. As a result, there was inflation which was responsible for the lower purchasing power. Tourism, like all other sectors of production and consumption, suffered the economic consequences of that crisis. The total international tourist arrivals in 1974 dropped by over two per cent in relation to 1973.

In the year 1975, as a result of efforts made by the governments of industrialised and developing countries to keep inflation within acceptable limits, there was resumption of production and consumption in the main generating countries. As a consequence, there was likewise a resumption of international travel. The total international tourist arrivals in 1975 amounted to roughly 213 million. The total number of international tourist arrivals in 1976 was estimated at between 218 and 222 million, which is a rise of between 2 and 4 per cent over 1975. According to the most recent estimates produced by the Secretariat General, World Tourism Organization, international tourist arrivals in 1999 were estimated to total 700 million, an increase of many folds over 1978.

Europe and North America continue to be the principal generating as well as receiving areas for international tourism, accounting for 70 per cent and 20 per cent respectively, of the international tourist arrivals. There is continuous trend of increase in international tourist arrivals in these areas since the year 1965.

It may be stressed here that intra-regional tourism— tourism between countries of the same region—has an appreciable influence on the distribution of world arrivals. Thus, while domestic tourist movements tend to increase more and more, holidaymakers and tourists tend at the same time to travel farther from their usual place of residence, first in their own region and afterwards beyond it. Of the total international tourist movements within Europe and North America, at least 74 per cent are intra-regional. For Africa, it may be estimated that nearly 40 per cent of the tourist flows are intra-regional.

In Americas, the United States and Canada alone account for nearly 50 per cent of all international tourist traffic in the region, where intra-regional international tourist movements are therefore predominant. In South Asia, intra-regional tourist movements may be estimated at between 20 and 30 per cent of the total tourist traffic in the region. In Europe, intra-regional tourism accounts for over 73 per cent of international tourist movements. However, a glance at the figures would indicate that most of the destinations are the same which were prominent in the year 1961. There is nevertheless a significant change in the number of arrivals in each of the destination. For instance, in 1961, France had generated 10.0 million tourists. This has been increased to almost 72 million in the year 1999. The big surprise, however, is China which received 27 million tourists in 1999.

The values are based upon preliminary data estimated for the full year supplied to World Tourism Organization (WTO) secretariat by the tourism authorities of the countries and territories concerned. Most countries and territories do not have the figures available for the whole year. However, experiences from the earlier years have shown that projections tend to be somewhat conservative. This implies that total figures might increase slightly when final figures are computed.

The most significant expansion of tourism has taken place primarily in the advanced industrialized countries, where tourism has become a part of life-style and consumption pattern of most people. Europe and Americas together account for almost 78 per cent of the total international tourist arrivals. The remaining

22 per cent is shared between East Asia/Pacific, Africa, Middle East and South Asia. South Asia's share is just one per cent of the total.

Fast Growth

The basic causes of this rapid growth of demand for tourism in the highly developed industrialized countries in the course of the recent decades are economic, social and technological in nature. Rising per-capita incomes leading to higher purchasing power and an increase in discretionary incomes have made tourism accessible to a large majority of people. Today in advanced countries, a large majority of people can afford an annual holiday. In fact, many can even afford to take 'second holiday' of longer or shorter duration. In the case of more affluent members of the society, establishment of what may be called "recreation homes", e.g., seaside flatlets, country cottages, caravans, cruising boats, etc., have become a fashion and a status symbol. Secondly, more and diverse types of holiday and recreation are becoming popular. For example, in addition to comparatively recent developments such as holiday camps, caravans and coach tour, there are even newer fashions such as yachting, trail riding, safari and archaeological holiday. Increased mobility as a result of use of motor car for travel is another important economic factor which is responsible for growth in tourism in Europe and North America. Ownership of private motor cars in these areas grew tremendously resulting in more travel, including travel for the purpose of tourism.

Societal Factors

The social causes of the rapid growth of tourism are linked with new attitudes towards travel and leisure. Traditionally considered a luxury, both are now held to be a normal, virtually indispensable part of the life-style and consumption pattern of all but the lowest income groups of the population. The entire concept of pleasure travel has changed quite drastically. Foreign travel in the pre-War days was reserved for the more affluent and leisured who enjoyed travel for its own sake and who were content to enjoy scenery and works of arts and theatres in foreign places. This concept has now changed with change in attitudes towards travel.

The present day tourist has a different kinds of background, and his ideas about travel are very different. He comes from a wider social mileu and his tastes and desires are much more varied. His leisure time is much more restricted and, accordingly, he desires to pack into it as much as possible. 'Democratisation' of leisure pursuits is yet another factor of growth in tourist traffic. Winter sports, for example, were an activity almost exclusively confined to wealthier members of the society until recently. Some of the other exclusive pursuits such as riding, boating, yachting, surf-riding, shooting, etc., are now available to an ordinary man who is interested in these. A large number of people are now going abroad to participate in more exciting and exotic activities like mountaineering, water skiing, trekking, underwater swimming and the like.

Technological Factors

The impact of modern transport technology, especially in the field of aviation, has brought about a completely new meaning to tourism. Travel to even remote destinations has now become a reality. During the last twenty years there has been a remarkable increase in the number of long-distance journeys undertaken by tourists. The technological developments in transport have made it possible for millions of people to travel to faraway places, places which only a few generations ago were regarded as being almost entirely inaccessible. Today holidaymakers can be transported a thousand miles or more in a matter of few hours. The gradual evolution of the originally homogeneous air-travel market into two separate and distinct segments—charters and schedule air travel—has greatly increased the demand.

The newer marketing methods like 'package tour' is a major contributing factor to the growth of tourism. By preparing organised holiday trips complete with all arrangements like transport, accommodation, sight-seeing tours, etc., and selling these on a large scale to the public, the average price per tour has been significantly reduced. This price is much below the price of the trip arranged individually. Opening up of new travel destinations, particularly in developing countries, creation of new facilities to receive larger flow of tourists, and increasing tourism promotion efforts by tourist-service enterprises and by official tourist organizations have increased the tourist flows. The participation of a large number of people in tourism activities, as seen in highly developed industrialised countries, is essentially a manifestation of prosperity. As great number of people in these countries enjoy higher living standards and can afford to set aside a proportion of incomes for holidays.

International tourism has now become one of the leading items of international trade and exceeds many other commodities including wheat, automobiles and machine tools. Tourism's importance was exemplified in the sponsorship by the United Nations of the Conference on International Travel and Tourism held in Rome in August-September, 1963. At this conference, which was attended by over 500 persons from some 84 countries, world attention was focussed on international travel and tourism "as economic and social force ot major proportions in the world". Many countries realized the benefits of tourism.

The most significant advantage which tourism has for many countries, more especially the developing countries, is the lure of foreign exchange. Most developing countries suffer from a more or less acute shortage of foreign currency. As a result, they have difficulties in obtaining the goods and services necessary for development. For a significant number of developing countries, international tourism has become a major and, in many instances, the largest source of foreign-exchange earnings. This has resulted in increased attention of these countries in the development of tourism. Presently in the developing world, over one hundred countries are getting increasingly interested in tourism. Some of these countries are calling upon international consulting firms to prepare their tourism development plans, asking the World Bank group to grant loans to finance tourism projects and also putting in requests to United Nations Development Programme to finance technical assistance projects for tourism.

Almost all developing countries set aside substantial financial allocations every year for the development and promotion of tourism. The dynamic efforts made by certain countries, especially the developing countries, both to build and strengthen the basic infrastructure and accommodation and to promote their products, have led to an intensification of tourist flows to those countries. Even the countries of Eastern Europe that were only a few years ago virtually closed societies have thrown open their doors to a large number of visitors in a bid to win a fair share of foreign exchange. The lure of foreign exchange has made China open its door to a large number of visitors. Though China was always a closed society, the country is now receiving a large number of foreign tourists from many countries of the world. Hoping to enlarge currency reserves with a large slice of tourist trade, the authorities have made travel in China more liberal and at the same time comfortable by building several new hotels, modernising airports and providing new accommodation at different tourist sites.

3

Progress and Growth

These are so many variables of marketing mix. Promotion is the most important and visible of the variables. Promotion is the mix of various communication activities which tourist firms or national tourist organisations carry out with a view to motivate or influence those target customers on whom their product sale depends. It is however, not only the target customers who need to be influenced by the various promotional techniques, there is the need to influence intermediaries like retail agents and suppliers as well as opinion leaders like journalists, travel writers etc. However, the primary target for promotion is the target markets, group of current and potential customers.

As applied to service industry like tourism, the most important function of marketing is to bring about an awareness of the product and its benefits in the minds of both current as well as potential customers. The message about the product must, however, reach the customer through a variety of channels. All this activity form a part of overall marketing communication. Systematic communication both with the actual as well as potential customers as also with trade intermediaries and opinion leaders is very essential with a view to bridging the gap between the producer of services on the one hand and the customer on the other.

Communication is therefore necessary like in any other industry, successful marketing in tourism cannot rely on a product of the right kind or a market related pricing policy or reliable and effective distribution network alone.

The primary role of the promotion thus is to convince the potential customers of the various advantages of buying or using the products and services of a particular enterprise, organisation or a firm. Coulson-Thomas in the year 1986 has defined the concept as : "The role of promotion is to communicate with individuals, groups or organisations so as to directly or indirectly facilitate exchanges by informing and persuading one or more of the audience to accept an organisation's products." Basically, the term promotion is interpreted to refer to informing, persuading, encouraging or more specifically influencing the potential customers and trade intermediaries like travel agents, tour operators, reservation services, hotel and charter brokers, about the benefits of the product. In other words promotion is creating awareness among the potential customers about the product. The question now arises as to how this awareness is to be brought about in the minds of consumers and intermediaries. Tourist enterprises use different methods of communication to achieve their objectives. However, there are certain identifiable methods which are being used by almost all the marketing organisations. Broadly these are:

(i) Advertising;

(ii) Press or public relations;

(iii) Sales promotions;

(iv) Publicity.

Different Methods

Advertising : Advertising is a paid form of non-personal communication about an organisation's product or service communicated through a message. The sales message is delivered through a paid medium for the purpose of influencing the buying behaviour of the purchasers. The term may be defined as "any activity designed to spread information with a view to promoting the sales of marketable goods and services." As such, it operates in two ways: firstly, by spreading information among consumers, about the possibilities of consumption, and secondly, by seeking to influence their judgement in favour of the particular goods which are the subject of the advertisement. Use of certain paid media space is, however, a prerequisite. It can also be defined as a "paid public message designed to describe or praise a product." Unless a communication has as its purpose a sale of a product or service, it is not properly considered to be advertising. For example, the publication of a message in a newspaper by a philanthropic organisation soliciting funds is not an advertising activity. It is only a public announcement as there is no sale of a product involved.

The Backdrop : The original advertisements, perhaps, were announcements written on public walls several thousands of years before the birth of Christ, offering various commodities for sale. As economic forces expanded with the rapid growth of population and the discovery of new worlds; so did the advertising activity prosper. Since the effect of advertising is directly proportionate to the strength of the channel of communication or medium carrying the message to prospective purchasers, it was not until the late seventeenth century that the subject took on any great importance. Printing process from movable type had been in existence, for about 200 years, and primitive newspapers were beginning to flourish.

As the various media were being developed particularly newspapers and magazines, merchants were able to offer their products to larger group of consumers, and expenditures for advertising increased correspondingly. Thereafter, the advances made in the sphere of photography, photo-engraving, and printing served to bring advertising into focus as a major economic force. Finally, the spurt in mass media magazines and newspapers with circulation in several millions, radio broadcasting facilities capable of influencing millions of people simultaneously have raised the business of advertising to a major importance in the world's economy. Added to all this the introduction of television gave a real boost to advertising in recent times.

Aims and Objectives : An advertising objective is a clear and concise description of exactly what the advertising programme is intended to accomplish in a given period of time. Very often the management is not sure exactly why it is spending money and time on advertising without realising what it expects to achieve from this in return. Advertising is an investment and like all investment should produce measurable results. Measuring results vis-a-vis inputs put in terms of investment is, therefore, very important and a crucial aspect which each organisation needs to take care of. The first and the foremost reason for setting advertising objectives is, therefore, to measure the return on one's advertising investment. The second reason is that organisations must seek the most efficient way of marketing the goods and services if they are to remain competitive. There is another important reason for setting objectives. An advertising campaign is the product of the combined work of an entire team of specialists. The team consists not only of top management, marketing, advertising and product managers, but also of agency copyrights, media personnel, art directors, TV producers, etc. It is, therefore, important that all these people are concentrating on a single product and putting their concerted efforts in the same direction. Without written and concise objectives all this would be difficult to achieve. Objectives, therefore, serve the purpose of coordinating, and integrating marketing and advertising efforts.

Professor Robert Buzzell of the Harvard Business School, in a written submission to the Federal Trade Commission during hearings on modern advertising practices in July 1971, gives the following example of possible advertising objectives for a manufacturer's consumer product advertising.

To increase sales directly by:

(i) Encouraging potential purchasers to visit dealers or distributors;

(ii) Announcing special sales, contests or other promotions;

(iii) Securing new dealers or distributors;

(iv) Inducing professional person's e.g. (doctors, architects) to recommend a product;

(v) Distributing coupons to be redeemed on purchases.

To create awareness and interest in the company's product by:

(i) Informing potential buyers about product features;

(ii) Announcing the availability of new products;

(iii) Demonstrating the benefits of a product's use;

(iv) Comparing a product with a competing product;

(v) Showing how a product should be used;

(vi) Informing potential buyers about the company's technical skills, production facilities, technical services, etc;

(vii) Informing purchasers about where products can be obtained;

(viii) Announcing changes in prices, packages, labels, etc.;

(ix) Publicising a new brand name or symbol.

Although the examples given above refer to possible advertising objectives for manufacturers, consumer product advertising, these are also relevant for tourism product advertising. The broad objectives in tourism advertising include making of the tourist product as widely known as possible and to make it attractive for the prospective consumer.

The Advantages : Advertising has several inherent advantages. The most important advantages of this method are :

(i) Wider coverage

(ii) Frequent appeal

(iii) Accessibility

(vi) Lower cost

Wide Coverage : Advertising is especially appropriate for communication with a large number of perspective purchasers of a commodity or a service. A uniform sales message is directed towards all prospective purchasers. An advertisement can be placed before a large number of prospective customers as compared with the efforts of a salesman. *Frequency* is another advantage. It can make its appeal frequently, whereas the calls of salesmen are usually not so frequent. Another advantage is its *accessibility.* It may reach prospects whom salesmen would find difficult to interview, owing to lack of interest or inaccessibility to salesmen. Advertisement may reach such prospects through many types of media and under a variety of circumstances, and may thus attract their attention and arouse their interest. *Lower cost* is another major advantage. Large numbers can be reached economically, i.e., at a lower cost per contact than in any other technique available.

Advertising may be used to do a variety of selling tasks. A great deal of advertising attempts to win acceptance for the product. Such advertising may produce few specific demands for the advertised brands, yet when retailers display or show advertised goods they sell more readily than non-advertised ones. Therefore, retailers often hesitate to handle non-advertised goods unless they are obtainable at low prices. Advertising thus directly stimulates sales to retailers. Advertising may at times be used to make the complete sale. Some direct mail and periodical advertising attempts to make sales by requesting readers to forward orders accompanied by the necessary payment. When the number of potential buyers is small and when they are widely scattered it could be extremely costly to reach them through salesmen. Advertising then becomes the most economic means of doing the entire sales job.

The Planning : Careful consideration must be given to the actual make up of the advertisement while planning. The headline copy, illustrations, colour scheme, size, layout, and method of printing or reproducing the advertisement must be planned very carefully. This is necessary in order to gain attention of the customer, maintain his interest in the message, and secure the action desired by the seller. Closely related is the question of periodicity of advertisement. How frequently to advertise? For instance, is it better to use a full-page advertisement once a month or a quarter-page weekly? A frequently presented thought is likely to force itself into our consciousness. People are inclined to believe statements they hear or see repeatedly and hence the logic of frequent repetition of advertisements. In starting a special campaign the advertisements should not be spaced regularly. Early in the campaign they should be used close together, while later on they can be issued at much longer intervals. This is desirable because consumers forget rapidly at first and much more slowly later on. After the facts are retained by the prospects, the advertisements can be presented at much longer intervals.

Selection of Media : The advertiser should give careful attention in planning to the selection of the medium or media especially adapted to his needs. The selection will depend upon the factors like the area to be covered, the type of audience to be reached, the appeals to be made and upon the services and facilities of the particular medium in relation to costs. The important factors which influence the media selection are:

(i) Media habits of the target audience;

(ii) Product characteristics: for example, TV may be the appropriate media for those products which may require a demonstration of their operation for effective impact on the target audience; and

(iii) Cost of the media.

Message Selection : The massage selected for use in the advertisement should be such that it retains the interest in the minds of the customers about the product. The customer must maintain his interest in the message, and secure the action desired by the seller of the product. The objective is to present the advertiser's message in such a way that the illustration may lead the leader to favourable considerations of the advertisement. The important characteristics of an effective message are:

(i) *Information:* it should be adequate for a decision,

(ii) *Interest:* it should be able to catch the attention of the largest audience,

(iii) *Authenticity:* it should avoid exaggerated claims,

(iv) *Persuasion:* it should be capable of creating a favourable conviction in the target audience, and

(v) *Memory value:* it should have something in it which can help the target audience to remember it.

Cost Effectiveness : The advertiser must relate the estimated cost of the objectives planned and the contribution expected from advertising. Can the advertiser carry on a campaign large enough to make it effective? Are the funds available or will they become available through the sale of the product. How much does the advertiser spend for the advertising? The various methods commonly used are :

(i) *Affordable method:* here, the advertising budget is set on the basis of what the agency can afford;

(ii) *Percentage of sales method:* in this case, the agency sets the advertising budget on the basis of specific percentage of sales;

(iii) *Competitive parity method:* here the agency sets its budget to match those of its major competitors;

(iv) *Objective and task method:* in this the advertising budget represents the outlay required to perform the various tasks which are necessary to achieve the properly defined advertising- objectives of the company. This method is considered the most rational.

Determining Effectiveness : Today advertisement through any media has become -extremely expensive. In view of this it becomes very important for the agency to ensure that the money spent on it does bring returns by way of increased sales. This could be done by way of evaluating or testing the effectiveness of advertising. Testing methods may be used to evaluate the results of an advertising campaign. By evaluating and analysing the effectiveness of advertisements that have been used, future advertisements may be improved. In addition, tests may be applied before advertisement has been run. Pre-testing of an advertisement prevents expenditure that would not be profitable and leads to expenditures that give the best results. In determining advertising effectiveness the commonly used methods are given below:

(i) *Inquiries:* Answer-back coupons, with some inducement, are incorporated in many advertisements. The amount of response is an indication of the effectiveness of the concerned advertisement.

(ii) *Recall tests:* Here the respondents are shown the magazine cover or any other media vehicle in which the concerned advertisement had appeared. They are then asked to tell which advertisements in that publication they remember.

(iii) *Recognition tests:* Here the respondents are shown the advertisement and asked if they have read them.

(iv) *Sales tests:* Here, the actual sales results before and after the concerned advertising are examined. The sales results in the selected 'test markets' are also compared to those in some chosen 'control markets', i.e., the markets where the concerned advertising is not done. This is done to eliminate certain factors, other than advertising, which may also have influenced the sales.

In the field of tourism, advertising is mainly used to create initial awareness and interest in the tourist service or a tourist destination to be promoted and it motivates the potential tourist to make further enquiries about the facilities, cost, bookings etc. As advertising requires careful handling and expertise it is normally handled by an agency which undertakes the job on behalf of an advertiser. A large number of tourist enterprises as also national tourist organisations assign the job of advertising to different advertising agencies.

By Advertisement

An advertising agency may be explained as an organisation consisting of one or more persons, the function of which is to provide advertising; merchandising, and other services and counsel relating to the promotion of a client's goods and services. The advertising agency is a service organisation which undertakes the planning and preparation of advertising. The agency service consists of interpreting to the public, or to that part of it which it is desired to reach, the advantages of a product or service. Originally agencies were media owners, service departments and not independent organisations as they are today, In the early days of advertising, agencies acted as representatives of newspapers and sold space in them to advertisers. At first, the agencies bought space in bulk, and made their profit by selling it in smaller units for as much as they could get. Later, agencies started to sell space on a commission basis, and a commission system is still the current basis for agency remuneration, agencies taking their profit from commissions granted by media owners rather than from advertisers.

The scope of the work of the agencies however expanded further. The agencies started a copy writing service and, soon after, design and art services were added to their functions. By this time agencies were really working more for the advertisers than for the newspaper proprietors and before long they became full-fledged service organisations giving their clients a complete range of advertising services.

The Selection : Selection of a suitable advertising agency is a major factor which determines the success or failure of a promotional work of an organisation. The choice of an advertising agency will depend on the size of a promotional budget, the range of services required and above all the objective assessment of the professional qualities of the agency. Most of the national tourist organisation and major tourist enterprises have appointed their own advertising agencies. The advertising campaigns of these organisations are run through the agencies. The national tourist offices usually hire the services of the specialised advertising agencies in various tourist generating markets to help them in market research, audience information gathering, designing messages and getting advertising schedules in well-selected media.

Scope of Work : Each major advertising agency has various departments whose area of work are well defined. The following are the major departments of an agency and their scope of work.

The Research Department: When the agency staff attempts to define their clients marketing problems they may decide that they lack sufficient information to reach a sound judgement and will take the assistance of the Research Department. A good amount of information is readily available in published form. Before any field research is undertaken there is always desk research which involves checking through existing sources of information. As soon as information collected has been checked, there are further meetings of the 'Plans Board' to consider the advertising and marketing campaign. Once this is done, the individual departments set to work to crystallize their ideas and to produce detailed proposals in accordance with the agreed broad plan.

The Media Department : Once the general strategy is agreed, it is now up to the media department to get down to detailed planning with the aim of spending the client funds in such a way that his advertising message reaches prospective buyers as effectively and economically as possible. The media-department then evaluates the media and selects the most suitable one in the light of clients' requirements.

The Creative Department: The Creative Department takes its work to a more advanced level. Copy is written for press advertisements or printed material and layouts prepared. For posters or display material, roughs and dummies are made and story boards drawn up for TV or cinema commercials.

Review of Proposals : As soon as detailed media and creative proposals are ready, the Plans Board meets again to review the progress of the work. The purpose is to check the proposals point by point to be submitted to the client to ensure that there are no discrepancies in the work of the individual departments.

Presentation of Proposals : Once the detailed proposals have been approved by the review board, they are made ready for presentation to the client. The media schedule is typed out in its final form as is the advertisement copy. The finished versions of designs are prepared by the creative staff. These are then presented to the client. Creative and media proposals are presented together. Where the presentation is on the major campaign, the agency may call on all those concerned to make a 'dry run' beforehand, amounting almost to a rehearsal. Some agencies even put the entire presentation on film or video-tape and screen this to the client rather than risk the possibility of error that is always present in the 'live' presentation.

Execution of the Proposal: Before giving an agency a go ahead' or a formal approval to proceed, the client checks the proposals to ensure that they are sound and that they dovetail with his company's marketing objectives. Once the agency has the client's agreement, the advertising proposals are put into effect.

Sources of Income : An agency's income is derived from media in the form of commissions and from clients in the form of service fees. The proportion of income derived from these two sources varies from agency to agency depending upon the pre-arranged agreement made with the client in any of the following ways:

(a) Receiving commission from media and billing the client for non-commissionable expenses plus a service fee;

(b) Charging the client a minimum fee and rebating all commissions to the client until the point is reached when commissions equal the fee, after which all commissions are retained and the fee is discontinued;

(c) Charging the client a set fee and rebating to him all commissions received, production expenses being billed to the client at cost;

(d) A cost-plus arrangement whereby the agency bills the client for a specified sum to represent the agency's profit, and invoices the client for all media and production expenses at cost.

However, in actual practice the most prevalent form of compensation is the first described above which is commission plus service fee.

Contacting People

In simpler terms, public relations involves measures designed to improve the image of a service, to create a more favourable climate for its advertising and sales support activities. It covers such a wide range of activities and is used for so many different aims that it becomes difficult to define it. Public Relations is the "art and science of planning and implementing honest, two-way communication and understanding between a company or an organisation and the many different groups with which it is concerned in the course of its operation." It is also defined as "continuous and consistent representation of an organisation's policies to the public at large and to sections of the public who have a special interest in the organisation's activities, e.g., to various strata of employees, shareholders, actual and potential customer as well as its local and national governments. Public Relations News, a weekly newsletter written for the PR profession in United States of America, defines PR as "a management function that evaluates public attitudes, identifies the policies and procedures of an individual or an organisation as they affect the public interest, and executes a programme of action, to earn public understanding and acceptance." The internationally accepted definition of PR however is that it is "the deliberate, planned and sustained effort to establish and maintain mutual understanding between an organisation and its public."

From the above definitions of Public Relations it is evident that its main function is to inform public about the activities of an organisation. In other words, it is a part of an organisation's total communication effort. Its purpose is to create best possible reputation for the organisation by way of presenting facts. Implicit in all the above definitions is the function of the professional public relations expert, which is threefold:

(i) To ascertain and evaluate public opinion;

(ii) To counsel management on ways of dealing with public opinion as it exists; and

(iii) To use communications to influence public opinion.

Public Relations is often confused with and used as a handy synonym for some of its functional parts, for instance, press agency, publicity, institutional advertising, propaganda, product promotion, and lobbying. The field with which PR is most closely identified is advertising. However, advertising pays for the print space, air time or electronic space in order to sell a specific product, while on the other hand public relations, which may include some forms of advertising as its tools, covers a much wider and broader range.

Generally, speaking, PR is the overall catchword for all of its functions.

Public Relations in Tourism : Public Relations in the field of tourism assumes special significance because of the peculiar nature of the product. Here the need for making complete information and facts available to both potential and actual tourists assumes special significance. It involves measures designed to create and improve the image for the tourist product, create a more favourable climate for its advertising and sales support activities, especially in regard to travel trade intermediaries and news media. Favourable acceptance of any tourist destination by the public is of utmost importance. In fact, no business is more concerned with human relations than the business of tourism. Public relations in tourism is used to create and maintain a positive image for a country, a tourist destination in the minds of people who are in a position to influence public opinion (journalists, editors, travel writers etc.), or in the minds of sales intermediaries (travel agents, tour operators, etc.). It is oriented towards creating and maintaining an atmosphere whereby travelling public at large is convinced of the advantages of visiting the country concerned.

Public relations is one of the important functions of the official tourist organisation. In fact, tourist organisations primarily are public relations organisations. The objectives of public relations in the field of tourism may be divided into two parts, firstly the dissemination of information, and secondly the creation of a favourable image for the tourist product.

The Techniques : Public Relations make use of several communication techniques. These include:

(i) News and feature stories
(ii) Press releases
(iii) Films and slides
(iv) Booklets and brochures
(v) Photographs, displays and exhibits
(iv) Advertising
(vii) House journals
(viii) Radio and TV scripts
(ix) Newsletters
(x) Stockholder reports

Public relations consist of a number of interrelated activities oriented towards creating and maintaining a favourable positive image for the tourist product. The main tools of public relations used by national tourist organisations in tourist promotion are as follows:

(i) Organising familiarisation tours for travel writers, editors, travel agents, photographers and other key personnel from different parts of the world as guests to visit the country and to get first-hand knowledge about it. These persons then write about the country visited in the well known travel and other general interest magazines.

(ii) Organising radio and television contests featuring the destination country.

(iii) Organising press releases and arranging press conferences with key personnel connected with the tourism field with a view to disseminate information about the destination.

(iv) Arranging seminars and workshops in the place where the tourist promotion office is located.

(v) Organising cultural programmes, musical and folk shows,

TV interviews, exhibitions and national friendship weeks in the country where the national tourist office is located.

(vi) Organising various types of contests about the country.

(vii) Encouraging large departmental stores, organisers of fashion shows and manufacturing companies to project the country or a part of the country as a promotion show case in their premises.

A Professional Public relations approach of a tourism organisation can develop and maintain :

(a) Positive image for a country;

(b) Increased visitor numbers;

(c) Investment in tourist plant;

(d) Interest of intermediaries like tour operators and travel agents.

It can best be achieved through:

(a) Professionally prepared publicity material distributed judiciously to main population markets;

(b) Arranging for key influential media representatives to visit the country on familiarisation tours;

(c) Promoting package holidays and transport services;

(d) Creating major events which will draw attention to the country.

Planning and organisation of public relations should be an integral part of a management strategy and must be conducted on a continuing basis. A public relations function of an organisation cannot be considered as an end in itself or something which can be introduced at a short notice to cope with a crisis situation. An organisation should have a positive and planned public relations policy. It is no coincidence that most of the national tourist organisations devote considerable effort to their public relations programmes.

Handling the public relations function requires the same expertise as handling advertising. The public relations functions of an organisation may be handled independently either by its internal staff members or by outside agencies. A public relations department within a company or organisation may consist of a single person, or a group of persons, depending upon the scope of work as also the size of an organisation. The larger the staff, the more specialised would be the work of each of the staff members. A number of organisations appoint Public Relations agencies outside of their organisation to look after their PR work.

Public Relations Agency : Public Relations agencies generally are retained as either an additional arm of an existing PR department or, if there is no PR department, as the sole PR wing. The agencies are hired either on a early retainer basis or on special projects/ assignments. In the field of tourism, a number of national tourist organisations have been taking the services of PR agencies to take advantage of the market. The tourist destinations have recently become increasingly competitive in the luring of tourists and visitors from various tourist-generating markets. It is a well known fact that all those countries which appear to be attracting the largest number of tourists are succeeding because they market their country's attractions, to the right potential audiences, professionally and systematically as well as positively. Much of their success can be attributed to a direct result of positive and competent PR efforts.

PR agencies play a significant role in assisting a country getting a larger share of tourist traffic provided they do their job properly. The selection of a proper PR agency, therefore, is very crucial. While advertising and other marketing tools increase the number of visitors to a country, the communications equipped to complement advertising, and thus fully realising a country's potential draw, can be accomplished through programmed media activity and with well-launched public relations support programmes. It is here that PR agencies come into the picture. Public relations, properly planned and executed through a public relations agency in a tourist generating market, can present a country in a favourable light and help in the country's efforts to attract more tourists. Public relations also go a long way in positioning a country as a nation whose people welcome tourists, whose hotels and resorts, transportation systems are accommodating and efficient and whose history and culture are fascinating.

Public relations agencies take up specific areas on behalf of their clients and apply public relations efforts to them. These are the basic areas of concentration on which a beginning is made in building an improved image of a country and its tourism environment. Given below in an outline format are specific areas to which public relations efforts are applied by PR agencies in the field of tourism.

Audience (Non-media)

1. Individual consumer travellers.
2. Special interest travellers.
3. The travel trade industry travel agents, in particular.
4. Business travellers.
5. Corporate travel managers.
6. Meeting planners as appropriate.

Media Audience

1. Consumer travel magazines and newsletters.
2. General interest publications (consumer).
3. Consumer newspapers (particularly those which contain travel sections) both metropolitan dailies and suburban weeklies and dailies.
4. Travel trade publications.
5. Broadcast both radio and television when appropriate and on a 'selected' basis.
6. Special interest publications which deal with recreational or sports activities, entertainment, architecture, and the like.

General Activities

1. In-depth discussion of the country's current and future plans, its marketing goals, its research findings, and its specific problems.
2. A review of the country's consumer and trade media placements over the past two years.
3. Coordinating public relations efforts with advertising, sales and marketing personnel.
4. Establishing methods of contact and information getting from all those entities which participate in the country's programmes of tourism.

5. Reporting actions and results on a periodic basis.
6. Writing with style, clarity and command of the country's many dimensions.
7. Determining media needs...apropos tourism to the country.
8. Providing media writers, reporters and editors current data and background information on the country.
9. Providing media with story ideas as well as with finished product news releases and feature stories.
10. Knowing consumer and trade media requirements so that information about the country is timely and presented in an understandable manner.
11. Arranging media interviews with key personnel.
12. Coordinating and advising on visits to the country by media personnel.
13. Assisting with travel agent familiarisation trips.
14. Participating in domestic and foreign trade and association shows, conventions, seminars and the like.
15. Updating and keeping current a country press/ information kit.

Media Activities

Trade Media : Ensure continued and complete exposure in all travel and tourism industry trade publications in the market. Among the many opportunities for editorial coverage:

1. Destination stories and reports (features)
2. Personnel announcements
3. Visiting tourism personnel
4 Inclusions in "business activity" stories and general industry round-ups
5. Reception photographs
6. Policy changes
7. Hotel renovations, redecorations and additions
8. Sales and marketing information
9 General news

Consumer Media Print works toward the placement of feature stories about the country in a variety of consumer publications with particular emphasis on travel and travel-oriented magazines and newspapers. The story ideas are limitless (destinations, resort areas, historical attractions and sites, architecture, beaches, skiing, wildlife preserves, hotels). Sometimes, such stories are agency-written, often, contributions and help can be given to writers and editors.

Electronic Media

More and more radio and television time is now devoted to travel subjects. With the penetration of cable-programming (television), there is now more opportunity to broadcast media placements concerning travel and tourism topics. Therefore, and as appropriate, monitor the broadcast situation and work on placements for the country's positioning.

Special Events

Travel Trade Events Participation : Advise on and assist with all the travel events meetings and conventions, both within and outside the country.

Tie-in Events and Promotions : From time to time, opportunities for charity events, fashion shows, athletic competitions and other events of a one-time nature arise. Sometimes such activities are worthwhile, depending on the publicity value and the business and/ or social importance of these varied possibilities.

Press/Information Kits : A well informative information package, in the traditional press kit form, is imperative for dealing with the media. Such press/ information kits are very often handy for supplying information about the country and its tourism resources to people and organisations outside the media.

Suggested Contents

(a) A good selection of black and white photographs, suitable for newspaper and trade magazine reproduction.

(b) Photographs of top executives.

(c) Two or three feature stories about the country (in press release format).

(d) Hotel and accommodation information (in brochure format or as lists).

(e) Airline information.

(f) Within country transportation information.

(g) Map of the country.

(h) Shopping, climate, currency and other pertinent information.

(i) Some typical giveaways

Sale Promotion

Sales support activities are all those activities and measures which establish personal or indirect contact with customers or trade intermediaries. In the field of tourism, it is considered to be all those promotional activities designed to transmit to the public and to the travel trade specific and detailed information on aspects like transport, accommodation prices, attractions etc. concerning the tourist services to be promoted in the tourist markets. In addition, the sales support is also a process of training employees of an organisation to be sales-minded.

In other words through the process of information dissemination regarding a product the sales team becomes motivated to participate in the product sale. Sales support has certain distinct closely related functions which neither advertising nor public relations can be expected to fulfil effectively. It is a channel of communications between the manufacturer or the 'producer' of a tourist service (accommodation unit, transport company etc.) and the 'distributor' or the 'seller' of that service. Secondly, it aids and assists the seller to do his job more effectively with the support of different techniques. The aim of the sales support activities is:

(a) To inform the customers (tourists-both actual and potential) or trade intermediaries, travel agents, tour operators, airlines, etc.) about the various services available, their price and quality, etc;

(b) To assist them in selling these services to the ultimate users;

(c) To motivate them to devote a sufficient level of sales activity to the service promoted.

Tourist service enterprises, tour operators, and national and regional tourist organisations, recognise fully well that their sales and profit depend to a very large extent on the support and assistance they provide to travel agents and also the way in which they motivate travel agents. This is done by way of sales support activities. In order to be able to sell a service (a room in a hotel, seat in an airline) or a destination to the prospective tourists, travel agents or other sales intermediaries need to be aware of certain factual information which includes:

(i) The country's tourist facilities such as, existing as well as new establishments, accommodation capacities, price schedules for various services.

(ii) Various travel regulations and formalities such as visa regulations including different certificates needed, custom rules, rates of exchange for currency.

(iii) The various transport and communication services available. The schedules of airlines, railways, road transport services, shipping services (where available), their rates.

(iv) Weather conditions at different times of the year, and types of clothing required during different seasons.

(v) The utilisation (occupancy rates) of existing tourist facilities at different times of the year.

(vi) Plans for opening of new destinations, hotels, transport routes (railways, airlines etc.) and also plans for expansion of existing tourist facilities.

Advertising creates a demand in the form of enquiries made by potential tourists, travel agents and other intermediaries. They now require, in addition to the type of information mentioned above, materials such as brochures, folders, booklets, guidebooks, directories, maps and illustrations in order to be able to transform demand into definite bookings. Most of the above material is meant for distribution to potential tourists by the travel agents and other sales intermediaries like tour operators, airlines, etc.; either directly or through mail. Almost all the tourist organisations and tourist service enterprises produce the material extensively and make use of it by way of distributing it to travel agents, tour operators, etc. Tourist sales intermediaries on their own also produce sales support material for distribution to potential tourists.

Sales Support Techniques : Sales support techniques can be grouped into the following two main areas:

(i) Printed material

(ii) Special offers.

Printed material includes brochure, folder, direct mail material, display material etc.

Handbills

The tour operator's brochure is the most vital marketing tool. Since tourism is an intangible product, which cannot be seen or inspected by the customer prior to purchase, the brochure becomes the principal means of both informing them about the product and also persuading them to buy the product. Brochure is a document bound in the form of a booklet. It is a voluminous publication with special emphasis on the quality of paper, the reproduction of illustrations, graphic design of the cover and the layout of the pages. Special emphasis is laid on the quality of the paper and the printing. In view of the quality, the brochure represents a major proportion of a tour operator's marketing budget. Larger companies get their brochure designed and prepared either in their own advertisement departments or in conjunction with the design studio of their advertising agent who negotiates with printers to obtain the best quotations and ensures that print deadlines are met.

The brochure contains a comprehensive and detailed information about a destination including cruises, bus tours, safaris, charter vacations etc., with colour photographs regarding all the destinations which a company is promoting. Detailed information about hotels, weather conditions frontier formalities etc. is also given. The price of various tours is invariably mentioned along with the dates when tours take place. Many established tour operators take great care with production of their brochures. There are, however, no travel industry standards or guidelines for the production of brochures. The following are some important areas which need to be taken care of while getting the tour brochure printed: (i) Quality of paper; (ii) Layout; (iii) Quality of printing; (iv) Photography; (v) Detailed itineraries; (vi) Special features; (vii) Weather conditions; (viii) Maps of areas; (ix) Tour conditions; (x) Tips.

Folder : A folder is a single piece of illustrated paper which can be folded. As compared to the brochures the folder is less voluminous and its production is less time consuming. These are usually printed on a single sheet and then folded ranging from a simple centrefold to more complicated folds. It is, perhaps, the most widely used sales tool by official tourist organisations and by tourist service enterprises. It can be used alone or in conjunction with a 'sales letter'. It is less expensive and can be used in a variety of ways. While producing, special care needs to be taken about the quality of the paper and printing. The folder as compared to the brochure is short, tastefully illustrated and attractively designed and produced.

Shell Folder : Shell folders are blank folders interspersed with pre-printed photographs and are provided free or at a low cost by airlines or national tourist offices to encourage tour operators / travel agents to run programmes using their services or destinations. Tour operators travel agents can overprint a suitable text describing their programmes. Since only the text needs to be added, a one colour print run at low cost meets the requirements of tour operators etc. The use of a shell folder is a convenient way to reduce printing costs and is suitable for limited capacity tour programmes or ad hoc special tours.

Sales Letter : Sales letter is a direct mail material. It is a tool through which an attempt is made to gain agreement or favourable action towards a product. The sales letter offers many opportunities for selling travel services. These could be used alone or in combination with travel brochure or folders. "These are sent out to those people whose addresses have been selected according to the likelihood of their being potential users of the services offered. A proper mailing list is a prerequisite for effective use of this tool. Sales letters require very little time to prepare and to distribute. The effectiveness of a sales letter can be measured very rapidly from the response it draws. This is done by way of a reply card which is included with which the recipient can request further information and also travel literature.

Display Material : Display material includes posters, dispensers for sales literature, cardboard stands, articles of handicrafts, exhibits, etc. This material is used in the agency's office or in the travel agent's sales-rooms. The material is displayed in such a way that it attracts the attention of a visitor as soon as he enters the office. In many cases, cinema slides are also used, either fixed or on an automatic projector for display purposes.

Some Special Offers : Temporary price reductions, free gifts, premiums and various types of contests are being used extensively in competitive industries like cosmetics, packaged foodstuffs, etc. The tourist industry has also started to adopt these techniques as an additional sales support tool. Reduced airfares for students, 'affinity group' special off-season rates at hotels and tourist resorts are the examples of some of the special offers in the tourist industry.

The Newsletters : Newsletter is yet another important promotional medium utilised extensively by tourism organisations. Its main purpose is to get the organisation's message across. A newsletter can be considered to be a major advertising medium. It is a personal reminder to regular clients that a company is still in business. Newsletters are also the best possible instruments for image building. The strength of the newsletters is in the continuity they create. Published monthly, a newsletter maintains a running dialogue with customers. It is also an inexpensive form of media to inform about staff etc. Similar information through newspapers and radio commercials may cost a lot of money.

A newsletter, however, has certain hazards. First, it requires a lot of time. It can also be quite expensive. With constant increases in postal tariffs and production costs, even a simple newsletter with minimal artwork and illustrations costs quite a lot. Besides, a newsletter must compete with a lot of other mail for attention. Because information changes so rapidly in travel today, a newsletter can be outdated even before its mailing is complete. In order to make full use of newsletters an organisation has to take into consideration certain essential ingredients for production. These are as follows :

Mailing Frequency: Mailing should go out often enough to maintain the agency's identity with readers. In fact, it should be so frequent and regular that customers look forward to it and, in fact, even miss it when they don't get it. At least four mailings a year are required to maintain identity and continuity.

Attractiveness: Newsletters should have short and crisp paragraphs with clear photographs to illustrate or document a story. Layout must have a good look so that the message is readable and pleasing to look at.

Relevance: In general, newsletters should address readers in their own frame of reference. Each idea or expression should be spelled out.

Simple Text: A professional journalist is not required to write a newsletter. However, a copy should be clear, crisp and colourful. The message should be clear and simple. Any grammatical errors or misspellings should be avoided as this can damage the image one is trying hard to develop.

Mailing Lists : Even the best newsletters will lose much of their impact if mailing lists are not kept up-to-date. There should be a proper system through which these could be regularly updated. A responsibility should be fixed on someone in the organisation for this. Feedback It is necessary to get a regular feedback from the clients regarding the newsletter. This would ensure whether the newsletter is being received or not as also the interest clients are having in it.

The Propagation

Publicity refers to the dissemination of information without charge or its news value in order to inform the prospect about a particular product. A publicity programme should include regular publicity, stories and photographs to newspapers, travel editors, contact with magazines on stories, ideas, and the preparations of story outlines and pictures in order to induce magazines to do feature stories on a particular destination. News releases to travel trade magazines on items of interest to the travel industry, such as opening up of a new area, total expansion, increased transportation facilities, development of a new resort, are measures which are adopted, together with other publicity through the media of radio, television, lectures, seminars, travel films, etc. Tourist publicity initially developed in an empirical way under the pressure of the growth of international travel, and to the extent that information had to be supplied to an ever-increasing number of tourists. Thus at its outset, it was simply informational publicity. With the growth in volume of commercial tourist publicity, particularly in the sphere of transport, and great increase in the number of tourists, various countries realised the importance of tourism in the national life. They recognised it, especially in economic terms and in the earning of foreign exchange This necessitated that countries organise their institutional tourist publicity with a new approach and employ experienced commercial publicity technicians to draw up a long-term publicity strategy.

Tourist Publicity Media : The publicity itself is carried out through media whose scope is that there are constantly new possibilities which suggest themselves to the resourceful publicity expert. This is of particular relevance in respect of tourist publicity whose new forms and scientifically based planning in publicity are not so frequently discernible. At any rate, tourist publicity media seem to be construed as a result of the fact that in general their publicity effect is limited to the visual and auditive sense. Illustration, copy and the spoken word are, therefore, the primary publicity media for tourism. They are multiplied through the media compounded out of them.

The greatest importance appertains to illustration, for it can achieve emotional effects in the reproduction of a landscape and its atmosphere and is also universally understood. Even if one is inclined to accept the psychological argument that every human being only projects his own personality in every consideration, the illustration retains from this standpoint also considerable publicity effectiveness, because it is viewed and perceived differently by different persons. Given the differences of individual tastes, the illustration naturally plays a decisive role. Consequently, the best illustration is just good enough for tourist publicity. It depends on the planning and shaping of the publicity medias to decide whether the illustration is to be employed in the form of a drawing, a printing or a photograph. Generally, the photograph is adjudged as possessing a greater objectivity in the statements. On the other hand, an artistic representation can be the expression of cultural activity and hence equally effective as publicity. Illustration can be developed through stylisation into a brand and thus create a concept which is derived from the meaning.

With copy as a publicity factor, there also arises the necessity for originality with the object of giving expression to the publicity idea. The purpose of every publicity media is to arouse and sustain attention. Illustration and copy must therefore create desires. In tourist publicity the tendency towards schematisation is extremely strong and counteracts necessity for publicity orginality. The similarity in the printed publicity material of hotels, travel agencies, tourist resorts, areas and even countries furnishes proof of this.

The spoken word is of importance in the case of personal publicity. The proper use of the spoken word is difficult but effective. "Words are not only conveyors of thoughts and ideas, but also of emotional contents and consequently they reach not only the intellect but also the psyche of the recipient and are expressed to this end." (Walter Hegeman on the Myth of the Mass). Thus the spoken word helps us to approach the imaginative world of the person addressed and this accounts for the importance of the information or sales talk as well as of publicity lectures, radio broadcasts, television speeches and publicity receptions. The spoken word is here supported by the appearance and presence of the speaker, as well as by his psychological capacity to adjust himself to the individual as also of listeners. The three primary publicity media mentioned - illustration, copy and the spoken word-form the basis of the composite publicity media which can suitably be arranged in the following groups: (i) Printed publicity, (ii) Advertising publicity, (iii) Projected publicity, (iv) Structural forms of publicity, (v) Personal publicity.

Printed Publicity Material : Printed publicity in the field of tourist publicity is mainly composed of the publicity leaflet, folder, brochure and poster. The publicity leaflet is used among others as inserts and enclosure in the case of conveying an information or communicating the knowledge to the largest possible number of persons. *The folder* is the most commonly used and the most important publicity medium for tourist publicity. We encounter it in numerous forms and multiple variations which leaves unsolved the question of the optimum effective folder. The question culminates in the investigation as to what the recipient expects from a folder, what he looks for in it, what he hopes to find in it and whether the folder corresponds to the imaginative conception of the country or region which it should advertise. The logical conclusion would be that account should be taken of the mental outlook of the recipient at the time of producing the folder. In the main, what actually takes place is that different versions of the folder are printed for different countries. This practice is further confirmed by the production of special folders like the cultural folder and those for motor tourists, mountain climbers, fishing and hunting enthusiasts, etc. These folders should deal with the special interests of the recipient and above all must be composed in "the idiom of the client".

The production of a general folder which has to be advertised for a whole country with its variety of attractions, specialities and circumstances requires much expertise. Here, there exists the danger of "too much" as well as "too little' besides the pitfalls of a dry description, superlative forms, over estimation and misappreciation of the points of attraction. A folder is not a travel guide nor a manual of geography. But it must not also be forgotten that the present day travellers are very often "illiterates in the field of tourism" who consequently require directions and help as well as information. This renders the page setting and composition of the text of an effective general folder, a task which has not yet been 100 per cent satisfactorily solved. "A folder has not incorrectly been compared with a representative. It is the silent representative of a firm, a resort or a country through which most often the first link is established with the future guest, the recipient"

The folder must also possess all the necessary qualities like proper appearance, faultless exterior, an unobtrusive and engaging presence, exact information about everything which is offered, truthfulness in assertions and no fanciful exaggerations. The text should never be long winded. A concrete and concise description containing exact comprehensive information corresponds to the quick rhythm of our time. To be adequately effective, however, the publicity medium of the folder needs to be not only well set up, but also to be produced in sufficient quantity and have a planned distribution.

The poster is the most important publicity medium of tourism. Difficulties touched upon in respect of the production of the general folder occur, especially in the case of the poster. The tourist poster should combine its effectiveness based on psychological factors with the task of depicting a country as tourist destination working on the limited means at its disposal. The tourist poster further suffers from the fact that there is no well considered distinction in the production of the poster for application as an interior or outdoor poster. In the majority of cases, there is an interior poster for the premises and show windows of travel agencies and information centres, whose use as an outdoor poster in the streets of large cities is consequently hardly discernible. Nevertheless, it should simultaneously satisfy the imperatives of a good outdoor poster and be designed as an eye catcher. The problem of publicity is further complicated by the discussion on the pros and cons of graphic and photographic posters. *The publicity* journal which is utilised at present by almost every national tourist publicity organisation is more representative than all other forms of printed material. As such it is expensive and therefore limited in its circulation. For the sake of comprehensive coverage, mention may also be made of the printed publicity material which really belongs already to the sphere of customer service, like maps, guidebooks, directories, inserts, etc.

Projected Publicity : Projected publicity media comprise film and slide publicity. Of particular importance is the film which is an outstanding medium, not only on account of its representational potentialities, but also because of its suggestive power. The colour film is assuming increasing significance within the framework of tourist publicity. The central idea of the film should be expressible in terms of motion and this accounts for the cardinal rule of all publicity films, short text but plenty of action which should captivate the attention of the spectators and also aim at influencing memory through emotional factors. Publicity effectiveness is a characteristic not only of the purely publicity film, but also the feature film as well as the instructional impact of the didactic film. In the United States of America and Western Europe the travel film with a commentary known as the "travelogue" has won extensive popularity. Television is a suitable medium to spread the interest in foreign countries and thus serves tourist publicity.

Structural Forms : Structural forms of publicity comprise publicity measures which manifest themselves in constructions and structures, as for example, in the establishment and equipment of a tourist publicity office abroad, in participation in fairs and exhibitions, in the preparation of show cases and window displays, etc. Here no restrictions are set on the inventive resources of the architects. There is also the possibility of publicity combinations whereby tourist publicity can be undertaken in conjunction with business publicity. For example, shops selling sports goods, fashion articles, travel accessories, etc. are willing to have such combinations in their show windows.

Similarly, at fairs the joint stands of a country procure publicity advantages for tourism because the exhibition as a whole shows tourism in relation to the country and succeeds in creating lasting impressions.

Personal Publicity : Personal publicity in tourism has various forms of application ranging from the informational and sales talk to publicity travel, which serves the need of maintaining contact with the travel industry and to support it in its sales efforts, and includes the publicity lecture. In all these spheres the personal effort holds sway. Also to this category belong interviews, radio broadcasts, receptions, etc.

The role of promotion in tourism is of paramount importance. The various promotional techniques like advertising, public relations and sales support are used together by tourism hospitality and leisure providers. All the three techniques are however, complementary to each other. The proper and judicious mix of these is very essential for the successful promotion of a product or a programme.

4

Schemes for Development

Tourism planning leads to tourism development. In fact, tourism planning is the process for tourism development. In general terms, planning refers to methods and means used in making decisions about the future. Planning not only guides actions to be taken in future but also helps in problem solving and arriving at decisions which help planners in achieving desired objectives. Planning is not static but dynamic and guides future actions. Tourism planning process involves creating a future that is acceptable to the host community as also to others who would be part of the host community as tourists for a short period of time. Since tourism involves hospitality, the planning for various tourism facilities must be based on the needs of the guests.

The need for planning arises whenever some rational thinking is required to arrive at a choice among a set of limited means so that certain ends are satisfied especially when the means are substitutable among themselves. In other words, planning essentially attempts to allocate scarce resources between different competing uses with a view to maximising output, income and employment and to ensure the balanced growth of different sectors. Such planning may be at an individual level or at a firm level or at an industry level or for the economy as a whole. There are broadly two economic systems prevailing—planned economy and market economy.

Planned economy is one in which each production unit (or a firm) uses only the resources of men, material and equipment allocated to it by quota and disposes of its products to person or firms indicated to it by simple order. On the other hand, a market economy is controlled by the forces of market, like demand, supply, prices, transport, etc. Plan can be applied to any type of economic system, whether centrally structured or built up of many units of purely market economy character. The different institutional frameworks will lead to compulsory planning under the first system and to indicative planning under the second.

Plan Coordination

In the field of tourism, the need for planned development is of paramount importance. Many countries in the world, especially the developing countries, have lately realized the importance of tourism and the benefits which it brings out. The use of macro economic planning techniques for tourism sector are, however, relatively new. The planning methods for national economic development, which have been largely utilized since the end of the World War II, did not always cover tourism development as a particular field.

The increasing significance of tourism as a source of income, employment generation, regional development and as a major factor in the balance of payments for many countries has been attracting the attention of many governments as well as others with an interest in economic development. Thus, tourism development became more and more a particular field of research in the economic planning undertaken by many countries. As far back as in the year 1962, the Secretary General of the United Nations had declared: "Impressive unanimity has been achieved regarding the potential value of development planning."

The United Nations Conference on International Travel and Tourism held in Rome in 1963 emphasised the need for planning in tourism and made several recommendations. Some of the important recommendations that the United Nations Conferences made in the area of planning in tourism were as follows:

(i) that the governments of developing countries should give high priority to projects concerning the development of tourism in their respective countries.

(ii) that the governments of developing countries should consider the possibility of seeking the assistance of the United Nations Special Fund for regional and sub-regional surveys of existing and potential tourist resources and for the preparation by experts of tourist traffic estimates and forecasts, with a view to the establishment of short-term and long-term plans for the development of tourist facilities and plant.

The conference endorsed the relevant comments of the group of experts who had pointed out that tourism was expanding swiftly as world economy improved and more and more travellers sought new places to visit. It further stated that to the extent permitted by its economic resources, a country should see a steady growth in the number of new tourist resorts developed. Existing possibilities of attracting tourists—mountaineering, winter sports, fishing, hunting, beaches, spas, national parks, game sanctuaries, national monuments, sites and shrines, folk traditions and customs, pilgrimages, festivals and sporting events—should likewise be developed and protected. Stress was laid on the importance of ensuring protection, not only for monuments, archaeological remains and buildings of historical, cultural or architectural importance, but also for the customs, traditions, art and folklore of indigenous peoples. The conference also agreed that a developing country which proposed to set up a national tourist organization should consider obtaining a preliminary survey in order to assess clearly what positive tourist attractions the country already had, what potential tourist attractions existed, and how they could most effectively be developed within the limits of the funds available.

The recommendations had far-reaching implications as far as planned development of tourism was concerned. All member states and the specialized agencies of the United Nations were called upon to consider and implement as appropriate the recommendations contained in the report of the conference. The recommendations of the conference were of particular interest to those countries which were just beginning to develop tourism. Until quite recently tourism was principally a feature of, and was largely confined to the developed countries. Many of the developing countries saw the possibilities in tourism development. Encouraged by the recommendations of the conference, many developing countries introduced tourism development programmes.

In 1965, the United Nations Conference on Trade and Development (UNCTAD) also emphasised the promise which tourism held out for the developing countries. For some countries, tourism offers a major opportunity since it provides employment for many; it stimulates investment and is an important source of foreign exchange. The third International Union of Official Travel Organizations (IUOTO) Travel Research Seminar held in Prague, the Czech Republic, in 1964, examined in great detail the many problems involved in the development of tourist industry and concluded that planning, whether at national, regional or local level, was indispensable. It concluded that all tourist planning should be based on two types of preliminary surveys: (i) detailed survey of the characteristics of the area being considered for development and, in particular, of its tourist resources; (ii) studies of future customers based on surveys and forecasts.

Careful planning is a prerequisite for complete success of any programme. The haphazard development in many countries had made the planners aware of the need for planning of tourism development based on scientific research. Every country, whether it already has an active flourishing tourist industry or is thinking of developing a tourist industry, has to decide on many crucial issues before launching a tourism development programme. The agencies responsible for tourism development have to consider the various issues. The official government agencies, especially in the developing countries, have to be extra cautious as they cannot afford to waste scarce resources on developmental plans which do not bring benefits. The governments in these countries have to decide on the following issues:

(i) rate of growth of the tourism sector, whether it wishes to encourage mass tourism or develop it more slowly, gradually and selectively;

(ii) the importance of the tourism sector to the national economy and how its development and growth is to fit in with the plans for national, regional and local development;

(iii) the respective roles which it assigns to public and private sector in the development of the industry;

(iv) the respective roles to be played by domestic and foreign capital (whether foreign investments are to be encouraged in case the country's financial resources are limited);

(v) decision as to whether the tourist industry should be treated in the same way as other industries or whether the peculiar character of the industry warrants it being given special treatment; and

(vi) decision as to whether tourist industry is to be developed on a continuous long-term basis or only as a short-term arrangement to overcome the trade deficit.

The Organization for Economic Cooperation and Development (OECD) in a seminar held at Estoril focussed its attention on all the above issues. According to the report "much of the discussion turned on the fact that tourism is by its nature somewhat different from other sectors of the economy, since it is an industry based on movement of people rather than goods. For this reason it is particularly susceptible to subjective considerations quite apart from the play of the economic forces. Political and social pressures, psychological attitudes, changes of fashion, may all influence the course of tourism development markedly and unpredictably. It is essential therefore that tourism industry should be as flexible as possible to be able to adapt to changing conditions and requirements."

The discussions at the OECD seminar also drew attention to the fact that tourism involves several considerations which are essentially of non-economic nature. The report of the seminar stated: "Tourism often has significant cultural implications (for example, the restoration of ancient monuments); aesthetic (the preservation of beauties of landscape and the safeguarding of the nation's heritage); social (the provision of recreational facilities for the health and welfare of the people); and political (the improvement of international understanding)."

The fact that tourism is by its nature somewhat different from other sectors of the economy necessitates careful planning. This is much more important for the developing countries which cannot afford to waste scarce resources. The various issues involved in the planning and development of tourism show how necessary it is for these countries to adopt growth plans in this specific branch, duly relating to their political and economic institutional framework. Just as a country will adopt a monetary policy, a policy of agriculture, of public works, of health, of transport, and so on as different elements of its national economic plan, so it should on the same grounds, adopt a specific policy of tourism development.

Coordination in Planning : The peculiar characteristics of tourism make it particularly beneficial in terms of general economic development. From this follows the necessity of adopting a development policy, which will take into account all the country's economic sectors which have a direct or indirect interest in its expansion. On the other hand, tourism, as an integral part or specific sector of the general plan of economic development, can only prosper within the context of the country's overall progress even though it calls for its own particular policy. Tourism, like other economic activities, flourishes best when it fits into a context of general economic policies and programmes designed to lead to the optimum growth of the economy of a country as a whole. This calls for coordination. Coordination between tourism planning and the general plan must therefore be based on coordination of effort in all the sectors concerned. Tourism policy must therefore be a global policy of development, taking into account the important implications, affecting the progress of this activity. In addition, the overall tourism development plan must take into account the social and cultural components of the phenomenon, for these also acquire prominence in the development process.

The planning of tourism, whether at the national or the regional level, must be regarded as an integral, and therefore, coordinated part of the country's general economic and social planning. This coordinated approach has a direct bearing on the success of the tourism industry, more so in a developing country. It is also to be remembered that tourism is not one business but involves many industries and a whole range of complex processes. A plan for tourism can only survive and serve its stated purposes if there is coordination among all the processes. A first requisite is the need to ensure that the government organs specifically responsible for the tourist sector play their important role, which is that of cooperating with all those governmental departments responsible for other branches concerned with the expansion of tourism. The essential aim of the tourist plan is to arrive at a balanced growth of demand and supply. In other words, to arrive at an optimum harmonization of the interrelations between the two poles of market while avoiding the creation of serious economic, territorial or social imbalances. Hence, the basis of planning in a sector must be viewed globally and mutually arranged with country's economic and social development and with the overall policy of planning for the territory in which the location of tourist centre assume primary importance.

Process of Planning

A process for tourism planning or the subjects of analysis of a plan of tourism development must be correlated with all the elements noted above, in order that they can achieve an optimum level of expansion without creating serious imbalances of various kinds. If a country, region or an area possesses attractions and provides some hospitality for prospective tourists, tourism will probably develop. If this tourism development is to benefit the host area, a formal forward-looking planning is essential. If tourism planning is to happen in a specific area, someone or some entity must stimulate and enunciate the original idea. This basic inspiration must be shared by some entity which holds controlling interests and responsibility for the resources to be utilized by the tourism industry. This principle holds true for planning a programme of any scope or dimension. For instance, there may be an existing resort, hotel or industry in a region. The stimulus may be realization that there is potential for growth if only existing facilities can be expanded or new ones generated. At the other extreme, an area may have potential but underdeveloped resources. No matter what the situation, for effective tourism planning, there must be active involvement and participation by persons or entities controlling the essential resources.

A description of various planning processes or analysis of a plan of tourism development is very essential. A description given here can only be briefly indicative and is limited to mere suggestions of the topics or the steps without entering into detailed analysis. The plan must take account of these various processes in quantitative terms, if it is to outline the optimum objectives to be attained in a given period of time. The objectives must be related to those of the overall economic development plan. The key steps, or phases in planning, can be as follows: (a) assessment of tourist demand and supply, (b) establishing objectives, (c) territorial planning, (d) basic infrastructure, (e) financial planning, (f) human resource planning, (g) administrative structure, (h) marketing and promotion, (i) monitoring progress, and (j) the time factor.

Assessment of Tourist Demand and Supply : One of the early steps in planning is gathering information on the things the way they are and on the potential available for desirable growth. One of the main problems in investigating the potential of tourism can be the simple lack of information. Recording of information and the development of statistics is therefore of utmost importance. The important initial steps in evaluating a potential for tourism development lies in determining present status. An analysis of the present structure of demand and supply in tourism is a pre-condition of any other estimate. This information base is a prerequisite for initiating tourism planning programme. In the first place, there must be a survey of the tourist attractions of various types which the country has to offer. Without a full study of the attractions a country possesses, it is not possible to plan for future expansion. It is, therefore, of fundamental importance that a very careful assessment be made of all attractions—physical, cultural, historical—that a country possesses.

According to Peters, there are a number of principles on which assessment should be based. First, it is highly desirable that the attractions should be developed progressively throughout the entire country so that tourism is spread as widely as possible. In this way, the benefits which accrue from the industry are also widely spread and most parts of the country benefit. Second, areas and attractions which are singled out for special development should appeal to the widest possible cross-section of tourists over the longest possible season. By adhering to this principle, over-dependence upon a particular season of the year will be avoided. Third, priority should be given to those attractions which can be most easily and most successfully developed. Those attractions which can be based upon the existing infrastructural services should be given priority as these would require less finance. Fourth, since it is very difficult, rather impossible, to develop all the potential attractions at the same time, it is important that similar or competing attractions should not be embarked upon until the volume of visitors can justify them. Finally, it is important to know that the tourist is usually looking for something new: he desires new experiences, different environments, new thrills, etc. Any country possessing attractions which are unique or out of the ordinary should attempt to capitalise on these for they are likely to have a great drawing power.

Demand must then be estimated, for both national and foreign tourists. Both internal and external data on tourism activities affecting the area under consideration should be assembled. This task should use published statistics on travel and tourism which are readily available from international and regional organizations. In addition, travel and accommodation statistics can be assembled from the region under study. Next the tourist supply must include all the different types of facilities additional to various types of accommodation establishments. Special attention must be given to the seasonal factor, i.e., the annual fluctuations in the demand as related to the country's tourist attractions.

Establishing Objectives : The information or the initial data thus gathered should develop a composite picture of what tourism can do for and to a particular area. In order to relate these projected results to a decision on whether to proceed with tourism development, there must be a basis for comparison. This basis is the cumulative set of objectives which should be developed concurrently. Basically, objectives for tourism should be a subset of the overall objectives (either implicit or documented) for the nation, the economy, the people and the social structure within an area. There are, however, no set rules as to what the objectives should be. In general, tourism objectives should deal with growth leading to increased standard of living, employment levels, opportunities for intellectual growth, enhancement of the investment potential in an area or country. Cumulatively, tourism objectives should describe the set of conditions under which a favourable decision should be made.

If the data indicate that reasonable objectives for tourism development can be met, this will generally lead to a decision to proceed with a conceptual planning study. As a basis for moving ahead with a conceptual planning study, a request for proposal (RFP) should be prepared. This is a detailed description and a set of guidelines for the study which will be used by prospective organizations as a uniform basis for submitting proposals. As a first step towards preparation of conceptual plan for tourism development, a market study and resource analysis should be performed. The market study begins with a determination of the type of tourism business which exists and can be expected. Market study provides the basis for conceptual planning. The conceptual plan provides a general view of the future tourism development programme and the steps necessary to achieve targeted results. The various steps: involved in conceptual planning, once the market survey has been performed, include (i) statement of objectives; (ii) selection of site, (iii) requirements of various facilities, (iv) supplementary attractions, (v) land use allocation and control, (vi) budgets, and (vii) legislative requirements.

Preparation of a master plan is another important step in planning. Master planning is a process for completing and detailing additional work on the portions of the conceptual plan which are approved for further development. The differences between conceptual and master planning lie largely in the level of details-involved. Where conceptual planning, for example, might indicate the need to expand airport runways and terminal facilities, master planning would go into specifics on land and construction.

Planning for Territory

The need will arise of locating each pole of tourism development so as to fit in with the general policy of territorial planning. Particular attention must be given here to natural and cultural assets of the country, while avoiding the damage which results from an unbalanced exploitation of their economic value. The need for tourist territorial planning must be reconciled with the limits in pace of industrialization and urbanization which, even though complementary to tourism, can constitute a serious danger to it. It will also be necessary to plan further tourism development in the selected zones in order to avoid excessive concentration in one area.

Basic Infrastructure : If a tourism development programme is to succeed, it is necessary to provide life support through a number of infrastructural facilities and services. Infrastructure elements comprise the system of services and utilities which are necessary to the operation of a tourism destination. The estimation of the basic infrastructure required for tourist expansion accordingly becomes a key economic factor in proceeding to the active phase of implementation. This infrastructure will be either specifically tourist in nature, e.g., transport, or more general, such as energy-producing units, and will in any case vary with the type of tourism envisaged. The requirements for infrastructure will vary for different areas. The requirements, for example, will be different for a mountain resort and for a tourist pole adjacent to some cultural attraction. The requirements will be for both tourists and local residents. As various agencies are responsible for development of infrastructure services, coordination is very essential. Without coordination, different elements of infrastructure may infringe upon each other resulting in wasteful expenditure. Specific areas of infrastructure are power, water, communication, sewage and drainage, roads and highways, parks, recreation and health-care facilities.

Financial Planning: Financial planning is very essential for a successful tourism development plan. Before any major attraction, facility or destination gets into full swing, considerable expenses are involved. There follows the study of a vital element in tourist development, that is, the financing of both infrastructure and superstructure. Assessing the cost of the project is relatively easy when compared to assessing benefits. There may be a choice of locations or a choice of techniques. Estimates must be made for each choice within a feasible range. Each proposal must be assessed separately to establish its feasibility, cost-benefit and degree of priority in making a plan. Agencies concerned with the development of an optional national investment programme should compare investments in tourism facilities and related infrastructure with alternative investment opportunities in other sectors. In World Bank Group Operations, this comparison is attempted on the basis of economic rates of return for well-defined investment proposals. In evaluating tourism investments the World Bank Group pays very close attention to the projected financial results. In general, tourism projects financed by the World Bank Group are justified in terms of both their economic impact and their financial viability.

In the case of those countries which already possess an active tourist industry or have potential for increased tourism development, finances for investment will usually be available readily. However, in the case of developing countries, which are anxious to develop tourism, due to financial constraints, the provision of adequate resources of capital may be difficult. The development of tourism sector will be only one of the number of options for development before a government, since government resources will inevitably be inadequate for all the competing claims upon them. In view of this, the proposed investment in tourism must be justified in terms of its anticipated contribution to the economic development of the country.

Except in centrally planned economies, such as in countries like Russia, Poland, Yugoslavia, public investment will be supported by private investment as happens in the mixed economies like France, Italy and India. The government may take the initiative in project development, but it will expect private investment support. If the government is anxious to develop and promote an active tourist industry it will help the private investor to the maximum extent. This can be done, first, by creating a favourable climate for investment and, second, by assisting private investor to consider tourism development as an attractive investment proposition. This could be done by way of offering special financial inducements such as subsidies, tax concessions, preferential rates of interest credits, special facilities for purchase of land, etc. All these investment incentives in some form or the other encourage private investment in tourism sector.

In addition to the public and private finance, foreign capital also plays an important role in tourism development programmes. Attention will have to be paid to financial means and facilities designed to attract foreign capital. A basic obligation at this stage will be the calculation of the output capital ratio, which will depend for the most part in the external economies that can be achieved. Foreign investment is usually welcome by many developing countries, largely because of their own acute shortage of capital resources.

Human Resource Planning : Professional and efficient management is an obvious prerequisite to successful tourism development. Of equal importance, however, is the quality of staff training, which is often relatively neglected during the early stages of tourism sector development. Tourism basically being a service business, a developing destination must take the necessary steps to build a pool of efficiently trained people to fill various jobs which will be created subsequently. A variety of jobs will have to be created to look after and manage various tourist services. Special attention, therefore, will have to be given to needs in manpower and personnel to be trained and rendered qualified for the various tourism professions. Special care has to taken to ensure that there will be no shortage of trained manpower in case there is expansion of facilities and services. In the case of a developing country, it will also be appropriate to study at this stage the volume of manpower required for activities complementary to accommodation industry, in particular in the commercial sector.

In planning for human resources development, programme should be established to screen and train prospective employees so that they could acquire both attitudinal as well as technical skills. Attitudinal characteristics contribute to an employee's success in tourism position and include pride, flexibility, adaptability and judgement. Technical skills required include facility and equipment operation and maintenance, financial management, food and beverage production and service, personnel management and administration and system analysis and design. In order to determine the need for various personnel required, a staff planning exercise may be done. This involves a series of steps which include job analysis, preparing job descriptions, job specifications and preparing staff forecasts. This sequence of activities leads to a detailed forecast of exactly what types of persons, with which specific qualifications and skills, will be required at all major facilities within the tourist destination. All this helps in determining the development of requisite education and training programmes within the country for local residents. This will also help in determining whether there is a need for trained personnel from other countries and also whether local people are to be sent for training elsewhere.

Administrative Structure : Next comes the necessity of setting up an adequate administrative organization to look after various aspects. If a tourism programme is to succeed, the responsibility of success must be assumed by some entity in the form of an organization. This organization should have a charter and resources appropriate to carry out various functions. Many countries have established special departments or agencies to manage and coordinate tourism programmes. Depending upon the economic, social and political structure in the country, the tourism organization may be a governmental department, a semi-governmental agency in the form of corporation supported by government but operating outside its organizational structure. It may also be a private-sector organization with government support and recognition. Whatever form the tourism organization takes, it needs to exercise its authority and responsibility in the sphere of tourism development. The administrative organization looks after the legal aspects, i.e., the preparation of the legislation required for the installation of the various tourism services, dealing with such matters as the classification of hotels or the control of travel agencies, etc. It has various departments for planning, marketing, research, training, and legal and administrative services.

Marketing and Promotion : The final stage of the plan is concerned with, the preparation of promotional activities aimed at launching the new tourist industry both within and outside the country. The main concern of tourists is having an enjoyable and pleasant experience rather than details associated with planning their journeys. Most of the tourists leave these details to travel professionals and intermediaries who look after all the details of the travel plans. Contacts with and support of travel professionals and intermediaries are among the most important factors for successful marketing and promotion of tourist destination. Facilities and specialities of travel professionals include national tourist offices, regional travel promotion organizations, airlines including other carriers, tour wholesalers, tour operators, travel agents, travel clubs and convention and conference organizers. The various channels of communication used to inform and stimulate include tourist literature in the form of catalogues, brochures and folders, direct mail, advertising, public relations and publicity. All these media are selected and organized into promotion campaigns aimed at selling to consumers and travel professionals and intermediaries. The media campaigns are timed in such a way that these correspond with the selling effort supporting a destination. It is very important to ensure that these activities match the level of tourist development aimed at.

Monitoring Progress : Monitoring the progress periodically is very crucial to get the best results. Preparation of a plan document is not an end in itself. The task of the planner does not end when a plan for three years, five years or seven years has been prepared. A system of constant revision and monitoring of the plan progress should be a part of the exercise of planning. Targets must be revised continually in the light of changing resources and other circumstances. The error is to mistake a plan for planning. To use a more elegant vocabulary, a plan is static and planning must be dynamic. Plans are interesting mathematical or literary or technical exercises that can be formulated with a great variety of methods and degrees of perfection. Planning, on the other hand, is a diffuse but coherent process of making and revising decisions that must be closely attuned to the implementation of planned action. What is needed is a system of monitoring progress and mechanisms for constantly and rapidly adjusting to the changing conditions and circumstances.

Time Factor : Time factor is a very important element. The main purpose of development planning is to move towards self-sustaining growth, that is, to create a cadre of trained manpower, to increase knowledge of natural resources and their effective utilization and to create institutions for enterprising investment. All this takes time. The duration of the plan could be for 25 years, 10 years, seven years or five years. Many planners are of the view that the first development plan should be a 10-year plan, as it requires an assessment of long-term perspective. Time is a fundamental factor in the preparation of the plan and in the identification of the objectives to be attained upon its termination.

The medium-term plan ranges between three and seven years with five years as the most popular choice. The long-term range upwards from 10 years to 25 years.

The short-term plan on the other hand is an annual plan. The annual plan is the controlling plan as it is the authorised document to check its possible achievements being matched by available resources year by year. It is governed by medium- or long-term plan, which sets its direction. The annual plan in the operative document, while long-term or medium-term plans are merely a set of intentions. Thus the need for orienting the short-term plan budgets with the long-term or medium-term plan budgets is the core of planning process. Time factor is the main element in the planning, including planning of tourism in any nation. It is vital to the prospect of achieving the economic and social expansion which is linked with tourism.

Tourism is receiving ever-increasing attention from national governments and from international development agencies. It can generate much-needed-foreign exchange for financing other sectors of the economy of a developing country and also for bridging the trade gap. In its broadest sense, tourism can do more to develop understanding among people, generate employment and raise living standards than any other economic force known. There is unlimited potential for tourism development. If properly conceived and executed, such development will prove not only to be financially viable but will also prove to be of immense benefit to a country. Inadequate planning and development, on the other hand, can increase probabilities of failure resulting in great loss.

Some degree of planning is very essential. It is perhaps much easier to have planned development in countries where there is a potential which is only just beginning to be realised. However, even in those countries having a long established and a highly developed tourist industry, some measure of planning is essential. Planning is essential for three main reasons. First, most countries, to a lesser or greater degree, have planned economies, and if tourism development is to be a part and parcel of national economic development, then this sector of economy also should be subjected to planning. Second, the success of tourism development depends very largely upon appropriate facilities being available in the right place and at the right time, and these can only be provided by adequate research into national tourist assets and markets. Research has a very important part to play in the future planning of tourism development. Third, planning is required to ensure that the natural and man-made assets are conserved and protected to maintain tourist appeal, for lack of care and coordinated development may impair and even ruin those assets upon which the tourist industry is founded.

Planning for Environment

Tourism is the world's largest industry. This fact has now been recognised all over the world. Although a 'smokeless' industry, it has environmental implications. Expanding tourism has the capacity to pollute the environment as would any smoke-ridden industry. A few years back, the United Nations organized a conference in Stockholm on human environment. This conference symbolized the growing importance that the people of the world attach to maintaining and improving the quality of human life and to enrich the human environment. It is a fact that all over the world man has been using the natural resources without any thought for the future. It is the wrong use of these resources which causes problems. Today environmental pollution poses a serious threat to life on earth and this is true not only of the areas where there is a great concentration of industries, but also areas where there is a great concentration of tourists.

The disadvantages of haphazard and unplanned development of tourism are well illustrated by many areas in North America and Western Europe and also to a greater or lesser extent throughout large parts of Asia's tourism circuit. Yugoslavia's Adriatic coast and the Seychelles are other examples. Many of the world's finest resorts have become ugly. Sochi, Russia's popular Black Sea resort, has proclaimed itself the world's first 'no-smoking city'. New laws ban smoking in all restaurants, cinema theatres, public transportation, hospitals and on the beaches. In India, there are many examples of uncontrolled growth of industries, shops and also slums near tourist spots creating problems of environmental pollution. Many of the beaches of North America and Western Europe bear a mute testimony to the havoc that can be wrought by uncontrolled development of tourism. Destinations once noted for their particular character are reduced to unattractive showpieces as many countries endeavour to keep pace with the visitor inflow. Despite a measure of governmental control during the development, the great increase in number of visitors to these areas resulted in rapid, unplanned construction of hotels and dwellings for tourists and for migratory service employees. These expansions threaten to destroy the very environment that is the tourist attraction. A prominent leader in the Seychelles objected to seeing his country become a "nation of maitres d'hotel." These examples underline environmental threat, both aesthetic and biological, from overcrowding of particularly attractive areas.

Tourism development germinates special ecological problems not encountered in other types of economic activity. The environmental resources 'exploited' for tourism attract tourists because of their outstanding beauty, recreational possibilities or educational and cultural interest. Modern tourism's most paradoxical trait is its capacity to destroy those attributes which attracted the visitor in the first place. The well-known economic analyst and futurologist, Herman Kahn, described the rapidly expanding tourism as "next only to atomic power in its potential for environmental destruction." Mass tourism has brought in its wake certain ecological and environmental pollution problems.

The environmental amenities which attract tourists have tended to be taken for granted. Preservation of their quality has only recently begun to concern tourism development planners. For tourism the quality of the environment is the basis for attracting visitors and needs to be conserved. Tourism development can become a positive factor for improving environment if some amount of intelligent planning is done. In fact, the quality of the tourism product depends upon a high quality natural environment. The interrelationship was pointed out by the International Union of Official Travel Organizations (IUOTO), the predecessor of the World Tourism Organization, as long ago as the 1950s. It was reiterated during the 1960s in the face of growing interest in environmental conservation.

The major social benefits accrue to tourists themselves. But tourism also has valuable spill over benefits for tourist-receiving countries. Notable among these is the contribution of tourism to the preservation of historic and cultural values. Careful maintaining, cleaning and beautifying the monuments, clearing the areas around the monuments, improving them for tourism purposes is a case in point. Through tourism development, the environment is not degraded but, in fact, can be improved. So great has been the national and international demand for tourism and recreational facilities that governments have increasingly to face up to the choice between extending public access and availability of sites and conservation and protection against over-development. Governments are increasingly aware that future growth of the industry will necessitate careful management and avoiding over-development of regions of natural beauty. Moreover, saturation in principal destination areas will require a more active policy diversification and redistribution of tourist flows.

Regional Concern

The potential of a region for tourism may be so great that its development will be central to economic goals and plans. However, regional planning for tourism more often will be considered as a separate and distinct planning effort, aimed primarily at determining the best location of facilities, hotels, resort facilities and transportation networks. Such planning views tourism primarily as a source of foreign exchange earnings. This approach would recommend development to accommodate maximum possible number of projected visitors and to design facilities to generate the maximum possible spending by the tourists. However, this approach of profit maximising to tourism development can result in deterioration of fragile environment and attractive landscapes through over-building and excessive number of visitors.

Every tourist site has a carrying capacity for the tourists as well as well as for any other type of use. This will vary with the fragility of the area concerned and the nature of the tourist activity contemplated. For instance, an island rainforest is a fragile environment which could be easily endangered by excessive number of people. By contrast a recreational beach is not easily damaged by sunbathers or swimmers. Planning facilities for tourism development in the first case would require limitations on construction of hotels and similar other installations in the region in order not to encourage excessive numbers of tourists. In the second case, high-density accommodations for tourism might well be tolerated.

There have been various attempts to define carrying capacity. Some of these are given below:

> The maximum number of people who can use a site without an unacceptable alteration in the physical environment and without an unacceptable decline in the quality of experience gained by visitors. [Mathieson and Wall, *Tourism: Economic, Physical and Social Impacts,* 1982.]

The concept of maintaining a level of development and use that will not result in serious environmental deterioration, socio-cultural or economic problems, or be perceived by tourists as depreciating their enjoyment and appreciation of the area. [World Tourism Organization, *National and Regional Tourism Planning,* (Madrid: WTO) 1994.] The level of tourist presence which creates impacts on the host community, environment and economy that are acceptable to both tourists and hosts, and sustainable over future time periods. [Cooper etal., *Tourism: Principles and Practice,* 1993.]

Types of Carrying Capacity : Following are various types of carrying capacity:

Physical

- Acceptable levels of visual impact and congestion.
- Point at which ecological systems are maintained before damage occurs.
- Conservation of wildlife and natural vegetation of both the land and marine environments.
- Acceptable levels of air, water and noise pollution.

Economic

- Extent of tourism that provides optimum overall economic benefits without economic distortions or inflation.
- Level of tourism employment suited to the local community.

- Extent of tourism development that can be absorbed without detriment to the life-styles and activities of the local community.
- Level of tourism that will help maintain historic and cultural monuments, arts, crafts, belief systems, customs and traditions without detrimental effects.

Socio-cultural

- Extent of tourism development than can be absorbed without detriment to the life-styles and activities of the local community.
- Level of tourism that will help maintain historic and cultural monuments, arts, crafts, belief systems, customs and traditions without detrimental effects.

Infrastructure

- Adequate availability of transportation facilities and services.
- Adequate availability of utility facilities and services of water supply, electric power, sewage and solid waste disposal and telecommunications.
- Adequate availability of other community facilities and services such as those related to health and safety, and of housing for employees in tourism.

Psychological

- Refers to crowding and the psychological impact of being with too many other people for comfort/enjoyment.
- Congestion

Carrying capacity, however, may change over time. Technological advances, for example, may increase the amount of sewage which may be treated, thereby increasing carrying capacity. Improvements to infrastructure, modes of transport, etc., may also increase carrying capacity over time. An important point to recognise is that the overall carrying capacity of a destination is often determined by just one factor. That is, one factor becomes the limiting factor. For example, there may be enough hotel beds to cater for 10,000 tourists per night, but if the sewage system can only cope with 5,000 then the carrying capacity will be 5,000.

Factors Affecting Carrying Capacity : A wide variety of factors will affect the carrying capacity. These range from the level of technological development to the type of tourist. Any factors which influence physical, economic, socio-cultural, infrastructural and psychological will affect carrying capacity. Major factors usually include.

Alien Factors

- The volume and characteristics of the tourist mass tourism will have a greater impact than independent/explorer type tourism
- The length of stay
- Geographical concentration of visitors
- The degree of seasonality

Local Factors

- The fragility of the local environment: sand dunes, marine environments etc. are more fragile than Trafalgar Square in London or Manhattan in New York.
- The social structure of the host economy: the more developed a country is, the less vulnerable to the influence of the tourist.
- The economic structure: developing countries are less likely to be able to reap the same benefits as a developed country due to the fact that they are likely to have to import more goods to cater for the needs of the tourist because they are not produced locally. They may also be dependent on foreign investment for development the profits generated from these developments will be repatriated (or at least some will be).
- The political structure: governments may encourage or discourage tourism. This will be reflected in the resources and support made available to cope with the impact of tourism.
- Availability of local resources: the greater the local resources, the lower will be the need for imports and the greater the benefit for the local community. Natural resources will also serve as an attraction for tourists.
- The policies adopted with regard to tourist dispersal.

Combination of Factors

- The difference between the tourist and host: the greater the difference the greater the impact. This applies to both differences in wealth and differences in culture.
- The amount of contact: fleeting contact will be less likely to allow hosts/tourists to learn about the other's culture.
- Segregation of the tourist reduces what is called the demonstration effect.

How to Maintain Sustainability : Sustainability is linked very closely to carrying capacity. Both are related to the concept of maintaining a level of tourism which does not cause irreversible damage and which allows tourism in a given destination to continue into the future. The WTO has described sustainability as follows:

The underlying approach now applied to tourism planning, as well as to other types of development, is that of achieving sustainable development. The sustainable development approach implies that the natural, cultural and others resources of tourism are conserved for continuous use in the future, while still bringing benefits to the present society. The concept of sustainable development has received much emphasis internationally since the early 1980's, although tourism plans prepared even before that period often were concerned with conservation of tourism resources.

The sustainable development approach to planning tourism is acutely important because most tourism development depends on attractions and activities related to the natural environment, historic heritage and cultural patterns of areas. If these resources are degraded or destroyed, then the tourism areas cannot attract tourists and tourism will not be successful. More generally, most tourists seek destinations that have a high level of environmental quality—they like to visit places that are attractive, clean and neither polluted nor congested. It is also essential that residents of the tourism area should not have to suffer from a deteriorated environment and social problems. World Tourism Organization, *National and Regional Tourism Planning* (Madrid: WTO), 1994.

It is difficult to pinpoint the responsibility to any one particular agency department for achieving sustainable development. Because of the nature of the tourism industry, i.e.., it is fragmented with many players, problems have arisen because of conflicting interests. Venice is a good example of where coordinated overall planning has proved difficult. There is no one government department that has responsibility for planning and conflicts have arisen between the needs of the locals and the needs of the tourists.

It could be argued that everyone involved should take responsibility. The government is usually involved, for instance, in terms of granting planning permission. Developers are involved, but do not always have long-term objectives, particularly if they come from outside the community in which the development is taking place. The local people have a vested interest in ensuring that their "home" is not spoilt, but often there are conflicts between hotel owners (or any one who benefits from tourism) and those who only "suffer" the tourists (e.g., traffic jams). Tour operators and travel agents have started to take a more responsible stance— in their brochures they try and "educate" the tourists to be more aware of local customs and save water. However, their main objective is to make a profit. Tour operators take options for hotel rooms, but if a resort does not prove popular, they can easily 'switch' to another resort and cancel flights. Two approaches to responsible planning for sustainable development are possible—a top-down approach, with plans prepared by a central authority (Central or regional government) or a bottom-up approach, driven by the community. Often a combination of the two approaches achieves the best results.

At Macro Level

Creation of "Honey Pots": This is the creation or development of popular resorts in one area, as a way to relieve tourist pressure from another area of a more sensitive nature.

Dispersion Policy: The use of "honey-pot" resorts may cause the depletion of resources in one area, and the exclusion *of* the rest of an area's population from the financial benefits of tourism. To prevent this, a policy of dispersing tourist resorts across a region or country may be adopted.

Zoning: This is the division or categorisation of land permitting only certain kinds of use on it. This may also be applied to lakes. Some lakes may be zoned for water skiing or fishing.

Encouragement of Green Policies: This is when green policies are adopted to protect and restore the environment or offset an environmental problem, and, at the same time, indirectly improve recreational resources. An example of this is the growth of urban forests which could in turn lead to these sites being used for recreation.

Provision of Urban Tourist Facilities: If there is provision of tourist or recreational facilities like urban farms, water splash·parks or access to existing facilities like rivers and lakes, it removes pressure from ecologically sensitive areas as the impact of tourism in urban areas is less. It fulfils the need of the tourists by finding a use for their leisure time and also benefits the local community by retaining income that would have been spent elsewhere. It also reduces the social and environmental cost of travelling to and from a tourist destination and also in a way substantially removes the need to desire for a holiday by reducing the demand for travel.

Create Environmental Awareness: Making people aware of the effects of tourism, providing tourists with information on scarcity of natural resources, information relating to cultural differences and advice regarding acceptable behaviour may be considered under this heading.

At Micro Level

Restrictive Entry : this is where access is controlled by the use of various means like permits licences, barriers across entry points, and quotas.

Use of Price Mechanism: To reduce the number of tourists high prices may be charged. This will create an image of "exclusivity" which in turn helps to justify the high price.

Signposting : By providing visitors with information and by the creation of signposted walks, behaviour may be modified and tourists may be kept away from sensitive areas. Signposting can be used in conjunction with information provision.

Protecting Footpaths: The sustained use of footpaths can lead to problems such as soil erosion or the widening of paths. In order to prevent this care has to be taken in planning footpaths and also consideration of what materials should be used in order to create a state of naturalness but which also sustains high levels of pedestrian flow.

Control of Access Points: It is similar to restrictive entry. The location and size of car parks, roads or hotels in relation to areas of sensitive nature can reduce the number and impact of tourists.

All the above steps, however, are to be taken very cautiously as many of these vary from one country to another. In a number of countries, especially in the West, these steps have achieved good results in protecting the environment of the areas and helped in achieving sustainable development. These steps have also helped in conserving natural and cultural resources of tourism for a long-term continuous use. Conserving the environmental amenities of a region and of advancing regional development through tourism are interdependent. The more local people benefit from tourism, the more they will benefit from a commitment to preserve the environmental features which attract tourism. Consideration of the region's ecological characteristics are essential to provide adequate criteria for the development of facilities and viable plans for the use and management of resources for tourism.

Of all the modern industries, tourism has the greatest need to protect the environment of the places of natural and cultural importance—be it a monument, a beach resort or a wildlife sanctuary. The planners must consider the environmental process wherever large investments are made in tourism development. The tourist has a strong desire to see and experience places of wonder and beauty in areas where nature remains essentially unspoiled. Destinations noted for their particular character and beauty should not be reduced to innocuous urban jungles in order to keep pace with the visitor inflow. Wildlife, which is deteriorating and vanishing so rapidly, can be safeguarded. The environment in which various animals live can be properly preserved. Similarly, many other tourist areas can be safeguarded against forces which are responsible for their degeneration. Tourism must be used as a positive factor in environmental improvement.

Physical planning and area development are therefore very essential for environmental improvement. Tourism development can become a positive factor for improving the environment if certain amount of basic planning and aesthetics are applied in the entire process. Whenever there is any major tourism development, environmental planning should be made part of that development. Any development without some controls, without any thought given to the environmental factors can, in fact, prove to be disastrous and will ultimately be counterproductive for tourism itself.

As many agencies are involved in tourism development, coordination is necessary among various segments responsible for environmental development and improvement. With a view to preserve the unique character, atmosphere and natural setting of monuments and other places of tourist interest, a coordinated approach needs to be evolved to exercise environmental control of tourist centres. In countries where there are town and country planning acts, these should be made effective enough and their provisions should cover legal protection to control environmental balance in tourist and development areas. In order to ensure that the act is properly enforced, it would be desirable to involve all those agencies which are responsible for tourism development. In countries having federal set-up, the authorities responsible for governing should carefully study the impact that the opening of a new area to tourists is likely to have on the cultural and social environment of the area. Master plans *or* area development plans should be formulated before permitting the tourists access to these areas. Concerned local authorities should be consulted at the time of working out of the proposals for area development with tourist potential. In order to ensure the implementation of the environmental control, it may be desirable for various regions to appoint coordinating committees consisting of various interests and departments to implement effectively environmental policies.

The United Nations Conference on the Human Environment, held few years back in Stockholm, recommended evolving a conservation policy within the framework of the resolution of the World Cultural Heritage. There was a unanimity of opinion that something radical had to be done to save the quality of human life and to enrich human environment. The conference was of the opinion that any development scheme of the particular area should be determined by the absorption capacity of the area; otherwise the environment would deteriorate and may in the long run create more complications than actually serve the purpose. This is true in the case of development of monuments, new tourist areas and resort towns.

A modern concept of conservation is that of science and ecology. The premise is that of man-environmental balance. The only way of striking this balance is to define conservation as protection of natural resources. Conservation means the exercise of rigid controls to prevent habitat destruction, habitat homogenization, reduction of species and natural resources pollution. Conservation, in the sense of preservation of the cultural heritage, is popularly supported today. Many man-made artifacts have a scarcity value that becomes as important to society's well being as do the natural resources. Therefore, conservation means their protection, restoration and interpretation.

Today the relationship between tourism and the environment has been receiving a growing level of attention from both public and private sector organizations all over the world. During the last decade various international bodies have cooperated in the production of great number of studies, programmes, plans and activities on tourism and environment. The degree of importance of the relationship between tourism and environment is cited in the Manila Declaration on World Tourism during World Tourism Conference held in Manila in October, 1980. The declaration states:

Tourism resources available in various countries consist at the same time of space, facilities and values. These are resources whose use cannot be left uncontrolled without running the risk of their deterioration, or even destruction. The satisfaction of tourism requirements must not be prejudicial to the social and economic interests of the population in tourist areas, to the fundamental attraction of tourism, and historical and cultural sites. All tourism resources are part of the natural heritage of mankind. National communities and the entire international community must take the necessary steps to ensure their preservation. The conservation of historical, cultural and religious sites represents at all times, and notably in time of conflict, one of the fundamental responsibilities of states.

The importance of the relationship between tourism and the environment is also stressed in the letters of agreement exchanged between the United Nations Environment Programme (UNEP) and the World Tourism Organization. The letters of agreement state:

> The protection, development and improvement of the various constituents of the environment of Man are among the basic conditions for the harmonious development of tourism. Similarly, intelligent tourism management can contribute in large measure to the protection and development of the physical environment and cultural heritage of mankind as well as the improvement of the quality of human life. It is, therefore, advisable that tourism development and sound environmental management should be integral concerns of national development policies.

Committee of WTO : The impact of tourism on the environment led the WTO Executive Council to form the Environment Committee. This committee held its first meeting at Madrid in May 1981. The representatives of various countries who attended the meeting attempted to define the relationship between tourism and the environment, and formulate guidelines and activities to be implemented by the World Tourism Organization in the future in the areas of the environment. Much of the discussion of the Environment Committee meeting centred on the theme "Tourism Development and its Effects on the Environment".

Tourism development can bring positive results to the countries that succeed in establishing an effective programme. It is important that the damage which can be done to the environment through a misuse of natural and cultural resources be avoided through the implementation of proper policies. Possible negative effects such as ecological deterioration in areas of good environmental quality, especially in mountain and coastal regions and in areas surrounding places of historical, architectural or artistic interest; speculative pressure on special sectors with the ensuing destruction of the landscape and wastage of natural environment, destruction of the traditional values of the domestic architecture and deterioration in the latter when the human dimensions of existing localities are exceeded; and saturation and overcrowding of the urban microcosm with consequent deterioration in the quality of the environment in these areas could then be checked.

Various positive steps have been taken with a view to preserve the natural environments. In the national and regional tourism plans compiled by World Tourism Organization, there is evidence of one or more of the following aspects receiving attention:

(a) Creation of natural reserves and national parks;

(b) Preservation of historical towns;

(c) Alignment of roads and highways so as to minimize environmental nuisance;

(d) Restrictions on the encroachment of the town into the countryside;

(e) Zoning of industry;

(f) Restrictions on dumping at sea, inland and in freshwater of household or industrial residues.

The formation of the Environment Committee by WTO Executive Council is the step in the right direction. The Environment Committee has adopted the following goals:

(a) To identify clusters of closely related touristic environmental issues specifically including: carrying capacity, ecosystem solvency, protection of cultural elements, protection of the built environment;

(b) To systematize field information;

(c) To define ways to involve tourists in the preservation of the environment; and

(d) To develop and disseminate guidelines for use by governments in assessing, controlling and minimizing adverse environmental effects in tourist activities.

With a view to achieve the above-mentioned goals, the Environment Committee recommended a programme of work that includes the evaluation and updating of existing studies and methodology and the general understanding of touristic environmental problems, cooperation between public and private institutions at the national and international levels aimed at developing touristic environmental guidelines and standards and finally, action by WTO and other international organizations to apply guidelines.

5

Socio-economic Aspects

Human behaviour can be understood by determining the motives, drives, or concerns which are being satisfied by the action, and secondly by the attitudes and information that the person uses to decide what response he should make in a given situation. A motive can be defined as a person's basic predisposition to reach for or strive towards a particular goal or combination of goals. Attitude, on the other hand, is a more restricted or a confined concept. It can generally be conceived of as an inner factor predisposing one to react positively or negatively towards particular objects, acts or institutions. A person's disposition or attitude towards an object is likely to be depend upon the basic motives with which the object is associated and the degree to which the object is perceived as instrumental in satisfying or blocking these motives.

The question of motivation is basically the question of 'why'. Why does Mr. X go to a temple every day? Why does his brother go on a strike and parade in the picket line four hours a day? Why does Mr. X's aunt religiously observe all the cultural taboos? Why has his cousin complained against him to his employers? The answers to all the above questions are usually given in terms of individual motivations. These are because Mr. X seeks social approval, his brother seeks more benefits from his employer, his aunt seeks status and security and his cousin seeks to express his open resistance against the family of Mr. X.

Besides some kind of an active driving force, in any account of the behaviours of people, has an important role. The individual needs, the individual wants, the individual fears, these play a commanding role in deciding individual motivations. The study of the relationships between these two variables, the driving force and the object or condition towards which that driving force is directed, is the study of the dynamics of behaviour and motivation. The basic principles or dynamics accounting for the behaviour of going to a temple, joining a particular association, seeking status and security etc., are the same, no matter how simple or how complex the activity.

In order to make accurate predictions of individual behaviour and in increasing our understanding of social phenomenon, certain questions need to be answered. The questions such as what induces these driving forces of wanting, seeking, fearing in the individuals? What determines for different individuals the specific nature of the objects or conditions towards which these driving forces are directed? What happen, for instance, when an individual, no matter how strong the driving force, fails to achieve his goal? To know the answer to these questions, certain other important questions arise. Does each individual have similar wants, needs and fears? Can an individual's wants, needs and fears be altered or changed? Can one goal be substituted for another goal to satisfy the same want? How can individual conflicting demands be resolved? The answers to all these questions' involve basic principles of perception, thinking and learning as well as that of motivation.

Role of Motivators

Before analysing various travel motivators, it is necessary to recapitulate as to how the evolution of demand for tourism came into being. Tourism and holiday making are only a part of the much wider field of leisure. Increased leisure, however, is an important factor in the growth and development of tourism and is likely to stimulate tourist demand. The implications of the growth of leisure in the twentieth century are manifold. Prior to the industrial revolution, it was only the aristocratic class who were able to afford leisure and had virtually a monopoly of it. The leisure activities of the artisan class were, however, confined to their homes and within the limits of the town. Longer holidays for them were not known. Gradually, as time passed and the working conditions improved, the workers were able to get more leisure time and managed to arrange short holidays. The first significant change, however, came in England in the year 1871 when Sir John Lubbock's Bank Holiday Act came into force. The Bank Holiday Act introduced the "August Bank Holiday" break to give four recognised annual public holidays to the workers.

As the tempo of industrialisation grew, so did the workers' demand for more leisure time. Holidays gradually became an essential part of amenities for the working classes. Various acts were passed by which it became obligatory on the part of the management to grant holidays to its employees. However, it was a gradual introduction of the system of 'holidays with pay' which heralded the era of what is today known as "mass tourism".

Increased leisure alone is not sufficient in the evolution of the demand for tourism. There are, in fact, many socio-economic factors which are important. These factors include: (a) Income; (b) Mobility; (c) Age; (d) Education; (e) Sex; (f) Travel cost.

Income is, therefore, the second important factor in the evolution of demand, after leisure. Level of income forms an important factor in influencing tourism as well as participation in recreational pursuits. The more affluent members of the society are the ones who travel most. *Mobility* is the third important factor in the evolution of demand. With the advancement of modes of transport, the mobility has increased greatly. People are no longer restricted to a particular holiday centre as they tended to be when they mostly travelled by train. The communication systems have advanced tremendously. With the building of the new and fast roadway networks, the mobility has certainly increased manifold. There are also great advances made in air travel, more particularly for overseas holiday-making. Tourists now can reach far off holiday areas in a matter of hours.

Age and sex also affect demand. More and more younger

people are taking holidays now. Younger groups participate more in travel because of more income. *Education* is yet another important socio-economic factor which influences the demand for travel. Broadly speaking, the better educated members of the population have higher propensity to travel. Besides, those with better education, travel more often. Cost is another crucial factor which influences the demand for travel. Holidaying abroad is particularly influenced by it. The price levels for various tourist services are specially significant. Countries receiving tourists should be able to compete with the costs of holidays in the generating countries. In Europe, a large number of tourists are attracted to Spain, Italy and France. In fact, these three countries receive the maximum number of tourists. One of the reasons for this is the low cost of Spanish and Italian holidays. Germany and Holland, on the other hand, do not receive as many tourists because of the high cost of food and accommodation. In South-east Asia, Singapore and Bangkok offer low-cost holidays and, therefore, are very popular among tourists.

Socio-economic factors like income, mobility, age, education and cost are thus crucial in the evolution of demand. Together with leisure, these are responsible for determining the growth of international tourism. The most comprehensive list of factors influencing the growth of tourism, however, comes from Louis Erdi of the Swiss Federal University. The list includes:

(i) Greater affluence and more leisure for an increasing number of people, particularly in the developed countries.

(ii) The emancipation of the young, and the relatively higher wages they possess (when they have no family responsibilities), enabling them to travel.

(iii) Transport facilities, especially air, very much better and cheaper, and there is a high rate of car ownership.

(iv) An enormous growth in international business, necessitating travel.

(v) Package tours allow people, not used to making their own arrangements, to travel with an easy mind, and are good value because of bulk buying of transport and hotel accommodation.

(vi) Relief from adverse climatic conditions in the home country may be found abroad.

(vii) Travel has become a status symbol.

(viii) Conferences and business meetings are proliferating.

(ix) Better education has interested a large section of the public in-cultural tourism.

(x) World exhibitions and trade fairs have become very popular.

(xi) Publicity has become more and more aggressive, whetting the appetite of even those most unwilling to travel.

(xii) Ideological pressure groups (Political, Cultural, Scientific, etc.) organise more and more annual conventions and conferences etc.

Travel Motivation

Without people's motivation to travel, there would be no tourist industry. The prospective traveller's selection of a destination is sometimes likened to a trip to a travel supermarket, where the shopper walks in and selects the destination from any one of the thousands of choices. Although there are hundreds of thousands of possible destinations, the perspective of the traveller is usually circumscribed by a number of factors. These include time, attitude, family responsibilities, finance, education, physical health and well-being. The basic question of motivation as applicable in different fields can similarly be applied to travel. Why do some people travel and not others? Why one particular member in a family takes to travel while others do not? Why in a particular country or a region, more people engage in tourism activity than in another? The answers to all these questions have been explained in the preceding paragraphs. Several Studies concerning psychology and motivation for tourism have shown that individuals normally travel for more than one reason. Tourism is the outcome of a combination of motives or motivators.

Travel motivators can be defined as those factors that create a person's desire to travel. Motivators are the internal psychological influences affecting individuals choices. Motivations operate on individuals travel purchase choices within the framework already set by the determinants of demand. Several attempts have been made to study as to why people wish to travel or become tourists. McIntosh has stated that basic travel motivators may be grouped into the following three broad categories.

Physical Motivators : These are related to physical relaxation and rest, sporting activities and specific medical treatment. All the above are concerned with the individual's bodily health and well-being.

Interpersonal Motivators : These are related to a desire to visit and meet relatives, friends or forge new friendships, or simply to escape from the routine of everyday life.

Status and Prestige Motivators : These are identified with the needs of personal esteem and personal development. These motivators also relate to travel for business or professional interests, for the purpose of education or pursuit of hobbies.

Motivations for travel cover a broad range of human behaviour and experiences. Breaking down and elaborating these will give reasons as to why more and more people engage in tourism. The breakdown of broad categories would include the following sub categories:

Outgoing Routine

Getting away from the routine of every day life is perhaps the most important motive of all in recent times. The individuals desire and need for pure pleasure is very strong. An individual likes to have fun excitement and a good time whenever possible. The significance of the pleasure factor is widely utilized by travel agents and tour operators who are astute psychologists when it comes to selling tours. Various brochures and folders particularly emphasise the pleasure aspect of holidays and travel.

Relaxation, Rest and Recreation : Industrialisation and urbanisation has created great pressures on modern living. The stress and strain of modern city life has made it more necessary than ever before for people to get away from all this and relax in an atmosphere which is more peaceful and healthy. Relaxation is very essential to keep the body and mind healthy. There may be various forms of relaxation and rest. To some it is secured by a change in the environment. Others seek relaxation in seeing new places, meeting strangers and seeking new experiences.

Health : The development of spas during the Roman Empire was the result of people's desire to seek good health. The subsequent establishment of many sanatoria in Switzerland was the result of an awareness of the various benefits of good health. These sanatoria laid the foundations for future resort developments. Many travel to spas-and clinics for curative baths and medical treatment. In some countries like Italy, Austria and Germany in Europe, great importance is given to spa treatment. In the Russian Federation along the Black Sea coast and in the foothills of the Caucasus, there are numerous world-famous sanatoria where every year millions of Russian citizens and international tourists come and avail of the facilities.

Participation in Sports : There has been an increasing participation in a wide variety of sporting activities such as mountaineering, walking, skiing, sailing, fishing, sunbathing, trekking, surf-riding, etc. More and more people these days are taking holidays involving physical activities. In recent years there has been a big increase in sporting holidays. The visitors go to places primarily to indulge in a sporting activity to which all their energies are directed.

Curiosity and Culture : An increasing number of people are visiting different lands, especially those places having important historical or cultural associations with the ancient past or those places holding special art festivals, music festivals, theatre and other cultural events of importance. Curiosity has been one of the major reasons for tourism. There has always been curiosity in man about foreign lands, people and places. In the present day world, technological developments in the area of mass media have made it possible for people to read, see and hear about different places. The increasing interest shown by many in architecture, art, music, literature, folklore, dance, paintings and sports, in other people's culture or in archaeological and historical remains and monuments, is but another aspect of man's curiosity to seek more knowledge. This curiosity has been stimulated by more education. International events like Olympic Games, Asian Games, national celebrations, exhibitions, special festivals, etc. attract thousands of tourists.

Ethnic and Family : This includes visiting one's relatives and friends, meeting new people and seeking new friendships. A large number of people make travel for interpersonal reasons. There is considerable travel by people wanting to visit friends and relatives. A large number of Americans visit European countries in order to see their families or because they feel they are visiting their homeland. Every year thousands of people visit India for ethnic reasons. Many friendships have been made as a result of holiday acquaintances.

Spiritual and Religious : Travel for spiritual reasons has been taking place since a long time. Visiting religious places has been one of the earliest motivators of travel. A large number of people have been making pilgrimages to religious or holy places. This practice is widespread in many parts of the world. In the Christian world, for instance, a visit to Jerusalem or the Vatican is considered to be very auspicious. In the Arab-Muslim world, the pilgrimage to Mecca or some other holy centres is considered to be a great act of faith. In India there are many pilgrimage centres and holy places of all the major religions of the world where every year a large number of pilgrims from all over the world congregate.

Status and Prestige : This relates to ego needs and personal development. Many people undertake travel with a view to talk about it to their relatives and friends. They like to impress them by relating their experiences in the various places visited. They also travel because they think it is fashionable to do so and, perhaps, show that they can afford to do it. 'Foreign tour' is a magic word and people like to mention it to their friends and other acquaintances.

Professional or Business : Attending conventions and conferences related to the professions, industry or commerce or to some organisation to which the individual belongs has become very popular. The 'convention travel' has made great strides in recent times. Many countries, in order to attract more tourists, have established grand convention complexes where all kinds of modern facilities are provided for business meetings, seminars and conventions. Large hotels also provide facilities for conventions as a large number of people travel for business and professional reasons. Conventions and conferences associated with education, commerce, industry, politics and various professions are increasingly being held in various parts of the world. Although some people travel strictly for business purposes, the majority link business travel with pleasure.

Professor Krapf cites in his summary to the history of tourism a series of motivations which he considers as the determining impulses of tourism in the past and present. As the *first* motivating factor, Krapf mentions the exploration of the close and distant neighbourhood. If we proceed from the fact that foreign lands and people were originally looked upon as dangerous and even hostile, it is obvious that considerable personal courage was required to visit or confront them. Only a strong man with initiative could dare to forsake the security of the family or the clan and travel to nearby or distant places.

The *second* motivation advanced by Krapf is divine service. Originally this also implied an exceptional social position for it was a prerogative reserved for priests to visit places considered as abodes of the deities and it was only gradually that the worldly high-ranking persons were able to approach them. The same held true for the *third* motivation which is participation in events of religious or secular authority. Such participation was again reserved for the selected few, i.e., those of higher social positions. The utilisation of natural medical cures or journeys to watering-places, as the *fourth* motivating factor, is again characterised by being restricted to particular social classes, at first the nobility and later the well-to-do bourgeoisie. Here the restriction flowed from the fact of long distances and the related high costs of travel and sojourn.

The final motive force mentioned by Krapf is the enjoyment of nature which must however be regarded as of relatively late validity at a time when men began to take pleasure in nature and did not look upon it as something to be taken for granted or even, to some extent, dangerous. It was the intellectual call for a "return to Nature" which first exercised the spell and made trips into what is now considered as "magnificent Nature", a favourite social practice. But here again the high costs resulted in this practice being restricted to the well-off, that is the higher social classes. Thus we see that there is no ground for modifying the argument that the spread of the need to travel outside one's habitual place has its roots in the striving for social influence and that the expansion of tourism or the satisfaction of this need is the logical consequence of social progress.

The democratisation of travel, this being formerly a sign of distinction, developed through holiday stays, the travel flow which we encounter at present. Consequently, we must enlarge the test of motivations drawn up by Professor Krapf with a tourist motivation, namely, the enjoyment of travel. It is not the fact of sojourning but of motion, not the destination but the journey, the innumerably multifarious, though often momentary impressions, which account for a part of modern tourism. It is the joy in motion, especially motorised motion, which has become a major motivating force while the landscape which is traversed has become a side-scene. Some of the motivations cited in respect of modern tourism are enumerated as follows:

(a) The exploration of the close and distant neighbourhood, knowing other countries, regions or people, and also travel for studies and cultural ends.

(b) Divine service as a travel motivating force subsists in journeys to sacred religious places and in pilgrimages.

(c) Participation in events of religious or secular authority manifests itself today in the form of travel to political meetings and ceremonies.

(d) The utilisation of natural medical cures comprises in the widest sense all travel undertaken with the object of rest and relaxation, medical care or treatment of diseases.

(e) Travel for the enjoyment of the beauties of the landscape has undergone modifications both in the conception of what is beautiful and in the expression of sentiment.

(f) A further motive force of tourism is constituted by sports travel. This includes travel for the sake of travelling, the joy in motion. In fact, this is only one sports activity projected on the travel scene in addition to the numerous other motive forces connected with sports for which landscape and nature provide the setting for the best possible practice and exercise of sports.

Several reasons as to why people wish to become tourists have been considered. In considering the reasons we are thus dealing with the motivations. After examining the motivations two broad distinguishable groups of travellers emerge. The first group consists of those who have to visit a particular place and includes businessmen and some elements of those who may be described as common interest travellers such as those visiting relatives and friends. The decision to travel, when and where to go, how much to spend, etc., is to a greater or lesser extent outside the control of this group of travellers.

They are also less influenced by price or distance factor. Particularly business travel is relatively price-inelastic and is not susceptible to price inducements. The second group consists of tourists in the pure sense who have a freedom of choice. This group decides for themselves whether they should apply a part of their income and a part of their leisure time to participate in tourism. They also decide for themselves where and when to go. The demand for travel for this group as compared to the demand for the former group is highly price-elastic, that is susceptible to price inducements. The reasons for travel away from home in the case of businessmen and others in the first group are self-evident. Each may, indeed, be marginally influenced by those considerations which affect the second group, the pleasure travellers. This may be reflected in the frequency of visits or the consideration of alternatives as, for example, in the choice of venues for conventions and conferences. In pleasure or holiday travel on the other hand, the reasons are varied and not always clearly evident or easily identifiable.

The prime motive to engage in tourism is to be 'elsewhere' and to escape, however temporarily, from the routine and stress and strains of everyday life. From this prime motivation two principal and distinct motivations may be stipulated as dominant. These have been described by Professor Gray as: 1. Wanderlust; 2. Sunlust.

Wanderlust describes the desire to exchange the known for the unknown or familiar with the unfamiliar, to leave things familiar and to go and see different places, people and cultures or architecture of the past, in places famous for their historical monuments and also past associations. This also involves seeing current fashions. *Sunlust* on the other hand generates a type of travel which depends on the existence elsewhere of better amenities and facilities for a specific purpose than are available in the home country of the traveller. It is prominent with particular activities such as sports and with the search for sunshine. Wanderlust calls for facilities geared to short-stay visitors and for means of movement at the destinations. Sunlust on the other hand requires facilities for a longer stay and for recreation.

Tracing the history of travel over the centuries, it is quite evident that the main motives for travel have not changed much. These have remained the same in form. Only the scope and the intensity have changed. The principal motives continue to be the same. While wanderlust in ancient times manifested itself in the exploration and search of the unknown, today it has the same purpose with a different angle. Similarly Sunlust in the past was associated with pleasure travel of the Romans, today it manifests itself in exotic holidays around the beaches and the holiday villages.

6

The Administration

A few years ago, a survey was conducted in Germany to find out what people would like to buy most, if they had a choice. Travel for a holiday was the choice of the majority. It is true of most countries in western Europe, USA, Canada, Japan and Australia. It may not be true in India as yet because a majority of people in India have other priorities, like housing and other basic requirements of life to deal with, before they can even think of a vacation away from their home. But for the emerging new middle class in the country with disposable income, holiday away from home is a top priority.

Importance of Travelling

First, let us find out why people travel. Travel, was in the past limited to a few who were rich and venturesome. The people who were not rich had little time to travel, because they had no respite from their daily grind. And, if they had time, they had no disposable income. One starts thinking of holiday travel only when one has some disposable income after taking care of housing, food, clothing and education of the children. More changes have taken place in the structure of our societies in the last hundred years, than in the previous two thousand years. Industrial development has led to urbanisation. Urbanisation led to pollution and overcrowding in our cities. Industrialisation brought about some benefits too—more employment, increased leisure and paid holidays to the workers. The overcrowding in the cities led to people's search for the sun, sand, solitude and the fresh mountain air.

The revolution in transportation, specially the evolution of cheaper air-services, encouraged people to travel. In the developed industrial societies of the west, the urge to travel became irresistible.

In 1961, fifty per cent of British workers enjoyed fourteen days or less paid holidays in a year. In 2000, almost hundred per cent of the British workers enjoyed paid holidays for one month or more. Executives and workers in major Indian companies have also acquired similar benefits. Government servants in India have too many holidays—more than most countries in the world. Even if a political leader dies, government declares a holiday. What for? One wonders! There are too many religious holidays in India. If we count their privilege and sick leave, Indians are on leave six months in a year.

A holiday abroad, has become quite affordable and attractive within Europe for Europeans. Brian Moynahan, author of a book, *Fools Paradise,* says: "At its best the industry offers superb value for money. A fortnight can be had in a foreign resort, with rooms, meals and air travel for the cost of a suit." He was referring to the low prices of package tours available in London, for Spain and Portugal.

Establishment of National Tourist Administration (NTAs): The rapid spread of education led to the desire to find out how people live in other countries. Governments helped in the promotion of tourism by setting up National Tourist Organisations, initially to promote inbound tourism to their country. Some countries actively promoted the concept of overseas travel among their own nationals. Take the case of Japan—this small country of one hundred and twenty million people sends fifteen million tourists to foreign lands every year— more than one out of ten Japanese. The Japanese Government considers it a way of balancing their huge trade surplus with other countries. The Japanese who come to India, for instance, spend money in India. And, the Indian Government which has an unfavourable balance of trade with Japan, can balance the trade gap to some extent.

Over fifty-five million trips to foreign countries are taken by the US citizens every year—and the total US population is a little more than two hundred and eighty million. Domestic tourism, too is an essential part of the life-styles of Americans, Europeans and the Japanese. Two or three domestic holidays in one year are not uncommon.

Why Travelling ? : Anybody who travels has a motive of his or her own. On the basis of these motives or purposes, we can divide tourism into distinct categories.

Recreational Travel : The first and foremost is recreational travel. The purpose in this case is recreation—holiday or leisure. People want to get away from the humdrum of everyday life and move to beaches, mountains and the scenic countryside. It has been estimated that seventy-five per cent of international travel in the world and fifty per cent of domestic travel is recreational. According to an Indian Government Survey, done in 1999, seventy-five per cent of foreign visitors come to India for recreation or holiday and the remaining twenty-five per cent come for business, official visits and other purposes.

Adventure and Sports Tourism : The trips undertaken by people for playing golf, tennis, skiing, trekking, mountaineering, etc., fall within this category. Adventure tourism is becoming a popular form of tourism in India. The country offers many opportunities for an adventure holiday and it is becoming more popular.

Cultural Tourism : The third category is cultural tourism. When people are motivated to travel in order to see the cultural heritage of their own country or those of foreign countries, i.e., visit ancient historical monuments, places of religious interest, museums, art galleries, etc., it is termed as cultural tourism. Visits to Varanasi, Haridwar or Rameshwaram are part of cultural tourism.

Health Tourism : The fourth category is that of people who take trips to have medical treatment elsewhere, or to visit places where there are curative possibilities such as hot springs, spas or yoga institutes. This is called health tourism. People travelling to

Kerala for ayurvedic treatment or to the USA for major surgeries, fall in this category.

Conference and Convention Tourism

In recent years, two new, but very important categories of tourism have emerged—convention and conference tourism. A large number of people are now travelling within their own country, or abroad to attend conventions or conferences, attending meetings relating to their businesses. The purpose is to gain knowledge through other people's experiences. This is a fast-growing area of travel. In many countries like the USA and Japan, expenditure incurred by company executives on attending business-related conferences overseas, is tax-deductible. If a doctor from the USA or Japan comes to India to attend a medical conference, his expenditure on his Indian trip will be tax-deductible. The Government of India does not extend similar concessions to its professionals as yet.

Incentive Travel

The concept of incentive travel was developed to motivate workers to do a better job. The manufacturing companies or business corporations offer their good workers, sales executives, retailers or wholesalers with rewards of free holidays within the country or overseas which include transportation, hotels, meals and entertainment. People seem to prefer free holidays as a reward, as compared to material gifts like a TV set, refrigerator or a washing machine. In affluent countries, workers often do not need these items as incentives as they have already bought them from their own savings. So, the idea of offering free holidays as an incentive was discovered and has since caught on. Often, the incentive includes free travel, both for husband and wife. Every year, millions of people are travelling as part of incentive travel from their companies in different parts of the world. In countries like the USA, there are travel companies specialising in organising incentive travel only for business corporations. Incentive travel for workers and executives has started in India too—though the scale is as yet modest. Some companies promote foreign tours to neighbouring countries.

World-wide Organisation

Having determined what makes people travel, we can look at the organisation of tourism in the world. The travel agents act as coordinators of different segments of travel.

Travel has become a massive business enterprise. In some countries it has assumed the shape of mass tourism. Imagine, Spain with a population of ten million—had forty-eight million foreign visitors in 2000) had Even in Asia, Singapore has a population of 2.4 million and foreign visitors were seven million in 2000.

Government's Role : Governments, therefore, have to play a key role in the planning, development, regulation and marketing of tourism. Tourism helps every government because it provides employment to the citizens and earns foreign currency for the country. Therefore, practically every government in the world, irrespective of its size, has a NTA. It may be called a Department of Tourism as in the case of India, a Tourist Promotion Board as in the case of Singapore, a Tourism Authority as in the UK and Thailand or a Tourism Ministry as in the Philippines. The NTAs are involved in planning, development, promotion and administration of tourism. While planning a beach or mountain resort, an NTA tries to make sure that there is no overcrowding, pollution and destruction of historic or archaeological landmarks as a result of the new area development for tourism. To promote tourism, an NTA opens tourist offices overseas to attract foreign tourists to their shores. They also have tourist information offices within their own countries, to provide information to foreign visitors on arrival and also to domestic travellers who wish to travel within their own country.

In India, the Central Department of Tourism has eleven tourist offices in foreign countries and twenty-one within India. In large countries like India, there are several Government tourist organisations. For instance, almost all the twenty-eight State Governments of India and seven Union Territories have their Departments of Tourism and majority of them have Government-owned State Tourism Development Corporations. They operate at State levels. Although most States have their Departments of Tourism and Tourism Development Corporations, the level of tourism development has been uneven. Tourism is a State subject and the

Centre cannot enforce its decisions unilaterally on all the States. It was in this context that the National Committee on Tourism (NCT), suggested in 1988 that tourism should be brought on the concurrent list of the Constitution of India. The advantage would be that the Central Government could initiate a legislation in the tourism field for All-India application. Initially State Governments were not interested in tourism development. The Centre had to subsidise the State Governments to open such departments for promotion of tourism. Now most of them are reasonably active and are no longer subsidised by the Centre. The Centre, however, assists them financially to strengthen or streamline their infrastructure where needed.

At the All-India level, there is the public sector—India Tourism Development Corporation (ITDC), with a network of hotels all over India, transport units in various states, a chain of duty-free shops at the international airports and undertaking other tourism-related jobs. Several States have followed the ITDC pattern at their level. Now, a decision has been taken at the Centre that the Government should leave the tourism business to private sector. ITDC is, therefore, in the process of privatisation and the State Governments too are thinking on similar lines. In fact, these Corporations with so much public investments have become a burden on public exchequer, as they are no longer profitable. The Government has to put in money to run them.

Establishment of World Tourism Organisation (WTO) : In the organisational chart of tourism, World Tourism Organisation (WTO) is the apex body—representing at world level, the tourism interests of NTAs and working as an affiliate of the United Nations Organisation (UNO). Started as the International Union of Official Travel Organisation (IUOTO) in the first half of the twentieth century, it became an intergovernmental organisation in 1975 and named World Tourism Organisation WTO, for short. Presently, it has a membership of one hundred and thirty-seven countries and territories. Besides, there are some three hundred and fifty affiliate members like airlines, travel agencies, etc.

WTO provides many services to its members—principal one being the compilation of travel statistics and the publication of books and reports, to help member Governments to plan and develop their tourism. It works closely with several other international organisation with the objectives of helping develop tourism in the world. It offers expert help to developing countries to plan, develop and reorganise their tourism. It strives to improve the quality of tourism education. Presently, its focus is to create environment for sustainable tourism.

India is one of its founding members and is often elected to its Executive Council. Its Chief Executive is called Secretary General. WTO aims to create favourable conditions for free movement of travel in the world. For this purpose, it favours the passport-free travel in the world. To some extent, it has been achieved in all the European Countries (EU), where the citizens can travel without visa and passport. Besides, they have introduced a common currency called Euro making travel hassle-free. At present, if a visitor gets visa for one of the eleven European countries, it is valid for all the eleven member countries. WTO is based in Madrid, Spain.

Establishment of Pacific Asia Travel Association (PATA) : Among other world bodies which sustain and promote international tourism, Pacific Asia Travel Association (PATA) is notable. Although its active members are from the Pacific region, extending from Canada to the Indian sub-continent, (hundred governments, sixty-six airlines and cruise lines. Its presence, etc., worldwide is felt through its more than eighty chapters (seventeen thousand members). It is primarily a marketing organisation, promoting tourism to the Pacific region and assisting member countries in various ways.

Originally established in Hawaii in 1951, it was later head-quartered in San Francisco for four decades and is now based in Bangkok, with divisional offices in USA, Australia, Singapore and Europe. It membership exceeds 2000 and consists of governments, airlines, steamship companies, cruise lines, travel agencies, media, etc.

PATA is headed by a Chief Executive and managed by a large Board of Directors, representing many countries. Its annual conventions are a great draw, attracting some one thousand five hundred industry leaders from all over the world. The 2002 Convention was held in New Delhi.

PATA organisation is actively involved in developing ethos for sustainable tourism.

PATA programmes are designed to meet the needs of members, allowing each to remain competitive in the world market place. PATA offers to its members research and marketing services, product development and a variety of educational seminars and workshops.

Besides the above, there are world organisations representing hotels, travel agencies, airlines, transport, etc.

In the organisation of tourism, transport is an inseparable element. Tourism transport consists of aeroplanes, motor vehicles, railways, cruise lines, etc. Of course, governments are closely involved in the operation and regulation of the transport system.

Another essential element of tourism is accommodation—hotels, moteis, inns, tourist bungalows or lodges, youth hostels, etc., where tourists can stay.

Finally, the most important elements are the tourist attractions of a country—scenic beauty, historical monuments, rivers, lakes, parks, mountains, beaches, forests, wildlife, flora and fauna, climate, food and shopping. Tourists come to see and enjoy what a country can offer. Together, all the elements mentioned above, comprise the tourism assets or resources of a country. When these are packaged, the experts call it the 'tourism product' of a country. After all, this is the product a visitor wants to buy. Like manufactured products, the tourism product too has a lot of variety. You can package it in many interesting ways as preferred or demanded by the customers. It may be a holiday on the beaches, a peep into a country's past, a mountain vacation, wi!dlife viewing or a shopping tour. The visitors have several options and combinations of options at different price ranges.

There is, however, one difference. Tourism is a product which has to be bought unseen. Like manufactured products, you cannot bring them to the customer to see and feel. The customer has to go to it to experience and to feel it. The new technology however, can present to you, on a computer, 'virtual reality' of the tourism product.

Establishment of India's National Tourist Administration (NTA) : As mentioned earlier, every country sets up its National Tourist Administration (NTA) according to its own requirements. All countries or States of the world, have a NTA, supported and sponsored by the Government of the country. In the western world, most NTAs are sponsored and financed by the Government. In a few countries, private sector also supports it financially and is involved, to some extent, in the management of NTAs. This is not so in India.

The Department of Tourism which manages tourism at the Government level, is wholly dependent on the Government for financial support. No attempt has been made to involve the private sector financially in a supporting role. The private sector is not involved even in an advisory role, though it is sometimes consulted at the discretion of the Government.

The argument in favour of private sector participation is that since the private sector is the major beneficiary of tourism promotion undertaken by a Government, it is logical that they share part of the expenditure on tourism promotion and management. The Government of India, in its wisdom, decided not to involve the private sector. Or, when the Government of India mooted the idea of promoting tourism, the private sector was not strong enough to contribute any money. A successful example of the Government and the private sector being actively involved in the NTO affairs is Switzerland, where the private sector contributes almost forty per cent of the expenditure. USA does not have a NTA—it was disbanded in 1995 for economic reasons. Federal Government felt that the private sector should solely promote tourism as they were the primary beneficiaries. And, US tourism has not since looked back.

There were valid reasons for not involving the private sector. When the Department of Tourism was set up in 1958, the travel industry in India was so small and so shy that the Government did not think that the industry could contribute substantially. So, the idea of charging a fee from the industry did not appeal to the decision-makers.

In fact, the private sector in hoteliering and transport was so reluctant that the Government of India had to set up a company in the public sector to build and operate hotels at tourist centres, where the private sector was not willing to invest. Similarly, at major tourist centres like Khajuraho, Varanasi or Jaipur, there was no adequate tourist transport facilities. The public sector company, ITDC with its headquarters in New Delhi, had to step in to operate public sector transport units to provide good transport fleet.

India, therefore, is a unique case history in tourism development.

During the early years of independence, major business houses, except the house of Tatas, did not consider the operation of hotels and restaurants as an honourable business. There were only a few modern hotels in the country and those too run by foreigners. The Government's intervention became necessary to develop the basic infrastructure at major tourist centres to attract foreign tourists. This led to the Government building and operating hotels and transport units, through its public sector organisation like the ITDC all over India. State Tourism Corporations have followed the same pattern and built budget accommodation and have also operated tourist transport fleets in their respective States.

The tourism scene has changed drastically during the last thirty years and the private sector is now very active in tourism development. Indian hotels in the private sector compare favourably with the best in the world and some of the leading Indian hotel chains are operating hotels in developed countries under their brand name. The Government of India has recognised this fact and decided not to invest any rnore in the construction of new five-star hotels, leaving the tourism industry totally open to the private sector in India. In fact, there are moves to sell hotels owned by ITDC and Hotel Corporation of India. A few properties were sold in 2002.

India's NTA would, therefore, consists of a Department of Tourism which is a Department of the Ministry of Tourism and also the India Tourism Development Corporation which is a public sector company and implements Government's policy decisions in tourism field. The WTO has a new name for NTOs— the National Tourism Administration—NTAs. They prefer to call it NTA because an Administration has wider ramifications than the Organisation.

The private sector is encouraged by the Department of Tourism to operate tourism facilities under the overall policy guidelines of the Government. In fact, there is an excellent cooperation and understanding between the Department of Tourism and the private sector tour operators, travel agents, transporters and hoteliers in the area of tourism development. Historically, tourism development in India has suffered due to a lack of clear thinking on the part of political decision-makers in the country. Bureaucratic hurdles made it worse.

India became aware of the importance of tourism promotion as early as in 1946. Sir John Sargent, Educational Adviser to the Government of India, headed a committee to survey the potential of tourism in India and recommended that developing tourist traffic, both internal and external, will be beneficial for India. The recommendation led to the establishment of a Tourist Traffic branch in the Ministry of Transport and Communication, with a network of tourist offices in India and abroad. The branch later transformed itself into a department headed by a director general in 1958. The first overseas tourist office was set up in New York as early as in 1952, followed by similar offices in London, Paris, Frankfurt, Colombo, Melbourne and San Francisco. In retrospect, tourist offices overseas were opened too soon at too many foreign cities without providing them adequate budgetary support and without analysing the availability of adequate infrastructure at home, particularly accommodation suitable for foreigners. Besides, travellers from distant countries like USA, Canada, had a poor image of India as a holiday destination.

Establishment of Tourism Logo Department : The establishment of a separate Department of Tourism, helped considerably and the international tourist arrivals which were sixteen thousand in 1951 jumped to over sixteen lakh in 1990, and were twenty-six crore in 2000.

The importance of promotion of tourism for the economic development of India, was realised by the late Prime Minister, Indira Gandhi. She established in 1967, a separate Ministry of Tourism and Civil Aviation under Dr. Karan Singh. It was good to tie up tourism with civil aviation, as fast development of tourism is not possible without the total support of the Civil Aviation Ministry, in a country where ninety-eight per cent of foreign visitors come by air. Subsequently, all kinds of experiments have been done with the Tourism Ministry to suit the political needs of the Government in power. At times, the Ministry of Tourism has been separated from Civil Aviation to work in isolation. Later, it was attached to Commerce which made some sense. In 1991, it was tied to Agriculture which made no sense. In 1991, the Tourism and Civil Aviation ministries were again combined under a Cabinet Minister, Madhavrao Scindia. The Deve Gowda Government linked Tourism Ministry with the Ministry of Parliamentary Affairs in 1996. The BJP Government did the same in 1998. Presently, it is attached to Culture which again makes sense. It seems, tourism portfolio is the least attractive for politicians.

The Director General of Tourism in the Department of Tourism, is of the rank of an Additional Secretary and under him are various heads of divisions like planning, publicity, hotels, market research, supplementary accommodation, etc.

Sphere of Work

The activities of the Department of Tourism in India, and for that matter, all NTAs anywhere in the world, can be summed up as under the following broad heads:

- Compilation, collection and dissemination of tourist information in India and abroad; attending to enquiries from international tourists, tour operators and travel industry sectors such as airlines, steamship companies and hotels; production of tourist literature—posters, brochures, information directories, tourist guide maps— for wide distribution. Now, most NTAs including India, have set up their websites for travel information so that the people with internet connections can access this information and make their travel decisions. There website have to be updated from time to time;
- Cooperation with international travel and tourist organisations at the Government and non-Government levels;
- Facilitation, such as simplification of frontier formalities in respect of entry of international tourists;

- Development of tourist activities of interest to international tourists;
- Publicity at home and abroad with the object of creating an overall awareness of the importance of tourism;
- Regulation of the activities of various segments of the travel trade, such as hotels, youth hostels, travel agents, wildlife outfitters, guides, tourist car operators and shopkeepers catering to tourist needs; and
- Compilation of statistics and market research on international tourist traffic to India and on its utilisation for effective tourist promotion. Compilation of domestic tourism statistics.

Proposals for Reorganisation

In 1987, the Government of India under the late Prime Minister, Rajiv Gandhi, appointed a high-level National Committee on Tourism under the chairmanship of Mr. Mohammed Yunus. The Committee consisted of leading experts on tourism from the Government of India as well as the private sector. A major recommendation of the Committee was the reorganisation of the Department of Tourism, to make it a National Tourism Board like the Railway Board, with considerable autonomy in the implementation of schemes. The other recommendation was to have a cadre of professional tourist officers in the organisation instead of inducting Indian administrative service officers or staff from other ministries.

The recommendations were welcomed by the industry but implementation is not yet on the horizon. The vested interest of the entrenched officers is the major hurdle.

Establishment of India Tourism Development Corporation (ITDC) : Set up in 1966 as an autonomous public sector corporation, ITDC was entrusted with the task of helping to develop a tourist infrastructure and promoting India as a tourist destination. Over the years, ITDC has been playing a crucial, strategic role in ensuring:

- Proper dispersal of socio-economic benefits of tourism;
- Promoting national integration and international understanding;
- Removal of regional imbalances;

- Generating employment opportunities;
- Augmenting foreign exchange earnings; and
- Acting as a catalyst in the development of tourism by opening up new unexplored tourist areas.

ITDC's present range of operations is diverse. The package of tourist services comprises accommodation, catering, transport, publicity services, duty-free shops, an in-house travel agency—the Ashok Travels—entertainment, conferences, and providing management consultancy services within India and abroad.

Chain of Accommodation

The Ashok Group, ITDC's accommodation chain, is the largest in the country and offers accommodation in over three thousand and eight hundred rooms in its thirty-three hotels at twenty-six destinations, ranging from luxury suites to modestly furnished rooms and from beach resorts to moderately priced travellers/forest lodges. ITDC owns twenty-six hotels—six of its hotels are owned by its subsidiaries.

Accommodation is divided into three categories—Elite (six), Classic (sixteen) and Comfort (eleven). A few of the ITDC owned hotels have recently been sold to the private sector. It may be mentioned that a few of the ITDC-owned hotels were sold to private sector in 2002.

The Corporation's scheme of joint ventures/consultancy collaborations with the State Governments/Tourism Corporations, and private entrepreneurs, has had an enthusiastic response. Several States and private sector organisations have entered into agreements with ITDC, with ITDC operating their hotel properties under a management contract.

Duty-Free Shops : To facilitate shopping by international passengers, ITDC operates ten duty-free shops and a tax-free shop. The duty-free shops function in the arrival and departure lounges of the international airports of the country—Delhi, Mumbai, Kolkata, Chennai, Thiruananthapuram and Goa. The only tax-free shop is located at Ashok Hotel, New Delhi. Duty-free shops offer a product portfolio of over fifteen thousand. It is currently one of its few profitable areas, others are loss-making including accommodation.

Facilitating Conferences and Conventions : India's potential for convention tourism has been exploited by ITDC. ITDC's flagship—Ashok Hotel in New Delhi provides good facilities for holding international conferences for a thousand or more people at a time. It is still a popular venue for international conferences in New Delhi.

Network of Ashok : The Ashok Network, a centralised reservation service located at New Delhi, with four regional offices covering north, south, east and west India, ensures instant accommodation and transport confirmations for individuals and groups countrywide. An addition to instant bookings/confirmations is Ashok Internet, a hotel-to-hotel reservation system of the Ashok Group.

Ashok Travels and Tours : To provide back-up support to its hotels, the Corporation has its in-house full service travel agency—the Ashok Travels and Tours (ATT). From eleven units, located in various parts of the country, the ATT operates the largest fleet of coaches, tourist cars and air-conditioned limousines.

Entertainment : The French started a novel experiment in the late fifties—telling the story of old castles and palaces through the medium of sound and light. This was an additional source of entertainment for tourists.

In India, the first Sound & Light Show was mounted at the Red Fort, Delhi, narrating the story of the famous Mughal Fort beginning with the Mughal era and going on to India's Independence.

Subsequently, another show came up at Sabarmati Ashram, Ahmedabad on the life of the "Father of the Nation", Mahatma Gandhi. In the same year, a Sound & Light Show was mounted at Shalimar Gardens, Srinagar, based on the romantic story of the Great Mughal Emperor, Jahangir, and his intelligent and dynamic consort, Noor Jahan. After that, ITDC put up shows at the Cellular Jail (a national monument now) in Andaman and Nicobar Islands and at Golconda Fort in Hyderabad.

Sound & Light Shows provide good, wholesome entertainment and are so very informative. ITDC has now mounted a show at Chandragiri Fort in Chittoor district of Andhra Pradesh. Others in the pipeline are at the Somnath Temple in Veraval district, Gujarat and at the Sun Temple at Konarak, Orissa.

The world heritage site of Hampi in Karnataka—the Capital of the mighty Vijayanagar Empire; as also Katra in Jammu— nestling at the feet of the Goddess Durga, will also see Sound & Light Shows before long.

Modern dramatic techniques of lighting systems, are being used in mounting these shows with the help of digital technology.

Travel Packages : To promote domestic tourism, ITDC operates various tourism packages every year. These packages are moderately priced and sold at all hotels of the Ashok Group in the country.

Publicity Consultancy : ITDC has a publicity division which offers consultancy services to State Governments and other similar organisations. Their services include advertising, publicity and tourism communications.

Financial Success : ITDC with an authorised share capital of Rs 75 crore and paid up capital of Rs 675 crore has six subsidiary companies. It is one of the few public sector undertakings which has been making profits ever since its inception. However, in the late nineties, it started its downhill journey and has been consistently in the red mainly due to over-staffing and unionisation. The Government of India has decided in principle to disinvest in the activities of ITDC and let the private sector run the business of hotel-keeping. It is only a matter of time when ITDC will be out of the hands of the Government. Delay is mainly due to vested interest.

Establishment of India Convention Promotion Bureau (ICPB) : In a bid to promote convention and conference tourism, the Ministry of Tourism has sponsored the establishment of the India

"Wanted Ambassadors for India" : It is estimated that more than 20,000 of India's professional elite, attend over 10,000 conferences worldwide every year. Are you one of them? We need you as an Ambassador.

We need you to go beyond the role of a delegate to that of a dignitary, to present India as the Conference Destination of the 90s.

To bag the next conference at the next international meet you attend, and make India the prestigious venue.

The Booming Conference Business : Over 33,000 conferences are held around the world every year and generate an incredible US dollars 104 billion in revenue.

India's share is minuscule. We host around 170 conferences annually.

Imagine the opportunities and the pivotal role you can play in attracting this immensely prestigious, booming business to India!

India - New Destination : There is an international awakening.

There is a growing realisation that India is much more than a tourist destination. It is an unforgettable learning experience.

Contemporary facilities and the richest legacies.

That is the inimitable beauty of India you can offer with the greatest pride and confidence: Majesty, Mystery, Grandeur and above all our famed warmth and hospitality in comfort and style that will redefine international standards. Assure them of our prestigious conference venues in historic Delhi, in scenic Srinagar and several other centres, each especially planned and developed as a confluence for minds.

Convention Halls for ten to 10,000, Hi-Tech Communication facilities—Fax, Telex, Computers, International Direct Dialling, Administrative and Secretarial help, Staff with convention experience. In essence, you name it, it is there.

India Convention Promotion Bureau (ICPB) redefines you from Delegate to Host : To make you vie with the world.

To provide all the support you need to bid and win. That is the role of ICBP. A non-profit association sponsored by the Ministry of Tourism, Government of India.

In this endeavour, ICBP has the support and resources of its member bodies comprising Airlines, Hotels, Travel Agents, Tour Operators, Tourist Bureaus, Travel Associations, etc.

Count on ICPB to make your conference happen. ICPB is with you all the way.

Right from the ideation stage, discussing ways and means of getting your conference to India, preparing professional bid documents, assisting in the post-bid phase through member organisations, promoters, bookings, management of the event—everything.

If all this sounds amazing, talk to ICBP if you are serious about becoming an Ambassador for India.

ICPB has its office at Room No.233, Ashok Hotel, New Delhi-110021. Tel: 6874318.

Convention Promotion Bureau (ICPB). While a major part of the expenses is borne by the Government of India, the private sector also contributes its share. Its office is located in the Ashoka Hotel, New Delhi. ICPB tries to attract international conferences to India—by making presentations at the conferences regarding the facilities offered by India and the fun that awaits the delegates.

Extracts from the text of an advertisement issued by ICPB in major national magazines are reproduced on the facing page. It explains the ICPB's area of work.

Opening of Overseas Tourist Offices : The Government of India opened its tourist offices overseas, to promote inbound tourism to destination India as early as 1950— now they number seventeen in different parts of the world. Most of them are located in the affluent countries of the west— including the USA, Europe, Japan and Australia. Annual expenditure on the upkeep of these offices and promotion abroad exceeds Rs 75 crore. The expenditure is insignificant as the country earns over Rs 10,000 crore from foreign tourism and this small expense seems justifiable. The entire expenditure is funded by the Government of India—the private sector which benefits from tourism does not contribute to it.

But, there are examples of some successful experiments doing without overseas tourist offices with little adverse effect on their inbound arrivals, e.g., the USA, China and Russia. The USA once had tourist offices abroad but closed them finding that they did not add to the number of arrivals. There are countries like Pakistan, Nepal and others which too do not have overseas offices.

A WTO study done in 1997 revealed that, worldwide, Singapore was the destination which spent most in a year on promotion overseas through its overseas office—US$99 million, followed by the UK, US$78 million; Spain, US$71 million; Thailand, US$66 million and Australia, US$61 million. But, their tourism is much larger than India's.

However, the new technology and the availability of excellent websites of nations has made them redundant. Even at the time, this technology was not available, the percentage of visitors to India who got information from overseas tourist offices or through their advertising was less than two per cent.

Now, it will be much less. Questions, therefore, have been raised by not only the travel industry but also by the Tourism Minister, Finance Minister, etc., about the utility of these offices or at least so many of them. In India, it is not easy to think objectively on subjects where plum jobs are involved—involving extensive foreign travel abroad.

However, in 2002, the Government of India decided to close down five of its sixteen overseas offices.

Explosion of Domestic Tourism : An unfortunate feature of Indian tourism is that policy-makers in the past have always equated tourism with foreign visitors. There were two reasons for it—one, it was traditionally the foreign visitor who occupied hotel rooms, filled airline seats, frequented bars and restaurants and used the recreation and adventure facilities. And, during the days of short supply of foreign exchange, it was the foreign visitor who seem to be purveyor of unlimited money supply. Every aspect of Indian tourism was, therefore, arranged to suit his needs. Even the price mechanism seemed to tie with overseas costs, ignoring the average standards in the country.

There is, however, a hidden dimension to Indian tourism one that has figured little in the policy planning or thinking of most industry and Government players: almost unobstrusive and yet inexorable rise in domestic tourism. In the last ten years, domestic tourism has increased by more than hundred million travellers, up by, from 63.8 million in 1990 to one hundred and seventy-six million in 1999.

The explosion in domestic travel is an inevitable by-product of economic development in the country and various other factors like pilgrimages. An average Indian traveller is an avid sightseer too and his average spending is growing. Soon, many of them will be patronising star hotels.

Personal spending on travel and tourism in 2001, by the residents positions, puts India as the nineteenth largest spender in the world.

The forecast for personal travel tourism growth over the next decade, at 9.7 per cent annually, positions India as the second fastest growing country in this category. Business travel and tourism in India is expected to grow by 7.1 per cent per annum over the coming decade (Source : WTTC), and, that too without much help from the Government.

NTA's Success Story

Singapore : Singapore Tourism is an interesting success story.

In 1957, when Singapore and Malaysia were one country, an Assembly man, William Tan, argued against the allocation of a budget of US$300,000 for tourism promotion because, he felt, Singapore had nothing worthwhile to offer to foreign visitors. Singapore, he stated, had only three attractions: "Swamplands, some five buildings and the death houses of Sago Lane. Little else!"

Despite romanticism engendered by Somerset Maugham's exotic tales of the east, written in the gardens of the Singapore's old Raffles Hotel, there were not many visitors who wanted to come to the city for sightseeing. In 1957, some one lakh fifty thousand passengers had to stop in Singapore *en route* to other destinations, but not even half of them chose to visit the city, instead they preferred to staying in "transit". Such was the image of this city till the early sixties.

After 1960, tourists started arriving in Singapore for a different reason. They found shops on Sundays with unbelievably low price-tags on imported goods. Visitors from Australia and New Zealand discovered a new world, full of itinerant Asian hawkers selling dishes with strange names and stranger flavours, interesting food taken on stools outside the rickety shophouses, firecrackers erupting on festival days, touts promising 'best buys for you, Sir' and exotic night-life. For the less adventurous, Raffles Hotel offered a slice of England on the Equator with Asia beckoning at the doorstep.

The Government of Singapore realised the potential of tourism and set up an organisation to promote it. But tourism efforts got a real boost when in 1 August, 1965, Singapore seceded from the Malayan Federation and became an independent republic. Independence gave an impetus to tourism which was strengthened to generate more employment and the economic development of the City-State.

The Singapore Tourist Promotion Board (STPB) was born with a mandate to be the catalyst in the development of tourism. And, they did it effectively. The Government gave them enough funds to undertake the promotion of Singapore all over the world and also to develop new attractions by the simple method of giving back to them, a small tax, collected on hotel room rental charges and meals. Singapore has not looked back since then.

Although this port-city is often compared to Manhattan, New York, because of its high-rise buildings, it is essentially eastern and presents a mixture of four cultures: Chinese, Malaya, Indian and European. The cultural mix has been successfully presented by Singapore in its advertising campaign. They present Singapore as a mini-Asia to the western world.

Singapore has a population of only 2.5 million: seventy-seven per cent Chinese, fifteen per cent Malaya, six per cent Indians and two per cent others. It has an area of one thousand square kilometres, the same as Hong Kong. This is the only country in Asia where the number of visitors in a year is more than double its population—over seven million in the year 2000. English is the language for business and of the Government. People also speak Mandarin, Malay, Tamil and Hindi.

The port of Singapore, the world's second busiest, is used by three hundred major shipping lines. On an average, a harbour vessel enters or leaves the harbour every ten minutes. Singapore has emerged as an important financial centre in Asia and over hundred international banks are located in the City-State. Communication facilities are as good as in any advanced country. The central position of the island-state and its comprehensive tourist facilities have attracted an increasing number of visitors.

Promotional Strategy

Since its inception, STPB has involved the travel industry of the country in its promotional efforts. Singapore hotels spend over US$25 million annually on overseas advertising, independently of STPB. Similarly, the National Association of Travel Agents (NATA) and the Retail Shopkeepers Associations are involved in the promotional programmes of their own, complementing the work of the STPB.

Singapore's advertising campaign is an example of cooperative working of Singapore Airlines and the STPB. Their advertising is perhaps most noticeable in the USA and in Europe as compared to that of other Asian destinations. In the UK and USA, Singapore runs television commercials, which not many Asian countries can afford. Although STPB contributes ninety per cent of the advertising funds, their name does not appear in media advertisements. The name is only of the Singapore Airlines, which responds to the enquiries.

Now, they are using Indian TV channels too, for selling Singapore to Indians.

Singapore's tourism promotion budget is the highest in the world according to WTO (above US$100 million in 2000).

STPB is convinced that Singapore by itself cannot be sold as a tourist destination. It has to be a stopover point or an extension to a holiday in the region—average stay is only three days. STPB, therefore, works closely with Malaysia and its other ASEAN neighbours like Thailand, the Philippines and Indonesia. They jointly promote the ASEAN region.

STPB's marketing skills have been applied not only at the selling end of the marketing process, but also at the starting point, with an ambitious product development programme aimed at keeping Singapore in good shape. Promotion and product development have moved hand in hand. The Government encouraged the construction of hotels in the early seventies. It was then felt that Singapore was over-building, but the period of low occupancy was short-lived and hotels soon started enjoying healthy occupancies upto eighty per cent and more.

While modernisation is taking its toll in Singapore, STPB is making earnest efforts to retain the old-world charm of historical institutions, sites and streets as tourist assets of the country. The year 1986 was a momentous year for the Singapore Travel Industry as the US$1 billion Tourist Product Development Plan was launched which has resulted in reviving of the old Bugis Street at a new site near the original one, the redevelopment of Haw Par Villa into the world's first Chinese mythological high-technology park and the revitalisation of historic districts like China Town, Little India, etc. Old buildings have been restored to their original condition and where it was not possible, these have been replaced with exact replicas.

The latest attraction is a *Night Safari Park,* an artificially developed jungle where hundreds of animals imported from different climes roam in their natural surroundings. The Park opens at night and the animals are visible from windows of a slow-moving train in bright moonlight—again artificially created. Only land-starved Singapore could undertake such a project.

There is no danger of animals straying out of their respective jungle abodes as the high-tech park has fool-proof security.

Singapore has one of the finest airports in Asia. The new Changi International Airport handles take-offs or landings every two minutes, round the clock. Things move very fast at this airport. Customs checks are nominal and immigration clearance even faster. While one is waiting for the baggage, there are courtesy phones from where a person may make a local telephone call without payment. Tourist literature is placed at convenient locations to be picked up by incoming passengers. For visitors taking connecting flights but having time on their hands, short sightseeing trips are available free of charge—courtesy STPB. Such short trips create an interest among the transit passengers to come back for a longer holiday.

Tourist Attraction

In order to keep tourists occupied in Singapore, a number of tourist attractions have been added and promoted. Among these is the privately-run twenty hectare Junong Bird Park. The Park boasts of myriad birds and a thirty-metre high waterfall, all enclosed in a gigantic forested cage. Other areas to visit include a Chinese and Japanese Gardens, a Nature Reserve, an Orchid Garden, etc. But the most popular man-made attraction is the newly developed Santosa Island, which is reached by cable car or ferry. On this island, a fast and efficient mono-rail is used to move people.

Festivals have been revived and given an international flavour to bring tourists and these include the annual International Kite Flying Contest, International Dragon Boat Races, Bird Singing Contest, Orchard Parade, Chinese Opera, etc.

Commenting on Singapore's successful marketing, Graham Hornel, presently Executive Director, Indian Ocean Tourism Organisation (IOTO), said, "The selling of Singapore during the past years by STPB, SIA and the Singapore Hotel Association is a communication success story in itself and, I believe, all PATA destinations can learn something from the Singapore example." Indeed, it is a success story. They have created a wealth of tourist attractions out of what one of its leaders described as "Swamplands, five buildings and the death houses of Sago Lane".

Essence : People travel for many reasons: principal among these are recreation or holiday; seeking adventure or outdoor sports; cultural travel to see how people in other countries or in other parts of the same country live; health tourism to spas or resorts; seeking medical treatment; business travel. Another increasingly pressing reason for travel is to attend business and professional conferences. Travel is also offered as a reward to good workers or salesmen of a company as an incentive. This segment is called incentive travel and millions of people are travelling all over the world having been rewarded by their companies.

Modern tourism has emerged as a big business providing employment to millions of workers in the host countries and earning them foreign exchange for economic development. Governments, therefore, are bound to take interest and play an active role in tourism.

Tourism also has the potential to do damage to the ecosystem of the host country or change the cultural pattern of the host communities, if allowed to develop unplanned and unregulated. Therefore, Governments take keen interest in the planned and harmonious development of tourism.

How do Governments intervene? Nationally, each Government has set up a NTO or what WTO now terms it, NTA. Their primary functions are promotion and marketing of the country as a tourist destination, planning and development of tourist infrastructure and in regulating to some extent, tourism-related activities. A good, efficient, honest and professional tourist organisation can do a lot to promote and improve the development of tourism in a country.

In India, the Department of Tourism which is a part of the Ministry of Tourism, Government of India, can be described as the NTA of the country. Not all the countries have the same system. Britain and Thailand have Tourist Authorities, while Singapore and Ireland have a Tourist Board each. Authorities and Boards have greater autonomy and, often, they have the involvement of the private sector in its management. Major funding is done by the Governments, but organisations benefiting from tourism are also expected to give financial support.

India's Department of Tourism is totally funded by the Government of India and the private sector has no direct say in its policy-making.

The ITDC, a public sector organisation working under the Ministry of Tourism is also a part of the NTA of India. ITDC, set up in 1966, was entrusted with the management and operation of all Government-owned hotels, motels and other similar properties. In addition, it offers publicity and other consultancy services to tourism organisations, operates an India-wide tourism-related transport network and runs duty-free shops at international airports. The hotels operated by ITDC are called Ashok Hotels. ITDC has thirty-three hotels at twenty-six destinations—about three thousand and five hundred rooms—a few hotels have been privatised in 2002.

ITDC was set up when the private sector was shy of investing in hotels and similar tourism projects. The Government decided to fill up the gap. ITDC performed excellently during the early years. However, now the private sector has come of age, and there is a strong demand that the facilities run by ITDC may be best left to the private sector. Competition has made ITDC indifferent and today, this highly profitable public sector organisation has turned into red. The threat of privatisation hangs over it like the Damocles sword. At the time of writing this book, the Government of India had identified it as one of the public sector organisation to be put on the auction block and disinvestment has already started.

At the State level, there are State Tourism Development Corporations run on the pattern of the ITDC. Most of them manage State-owned hotels or guest houses, tourist transport and offer package tours, in their respective States. Many of these Corporations are in the red. They too are facing the threat of privatisation. But vested interests do not allow the State Governments to sell these loss-making companies.

At the international level, the WTO with headquarters at Madrid, is UN-sponsored inter-governmental organisation with one hundred and thirty Governments as its members. India plays an active role in the working of the WTO and has been a member of its Executive Committee. Apart from providing coordination among the member Governments in matters relating to tourism, WTO compiles international tourist statistics.

PATA is yet another international organisation devoted to the promotion and marketing of tourism in the Asia Pacific region, of which India is a part. Set up in 1951, it has membership of hundred Governments and two thousand other travel-related companies as its members. India is a very active member. Its annual convention in 2002 was held in New Delhi.

Established in 1958, the Department of Tourism, Government of India, has promoted India successfully as a tourist destination during more than four decades of its existence. Initially, the Government of India did not consider tourism as an important economic activity. In recent years, the Government has realised the importance of tourism as an economic factor and allocations for publicity and infrastructural developments have been steadily enhanced. It has also been declared as an industry, but implementation has yet to come.

There has been a demand for the reorganisation of the Department of Tourism. The National Committee on Tourism (NCT) set up by the Government of the late Prime Minister, Rajiv Gandhi, felt the need for change and recommended the establishment of a National Tourist Board on the lines of the Railway Board of India. The recommendation has not yet been implemented and its report is gathering dust in the archives of the Department of Tourism.

It is a shame that national issues are ignored with damaging consequences. No wonder India's share in the world tourism is a mere 0.38 per cent.

Various Modes

Travel and tourism involves the movement of people from their place of residence to a tourist place and, in consequence, the relationship between transport and tourism development is a vital area of tourism studies. For development of any destination, adequate and efficient transportation infrastructure and access to generating markets is one of the most important aspects. The destinations which can be reached by efficient transport systems are the ones which receive the maximum number of tourists. Within the country, efficient modes of transport are vital for movements of domestic tourists. On the other hand the demand the tourism stimulated the rapid development of transportation. Transport, therefore, is one of the basic components of tourism. A tourist in order to get to his destination, has to travel and, therefore, some mode of transport is necessary to make possible this travel. In fact, transport is the necessary pre-condition of travel.

In the ancient times the mode of transport used by travellers was a horse, a horse carriage, a hand-driven carriage or a boat. This was followed by a ship. It was, however, in the nineteenth century that mechanised transport was invented beginning with the introduction of railways, motorcar and thereafter the aeroplane, all of which revolutionised transport all over the world. Developments of road transport in the post-World War I period and air transport in the post-World War II period were the major factors which were responsible and continue to be so for the great support in modern tourism. For the greater part of contemporary tourism, transport means airlines and private cars. As a broad generalisation, it can be said that holiday makers travelling away from home to another country spend a major portion of their total holiday budget on transport. Transport costs as much as 30-40 percent of the total long-haul holiday expenditure. This fact has been brought about by a number of studies undertaken by various organisations. The war necessitated innovations in the fields of motor and air transports for the purpose of initially using them for the war itself. After the war was over they were utilized as modes of transport for travel. Many road systems and airports which were initially built for transporting men and material for use in the war were subsequently utilized for transporting passengers for the purpose of travel and tourism.

According to Burkart and Medlik transportation can be defined as "the means to reach the destination and also the means of movement at the destination". The pattern of the geographical distribution of world travellers as well as distribution of travellers within their own country is greatly influenced by the transport systems and services that enable the travellers to get from home to the tourist destination. Transport systems link the tourist-generating regions with the attractions tourists wish to visit (i.e. their destination). In general, transport routes and systems enable tourist movements to take place.

Transport in Different Modes : There are different modes of transport which have been evolved over the years. Technological developments have revolutionized various modes of transport and there is a continuous research to upgrade them. Each technological advance in a travel mode affects the other modes. Railways replaced the horse, the private ownership of automobile and public bus system replaced the railways and the airplane replaced the trans-oceanic ship and long-distance rail travel. There are four major modes of transport. These are:

(i) Road
(ii) Rail
(iii) Sea
(iv) Air

System of Road Transport : Up to the beginning of the twentieth century, tourists travelled almost exclusively by rail and steamship. The invention of the new transport medium, travel by a private car and coach received its first impetus in the ten years which preceded World War I. The entire shape of the tourist industry was therefore transformed by the invention of this new transport medium. The growth of the private car may be identified as a major cause of the decline of the railways. In both USA and the United Kingdom, passenger rail traffic almost halved in the first ten years or so after the First World War. The motor car gradually came to be the alternative means of transport for both short and medium range journeys. Subsequently, with the growth of a fine network of fast and superfast national and international highway systems, long journeys were also performed by motor car and motor coach.

The motor car revolutionlised the holiday habits. Although the first motor car had come into operation by the end of the 19th century, up to the time of the First World War their numbers jumped manifold. It became increasingly important in the pursuit of leisure and tourism. The actual number of holiday makers travelling by road increased tremendously as more and more people took holidays away from home. The provision of the good motor roads and road services were important factors in the development of both domestic and international tourism. With the tremendous increase in the road traffic, improved roads and dual carriage ways were introduced after 1930. In 1930s, Germans pioneered the development of motorways with their autobahn. improvements in road transport facilities stimulated tourism in many European countries such as France, Spain and Germany. Mention may be made of the great progress made in USA in building highways, expressways and superhighways. In many other countries of the world newer and faster roads were built which made movement of traffic by road faster and more comfortable.

Mobility can, perhaps, be considered as one of the major causes of the development of the motor transport. The motor car had provided the actual mobility so that people are no longer anchored to a particular holiday centre as they tended to be when they mostly travelled by train. Speed is yet another important factor which economises on time and, therefore, makes it possible for people with limited amount of time to travel to distant places. People with even one week of holiday considered it sufficient to travel. The gradual spread of the network of roads opened up many new areas and made many places hitherto not very accessible easy to get to. The railways, on the other hand, tended rather to concentrate and restrict movement to particular channels.

Road transport made striking advances in the subsequent years. Soon after 1950, when the difficulties and restrictions of the immediate post-war years had begun to make themselves out, there were rapid developments in transport; whereas the car ownership multiplied, the motor coach appeared in increasing numbers and the coach tour became popular. Greater use of motor car and coach is being made at present for the purpose of tourism. A great majority of people travel by the above modes in Europe. Increasing use of this mode of transport is being made in USA and Canada as also in other major tourist countries. The construction of motorways in many countries has made speedy travel over long distances by car and the coach easy and have made many remote places more accessible. The development of 'motorail', the carrying of cars and coaches over extended distances by train is making it possible for holiday makers to use motor cars in holiday areas.

Though economic conditions in the recent years, as a result of increasing fuel costs and the energy crisis, have not favoured travel by private motor car, road transport remains the mode most used by international visitors. The world economic crisis which brought about cut backs in the use of transport facilities, did not, however, seriously impair the growth of road transports. In many countries of Europe increasing emphasis is being given to the construction of new roads. Several countries are continuing to build motorways and highways and new road systems to cater to the increasing volume of road transport including tourist transport. There are large-scale highway programmes in the pipeline at present in different regions of the world. When completed, these, will cater to the ever-increasing demands of the tourists.

Some of the large highways programmes in the pipeline in different regions of the world are :

(i) The Trans-African Highway

(ii) The Trans-West African Highway

(iii) The Trans-East African Highway

(iv) The Trans-Europe North-South Motorway

(v) The Pan-American Highway

(vi) The Asian Highway

System of Air Transport *:* The role of air transport in the development of international tourism is becoming increasingly important. It has certainly been a key factor in the growth of international tourism, especially in respect of long distance and inter-continental travel. Although commercial air travel took place before the Second World War, air transport for the masses has essentially been a post-war phenomenon. The main period of growth was during the 1960s when overseas holiday became a symptomatic benefit of a society experiencing rising living standards.

In Europe, the years immediately after World War I witnessed the attempts to create commercial airlines. The war itself had a direct bearing on the development of air transport in a similar way as it had with motor transport. Certain commercial civil air services were inaugurated and developed in this period. Besides Europe, air transport, was developed in many other countries during this period. Although international air travel was born at the end of World War I and slowly grew between the two wars, it was only at the end of World War II that it made a tremendous breakthrough. It emerged into a practical mode of transport over long distances only in the late forties when the aircraft industry in America applied the technical and manufacturing resources it had developed during the war. This period saw the development of large pressurised civil aircraft like the Douglas DC-6s and the Lockheed Constellations followed by the DC-7s and the super constellations operating at twice the speed and flying altitudes of their predecessor war planes.

The removal of wartime restrictions on international travel and the tremendous speed, safety and comfort provided by the new aircrafts released the long pent-up wanderlust of the people the world over. In the year 1952 the two-class travel was introduced which was made possible by the larger capacity of the new aircrafts, which also resulted in lower airfares. The steady fall in the real cost of flying has been chiefly productive in traffic across the Atlantic and within the USA, stimulated by the introduction of tourist fares in the year 1952. This period also saw the first post-war attempt to build a "package holiday" around air transport, the model for most of today's global tourism. The growing willingness of tourists to take to air travel during this period was responsible for the annual flood of North Americans across the Atlantic to Europe. This trend continues even today. Within Europe, there has been the spectacular explosion of the Mediterranean resorts.

Air traffic between commercial sectors was now growing rapidly. In Europe before World War II, Swiss air was already flying twin-engine Douglas Dc-2s carrying as many as 14-16 passengers between Zurich and London. In the year 1920, KLM the Dutch Airlines, introduced the first commercial service between Amsterdam and London. The journey in a two-seater De Havilland DH-9 took about four hours. In the year 1929, KLM inaugurated another service to the Far East to Jakarta, and within the next few years it was flying to most major West European cities.

Travelling in these early commercial flights was rather an adventure than the pleasure that it is today. It was only after World War II that commercial air travel started surging ahead. More facilities were added for the passengers and travel was made more comfortable.

The commercial jet air travel, however, was pioneered by Great Britain in the year 1952 with the inauguration of jet flights, by BOAC. Thereafter Pan American introduced the Boeing 707 service between Paris and New York in the year 1958. By the year 1968 most of the European carriers had converted totally to jet aircraft. As a result of the introduction of jet air services, there was a tremendous boost to air travel from the year 1958. The most decisive development during this period was, however, the development of the concept of 'inclusive tours' in which travellers were carried on charter flights at rates substantially lower than those on normal scheduled services. Air transport can be considered to be responsible for the introduction of cheaper travel, especially long distance, enabling a large majority of potential travellers to think of visiting far off countries for the purposes of holiday.

Introduction of Jumbo Jets & Mass Tourism : It was, however, the introduction of 'Jumbo Jets' in the year 1970 which heralded the phenomenon of mass market international tourism as well as business tourism. The jumbo jets-the Boeing 747s, DC-10s and L-1011s made air travel convenient, comfortable and luxurious. Luxury air travel was made possible for business as well as non-business travellers as the big size of jets gave the airlines space enough to partition off a section of the plane for executives who were willing to pay extra for the luxury. Pan Am and the Japan Air Lines (JAL) were among the first carriers to offer passengers what came to be known as business class travel. The seats in this class were wider, giving more space to stretch and relax in comfort, making the long distance travel less wearisome.

As the popularity of business class travel grew, more and more airlines introduced the scheme. It became extremely successful on long-haul international flights. As an outcome of the success of business class, yet another class known as 'Executive Class' was introduced. As the size in the number of business travel grew and competition increased, the airlines started to further upgrade their services for their clients. This resulted in the introduction of 'Executive Class'. It was once again Japan Air Lines which in the year 1975 started an 'Executive Service' lounge in the Imperial Hotel in Tokyo, complete with conference rooms, having all the facilities for meetings. Lufthansa opened a lounge at Frankfurt and SAS at Copenhagen airports. Many other airlines such as TWA with Ambassador Club, Singapore with Silver Kris Lounges, Pan Am with Clipper Club, Air France with Le Club, Cathay Pacific with Marco Polo, British Airways with Supper Club, and airlines like Qantas, Air India, Air Canada, Singapore Airlines, Swiss air, etc., offer additional on-ground facilities to their clients. These include special check-in-counters, priority baggage handling and clearance, free transport to and from airport, free drinks, etc. The membership is open to those who pay a nominal fee or is offered free to travellers who have travelled frequently on the carrier.

The air transport industry, in spite of ever-increasing fuel costs and inflation, is able to control successfully fare levels as a result of economies of scale provided by the big wide-bodied aircrafts of modern times. The improved fuel efficiency of the later models of jet engines combined with ingenuity and marketing expertise of airlines, travel agencies and tour operators have made air travel accessible to an increasing number of people. This is also illustrated by the North Atlantic route the so-called golden route of traffic, which saw the successive introduction of excursion fares in 1948, coach fares in 1952, family fares in 1955, economy class fares in 1958, affinity group in 1963, group inclusive tour fares in 1967, youth fares in 1972 and apex fares in 1975. As a result of these innovations in air travel, fares per seat mile declined in real terms, between 1962 and 1975. Great advances have been made in air travel in the recent years, more particularly for overseas holiday making. Tourism in turn has had a significant impact on the aircraft industry and on the carriers. Factors like comfort, speed, and safety influence the tourists' choice of mode of transport. Now wide-bodied jets such as Boeing 747, the McDonnel-Douglas DC 10, the Airbus A 300, A 320 and Lockheed Tristar L-1011 are all part of the response to the requirements of the ever growing travel market. The technical brilliance of the supersonic aircraft like the Concorde and of the Tupolev 144 are remarkable landmarks in aviation history.

The future for air transport is very bright. It is estimated that for every million air passengers travelling today, about three million will be airborne in 2020. Ongoing advances in the aerodynamics and engine technology will inevitably push the range of new-generation aircraft towards a capability of nonstop flights anywhere on the planet. With the airport and airspace already at a premium, the only solution is larger aeroplanes. Both the world's biggest aircraft manufacturers Europe's, Airbus Industries and Boeing in the United States have already researched the future airline market and have started manufacturing new-generation aircrafts.

Airbus industries have already commissioned the manufacture of its 600-800 seater initially dubbed as AXXX, while Boeing is going ahead with its project of stretched variants of its increasingly popular and successful B 747 "Jumbo Jet". Airbus hopes to have its first AXXX in revenue passenger carrying service by about 2004. A number of airlines have already placed orders for the purchase of this new-generation aircraft. Another major company McDonnel Douglas is also planning a new generation aircraft, the MD-12 four-jet double-deck aircraft, with capacity between those of the Airbus and Boeing projects (over 500 seats).

In the next phase of development, which could well be advanced in concept by 2020, it is likely that an aeroplane of 1800-2000 plus passenger capability with six or eight engines could be under development. The air-transport industry has a bright future inspite of rising fuel costs and inflation. As far as long distance air travel is concerned the large majority of the aircrafts used will continue to be of wide-bodied generation. Air transport, thus is a single key factor which has been primarily responsible for the spurt in growth of tourism especially long-haul tourism. The future of air transport is bright and the airlines would continue to play a vital role in the growth and development of tourism in the coming decades of the present century.

System of Rail Transport : Although the first regular steam engine passenger run was inaugurated over a one-mile section on the 6.5 mile track from Canterbury to Whitstable, Kent, England, on May 3, 1830 hauled by the engine Invicta, railed tracks were used for mining purposes as early as 1550. These tracks were used at Leberthal, Alsace near the French-German border and at the Brosseley Colliery, Salop, England in 1605. The first self-propelled locomotive ever to run on rails was built by Richard Trevithic (1771-1883) at Salop in England. The first electric railway was Werner Von Siemens 600-yard-long Berlin electric track opened for the Berlin Traders' Exhibition on May 31, 1879. The oldest underground subway railway system in the world is the London Transport subway system whose first section was opened on January 10, 1863.

The birth of the organised rail transport, however, came in the year 1841. A Baptist preacher of Derbyshire on his way to a temperance society meeting in Leicester was inspired with the idea of engaging a special train to carry the friends of temperance society from Leicester to Loughborough and back to attend a quarterly delegate meeting. The man behind this idea was one Thomas Cook. He sold his idea to his friends. A few weeks later 570 passengers made the journey by the Midland Counties Railway at a specially reduced fare. And thus began a new era in rail passenger transport. Many other countries in Europe built and opened railway lines as a result of the success of railways in England. Railway tracks were laid in France, Austria and Switzerland.

Across the Atlantic the tracks were laid in America. This revolution in rail transport technology produced an immediate expansion in the European travel scene. The mobility provided by rail-roads encouraged a large number of people to move from the place of residence to another place for short periods for the purposes of travel. In the year 1881, the railways carried over 600 million passengers over lines operated by one hundred odd companies. The railways were now keen to stimulate travel and to improve the system. There was also an element of competition now and various railway companies tried to make travel as comfortable as possible for the travellers by introducing more and more amenities and facilities. In the early 1870s, first class railway travel was introduced by an American, G.M. Pullman, who developed the Pullman coaches with their luxury furnishing and dining facilities.

Long distance travel could now be undertaken in comfort and with pleasure. The longer distances in America necessitated the ensuring of greater comfort for passengers. The Pullman coaches manufactured in America were imported by some railway companies in England by other European countries. By the year 1872, the Pullman company had 700 cars working over 30,000 miles of railway under contract with over 150 different companies. The introduction of rail transport vastly increased the opportunities for escape from the rigours of city life. The railways can be considered as one of the most powerful motives for mass travel in the nineteenth century. Although the railways monopolised the mass travel market during the nineteenth century, they suffered from competition from coach and car transport during the twentieth century.

Today's rail transport market, however, is very different from that of a hundred years ago. Railway services compete not only with automobile travel, but with motor coach and airplane travel as well. In many countries rail travel offers a leisurely pace and unique views of scenic countryside along routes rarely seen by air or road. In newer passenger trains comfortable sleeping accommodations are available. European trains are among the most modern and comfortable in the world. The single most significant development in the European public railways took place in 1989 when the community of European Railways representing the 12 members of the EC, plus Austria and Switzerland, announced plans for trans continental high speed rail network. It is estimated that by the year 2015, some 21000 miles, (33600 Kilometres) of new track capable of handling trains at a speed over 200 miles (360 Kilometres) per hours would be in operation.

Arrival of Trains of High Speed : Lately an interesting development is taking place in the field of transportation. The energy crisis since 1974 which resulted in widespread recession and galloping inflation have rather adversely affected travel by air and by the private car. It is becoming increasingly expensive to travel by air and by the private car and coach. The fuel consumption per passenger kilometer is two to four times more in automobiles and ten times more in aeroplanes as compared to trains. This factor of increase in oil prices is responsible for the remarkable achievement in recent years in the growth of faster and cheaper rail transport. Besides the cost factor, the railways also have an advantage over the airlines in that the terminal stations are often located in the heart of the cities and the train timings are generally more convenient. To add to this the growing congestion on highways and airports has given a further impetus to this trend.

All the above factors coupled with advanced technology and an increasing need for mobility are leading to a renaissance of the rail transport. The railways which were pioneers in the growth and development of early mass travel and were relegated to a secondary place with the introduction of motor and air transport once again are assuming an important role. In almost all the European countries, the United States of America, Asia and elsewhere, revolutionary ideas for achieving higher speeds and comfort are being conceived and put into practice.

The trend, however, was discernible before the world was affected by the energy crisis. It was in Europe when the designs for faster and comfortable trains were first formulated. In the year 1960 British Railways electrified its London-Manchester line, a very busy line, to achieve the speed of 160 kilometres per hour. The new high-speed trains on this line reduced their running time by full one hour from the former three hour forty minute-trip. Passenger traffic almost doubled in five years. In West Germany, a new inter-city system introduced in 1971 provided a rapid train service at two-hour intervals between every major city in the country and brought over 30 per cent more passengers in the first twelve months. Passengers were provided with extra-conveniences like telephones, secretarial services, latest stock quotations and 'a la carte' dining-car service round the clock. Similarly, in France, the 160 kilometres per hour turbine train service, which began in 1970 between Paris and Caen in northern France, cut travel time by almost one-fifth. Passenger loads went up by 25 per cent in the first year. High speed train services elsewhere in Europe connect Paris and Lyons in France, Rome and Milan in Italy and Moscow and Leningrad in Russia.

In Asia, it was Japan which took the epoch-making decision to use the latest technology and convert the rail line between Tokyo and Osaka, covering a distance of 515 kilometres into a high-speed track. This ambitious project was completed in the year 1964. The superfast train known as Hikari Express-'bullet train - travels on the new Tokaido line at a speed of 210 kilometres per hour cutting the journey time to less than three hours against six and a half hours taken earlier. Encouraged by the success of its bold venture, it went further and built the new Sanyo line, 565 kilometres in length on which trains travel even faster at a maximum speed of 260 kilometres per hour. Elsewhere in Asia, new and faster rail tracks are being introduced as the number of passengers carried by rail have been increasing in Malaysia, the Philippines and Thailand. However, it is only in recent years that extraordinary developments are taking place in rail transport systems, especially in Europe.

It was in France that a world record of speed was broken in the year 1981. In September 1981, a new high-speed train owned by the State-run SNCF Railroad Company shattered the 26-year old world record for rail speed by clocking 380 kilometres per hour (236 miles). The record-breaking time was achieved near the central French city of Tonnerre during the test run of the French manufactured 'Train a Grande Vitesse' (TGV) train. It broke the previous record of 331 kilometres per hour (205 miles) that was set earlier. The commercial operations of this high-speed train began in 1981 first between Paris and Lyon. The fastest train in the world, TGV, was launched in September 1981 covering the 560 kilometres distance between Paris and Lyon in one hour and 48 minutes. In comfortable, sound-proofed cars the only noise heard is the quiet hiss of air-conditioning.

The newest and the fastest, the 'TGV Atlantique', had reduced an hour off journeys from Paris to main cities in the West of France from Brest to Bordeaux. By mid-1990 the French started running TGVs along half their long-distance routes, to bring London, Bordeaux, Rotterdam and Cologne within 3.5 hours from Paris. Several other new rail projects have been announced in the European countries. The Italian State Railways has inaugurated high-speed runs between Rome and Milan. The non-stop train makes the 393 miles (638 kilometres) trip in four hours and 55 minutes, about an hour less than the standard runs. Sweden has upgraded its four major lines to reduce the travel time between its major cities.

In the United States of America, the railways are coming back into the scene in recent years. Increasing number of railway lines are being built to carry a large number of passengers not only within the suburbs but also long distance. There is a great spurt in the urban rail system construction all over the United States. It is increasingly being felt that a mass transit system can reduce congestion in high density towns and that this may reduce the automobile pollution. Long-distance trains running on the Amtrak system between New York and San Francisco have been modernised. The Amtrak has also added new double Pullman coaches on the system with a view to encourage more rail travel. High-speed train services now connect highly populated Washington - Baltimore - Philadelphia - New York - Boston 'Corridor' in United States.

Trains of Super High Speed : After more than 25 years of research, the world of railways is on the verge of entering an exciting super high-speed era. Magnetic levitation (Maglev) technology will enable trains to run at supersonic speeds within the next decade. By about 2010 or so, commercial passenger trains will run at more than 550 kilometres per hour floating frictionlessly a few centimeters above the rails. It was Japan which first started working on Maglev in the late sixties. A milestone was achieved in 1999 April, on the new Yamanashi Maglev Test Line when a manned Maglev train clocked a record 552 kilometers per hour.

Super high-speed trains, independent of wheel and rail friction have been a long-standing dream of researchers. With Maglev, the train is magnetically-levitated (not supported by wheels) and is propelled by a linear induction motor instead of conventional rotary electric motor. The levitation method utilized ordinary direct-current electromagnets that are attached to the bottom of the vehicle. Their magnetic field lifts the train. An electronic circuit amplifier controls the current to the electromagnets in order to maintain the gap between rail and magnetic cores. The gap is measured by a sensor. Barring the air-conditioning system, Maglevs have no moving parts and therefore there is very little wear, no noise or vibration and low energy consumption.

Elsewhere in Asia new and faster rail tracks are being introduced. The new rail services are even giving airlines and the coach transport their greatest competition. The upgradation of tracks and advances in maximum speeds in railway systems in Europe and elsewhere have made possible for travellers to reach various city centres in almost the same time as air travel time. Many business travellers are being lured away from air travel especially in continental Europe.

System of Sea Transport : Shipping, like the railways, had made a significant contribution to travel during the nineteenth century. While railways were responsible for inland travel, especially in Europe, the steamship crossed the boundaries and made strides in intercontinental travel. The shipping technology made a number of innovations in the nineteenth century. In America a number of sailing ships were built which were considered to be superior to those built in England or elsewhere. The English felt a great need for improved communications across the Atlantic with America for the purpose of trade and passenger transportation. As a result of this there were great strides in the development of deep sea shipping.

The history of the Cunard Steamship Company in England demonstrates important features in the growth of North Atlantic Shipping. A subsidy in the form of an award of the mail contract represented a recurring theme in the development of passenger transportation. With the passage of time, toward the last quarter of the nineteenth century, emigrant traffic became an important factor in North Atlantic travel. America was considered at this time the 'new world' full of opportunities and fortunes for people in Europe. A great number of people from the continent started going to America in search of fortune. First Great Britain, and later Germany, along with other countries, became the principal generators of emigrants to the new world. Many travelled as tourists to see the new world. The opening of the Suez Canal in 1869 brought about the possibility of a much shortened route between the West and the East and in turn stimulated the introduction of better steamship carriage to the Far-East.

Recent Happenings : Use of the ships in the cruising fashion for the charter and operation of cruises on a limited scale dates from the mid-nineteenth century. One of the earliest cruises, perhaps, was that described by Mark Twain in his first book, *The Innocents Abroad,* published in 1869. Cruising, however, did not play a significant part in the world of shipping until the beginning of the twentieth century. The period just before the First World War can be considered the heyday of liner passenger service. It was an era of large and comfortable fast ships operated by a relatively small number of companies in various countries. The glamour of the deep-sea travel was, however, reserved for the wealthy Europeans and Americans. In the luxury liners, a big space reserved for the not too wealthy was used by the emigrant traffic. In fact, the biggest volume of trans-Atlantic passenger transport was the emigrant traffic.

In the first half of the twentieth century, the descendants of those migrants must have formed a large part of the transatlantic tourist movement. Transport by water makes a significant contribution to the development of travel on land and by air. Scheduled liner transport, formerly much used for intercontinental travel, has presently almost vanished. The expansion of international tourism has, however, led to an increasing use of ferry boats by tourists on short sea-crossings. Tourist sea transport on the whole does not seem to have a promising future. Long-distance sea travel may continue to contract, although there will always be a limited demand for sea cruising, since this leisure and attractive mode of travel has a great appeal. In the recent past one of the most important development in sea traffic has in fact been that of holiday sea cruises, especially in the Mediterranean and Caribbean and also in South-East Asia.

Introduction of Cruises : The advantage of travel by vessel, however, is the element of relaxation and entertainment of a voyage by sea which has resulted in the introduction of cruises. Since the beginning of the 1960s, passenger shipping industry has gradually shifted its emphasis from the voyage services to cruises. More and more rich and elderly people initially promoted the cruise as they wanted a holiday in a completely relaxed atmosphere.

Subsequently, many companies discovered the advantages of a cruise for their incentive-winners. Cruises became increasingly popular to motivate top producers as more and more incentive-winners wanted to enjoy the delights of life on the high seas. Cruise-lines aim to please as cruises offer everything which is a five-star luxury like gourmet dining, top class entertainment, and excellent service. In addition, they offer fascinating shore visits with unusual " shopping opportunities and enough activities to keep most athletic and energetic individuals satisfied.

Passenger sea transport, however, has not made much strides compared to rail-road and air transport. Because of the advances in air transport technologies resulting in reduced airfares on most of the routes, and especially across the Atlantic, most of the shipping lines were unable to compete, resulting in a decline in their services. Coupled with this, the higher labour costs, prohibitive cost of replacement of older and outdated vessels, operating costs etc., resulted in many companies closing their business, especially after the early sixties. During 1960s and 1970s most of the major shipping companies either reduced their services or discontinued their long-established routes.

The ocean liners, especially the passenger lines, could not withstand the competition with airlines. Cruising on the other hand did manage to come up to a point where it was necessary to diversify the product and change the marketing strategy in order to survive. On the other hand, short sea voyages or ferry services have managed to withstand competition and are doing well in many areas. Channel crossing between some European countries and England by ferry service or hovercraft has been a profitable business for many ferry companies. This could be attributed to the general growth of tourism in the region, lower prices due to competition as also shorter journey time. Increase in the private car ownership in the region is another very important factor in the success of short sea voyages. Transportation is very vital to the success of both domestic and international tourism. Mass tourism, as it is known internationally could not have existed without inexpensive and easily accessible transportation. Almost all the destinations in the world depend a great deal on efficient means of transportation being made available to tourists. The choice of a particular mode of transport, however, depends on several factors. Many theories have been put forward on mode selection decision processes. The choice of selection of mode of transport are affected by the following factors:

- Distance and time
- Comfort
- Safety and utility
- Availability and frequency
- Comparative cost price
- Ground services
- Status and prestige
- Geographical position and isolation
- Departure/arrival times
- Level of competition between services

The relative importance of the above factors, upon selection of different modes will, however, vary from one visitor type to another.

7

Latest Developments

The tourism industry is closely linked to the transport sector in every country. The tourist has to travel out of his normal city of residence. That makes him eligible to be called Traveller. Naturally, he would use one mode or the other that would help him move to the coveted tourist spot. Besides accommodation, transport is the most important component in the tourism industry. Transport systems must be comfortable, fast and reliable so that tourists may be able to enjoy safe and luxurious travel. They are not ordinary travellers. They are out to enjoy the environs of the countryside or the tourist spot. Thus, if they have bad experiences, they would not turn up again. They are not ordinary commuters, just like millions of people travelling in the cities and vast regions of the world. They want to have only good experiences; ordinary travellers become habitual of having bad experiences because they must travel due to the requirements of their jobs and businesses. Tourists travel for enjoying the time or new places they are visiting. This feature differentiates the tourist from the ordinary traveller. In this chapter, we shall study transport systems of India and also, give basic facts and data related to the transport system.

Important Modes of Transport : Let us look at the basic modes of transport in a nutshell. The modes of transport can carry passengers, tourists and freight. The airlines carry freight, passengers and ordinary travellers. We must point out here that the modes of transport used by ordinary passengers are also used by tourists. The idea of defining a sub-category in each one of the three major modes (rail, road and air) is to convince our readers that there are separate modes of transport available for tourists. However, these tourists can also use such modes of transport as are being used by ordinary travellers. Example: A family can go to Madgaon (Goa) by Mangla Express from Hadrat Nizamuddin. This family cannot use a taxi or coach to reach Goa. It must board a train to do so. But this train is also catering to the travel needs of ordinary passengers who are not keen to explore Goa as tourists. Some of them could be natives of Goa and it is just possible that they are going home for a few weeks. Thus, we cannot put tourists in water-tight compartments so far as modes of transport are concerned.

In the parlance of tourism, the tourist seeks pleasure even during the course of his journey. That is because he:

(a) is in a leisure mood;

(b) wants to enjoy the environs of the tourist spot and those that he comes across en route the spot;

(c) has spent a lot of money on his tour programme and so; wants to enjoy each and every moment of his itinerary; and

(d) expects that services provided during the course of transport would be at least equivalent to the money spent by him to buy these.

Time is another factor to be considered in this context. If the tourists does not have much time, he would prefer a faster mode of transport like aircraft. If he has a lot of time, he would not like to miss the pleasures of journey and thus, may opt for sea cruise or coach travel. If he has some time at his disposal but wants to be independent, he can hire a taxi.

The number of passengers also decides the mode of transport. If the number of people in a group is large, the group hires a 16-seat van or coach. Large numbers of passengers even hire buses. We have come across cases when people (nearly 70 in number) have hired buses to reach Vaishno Devi Shrine (Jammu & Kashmir).

They started from Delhi and completed the 10-day tour in comfort. They also carried gas cylinders and a cooking range along with them and ladies aboard the coach cooked as and when there was a need to do so. Such types of tours are not uncommon in northern India. From the south, coaches come to the north during summer holiday seasons. These buses come from as far as Chennai, Hyderabad and Coimbatore. Students prefer to travel by trains. They get entire coaches booked for travelling to distant tourist spots. The railways also offer them discounts in tickets.

Season plays an important role in selecting the mode of transport. Off-season discounts are available when we travel by rail. Students can avail such discounts if they prove that they are students of recognised institutions or universities. Children below the age of 5 years can travel free of cost in trains. Children in the age group of 5-12 years can travel at half the ticket price by rail. Children above the age of 12 years would have to pay the price of full ticket, however. Children below the age of 3 years can travel free of cost by bus. Children in the age group of 3-9 years can travel at half the ticket price by bus. Children above the age of 9 years would have to pay the price of full ticket. Children below the age of less than 2 years would have to pay 10 per cent of the basic adult ticket of fare in an aircraft. Children in the age group of 2-12 years can travel buy paying 67 per cent of the basic adult ticket fare in an aircraft. Children above the age of 12 years would have to pay the price of full ticket in an aircraft. Airport taxes and other surcharges would have to be paid by all the passengers. Families decide according to their convenience and time at their disposal. The overall cost of the budget is also a major factor that decides the mode of transport.

Rich people (who have money but no time) prefer to use faster modes of transport like aircraft, taxis, etc. They also spend more money on executive or luxury class of travel. Middle-income families and businessmen (who have some money and some time) prefer luxury trains, ordinary trains, cheap cars, auto-rickshaws, metro railway services and coaches. They spend on economy class or, in rare cases, on luxury class of travel. Poor people (who have lots of time but no money) prefer ordinary buses, trains with second class reservation, auto-rickshaws, cycle rickshaws, local buses and metro railway services.

Tourists do not want to use such modes of transport as are not reliable, or have been dubbed as notorious.

Example: Tourists would not use a cruise ship that has met with many accidents during the past. They would also not use such airlines as have been grounded time and again due to reasons associated with civil aviation safety. They prefer to board only those trains that are invariably regular. If some trains are generally late by 4 to 5 hours, they prefer not to use them. They do not prefer passenger trains that stop at every Tom, Dick and Harry station.

How to Manage Transport : In the parlance of tourism administration, logistics plays an important role in facilitating various functions. Logistics is the science of transporting goods in bulk from one place to another. It is a part of marketing or one of its 6 Ps (Product, Price, Promotion, Physical Distribution, Power and Political Influence). We must know about its basic framework because hotels and restaurants need to get vital inputs at their premises so that they could serve their customers (guests and tourists). Further, tourists can also use various transport services to move their personal effects and other goods in bulk from one place (or country) to another. Human transportation systems are integrated with logistics systems to assist the tourists during their itineraries. Heavy and bulky load is always carried by large vehicles or ships.

Varied Transport Task : The transport task is assigned to the transporter by the client. The executives of the transporter (or transport company) study :

(a) Requirements of the client;

(b) Details of materials to be transported (including their nature like fragile, liquid, perishable, etc) ;

(c) Quantities to be transported ;

(d) Packaging needs ;

(e) Station of origin (starting point or origin) ;

(f) Station of arrival (ending point or destination) ;

(g) Expected Date of Departure (EDD) ;

(h) Expected Date of Arrival (EDA) ;

(i) Expected Time of Departure (ETD) ;

(j) Expected Time of Arrival (ETA) ;

(k) Insurance requirements of the client; and

(l) Instructions of the client regarding the handling procedures of the goods- in question.

This information is given by the client to the transport executive of the transport company. This transport executive tries to have a look at the goods; in fact, he sends someone from his office to the godown of the client. Alternatively, the client can bring the goods to the office of the transporter (if these are not very heavy or bulky) . The idea is to understand the nature of the logistics assignment so that problems are not encountered while transporting it to its coveted destination.

Analysis of Environmental Impact : In this step, the executive needs to understand the general transport environment, which is unique as compared to other activity centres of logistics. Transportation is affected by five factors, as follows

(a) *Consignor :* He is the firm or firm that sends goods to his clients or consignee. In the parlance of tourism administration, he could be a producer of raw materials, foodstuff, clothes, garments, machinery, beverage, liquor, etc. The consignor could also be a tourist who may be trying to send his goods from one country to another. He must be aware of such factors as nature of goods produced by him, perishable nature of goods, etc. The organisation must also have a loading system and godown to facilitate efficient transportation of the products being produced by it.

(b) *Consignee :* He is the person or firm that would actually receive goods and consume these. Normally, it is a hotel, tourist resort, restaurant, disco club, bar, highway motel, theme park, etc. Goods received by it are used in various activities that, in turn, increase the influx of tourists. The organisation must also have an unloading system and godown to store the products being received by it.

(c) *State :* In India, the government influences the policies and activities related to logistics. It decides the rates of fuels, prices of automobiles (through various tax regimes), parts of automobiles, octroi duties and other taxes. The transporter passes these costs on to the client. Thus, the client is directly affected by the changes in transport policies of the State, which may be changed from budget to budget. Many transport carriers like the TCI are controlled by the government. Further, the government is also responsible for developing rail, road, water and air networks. Transporters cannot execute these Herculean tasks. Thus, the government builds the infrastructure that supports the activities related to logistics.

(d) *Masses :* The masses demand products at various locations. The firms that supply these goods to the masses must deliver the right quantities at the right places and at the right time. Moreover, the masses need the products at right prices. The natural corollary of this fact is that transport costs must not be very high, lest the ultimate customers should avoid buying these goods. If a marketer tries to reduce the delivery time, the cost of transportation increases and vice versa. Further, safety norms must also be adhered to during the course of actual physical transportation of goods. Finally, the government also regulates such activities of transport systems to generate pollution or other hazards. Note that provision of a healthy pollution-free environment to the citizens of a country is the responsibility of the State. That is why, Delhi has become the only city in the world to have a local public transport system with CNG as its basic fuel. In the context of logistics, the government can take steps to protect the ecology and environment of the country. It is quite natural that the transporter as well as the client would have to conform to such norms. Environmental Impact Analysis (technical facts) has been discussed in Chapter 9.

(e) *Transporter :* The carrier or transporter of goods is a private business firm in most of the cases. Its objective is to maximise profits and minimise costs. He has to pick the goods from a common collection point (at the origin) and deliver the same to a common delivery point (destination). Nowadays, door-to-door cargo services are being provided by many a transporter. These services are efficient, fast and costly. Goods are picked up from the godown or office of the client and delivered to the godown or office of the client at the destination city/town.

Objectives of Transport Activity : In this step, the order of preference in terms of functions (to be performed by transport firm as an activity centre) is defined in lucid terms. The client (consignor) has to achieve a balance between time and cost. It has also to consider factors such as flexibility desired during the course of transportation activities. Setting of objectives in this context would enable the client firm to choose an efficient mode of transport. The client (consignor) and the transporter have to interact a number of times to delineate such objectives.

Opting Mode of Transport : Various modes of transport are considered in this step. The logistics manager has to take a decision with respect to one of the modes available. There are two modes of transport—single mode and inter modal. In single-mode transportation systems, the transport executive chooses only one of the modes of transport. In inter-modal transport systems, the transport executive combines two or more modes of transport to achieve the objectives of transport. It is self-explanatory.

Selection of Transports within a Mode : The firm now decides if it wants to outsource the activity or insource it. The main types of modes of transport service are contract carriers, exempt carriers, freight forwarders, parcel post service, shippers' associations, brokers, etc. The firm has to carefully select the right mode, keeping in view the product to be carried, its nature, weight and its other features. The requirements of the consignor (client) must also be looked into while deciding the transport method with a mode.

Role of Transport

The type of transport mode selected by the transport firm would lead to definition of functions that need to be performed.

If the transport service is to be hired (outsourced), the following functions would have to be carried out (railways and private transporters are involved in this category);

(a) Scanning of transporters and discussions with coach owners/railway/ship officials.

(b) Getting quotations from transporters by giving them an idea of the assignment.

(c) Comparing quotations.

(d) Negotiating with executives or owners of transporters.

(e) Defining terms of insurance (an insurance firm or agency may step in).

(f) Defining modalities related to claims management and demurrage.

(g) Defining procedures related to diversion and reconsignment.

(h) Defining export/ import procedures in the parlance of transport.

(i) Finalising payment terms.

If the transport service is to be provided from in-house or private sources, then the following functions would have to be carried out (the personal transport fleet of the firm is involved in this category) : (a) Study of routes. (b) Study of costs associated with transportation. (c) Cost accounting and evaluation of the commercial viability of the transport activity. (d) Route selection. (e) Preparation of schedules. (f) Negotiations with executives of the client firm (consignee). (g) Defining terms of insurance (an insurance firm or agency may step in). (h) Defining modalities related to claims of management. (i) Defining procedures related to diversion and reconsignment. (j) Defining export/import procedures in the parlance of transport. (k) Raising of bill on the client firm (that would include the transport cost).

Execute Transport Functions : In this step, the transport actually takes place. All the plans are executed. Goods are loaded on trucks or four-wheelers. These can be loaded from the godown of the consignor or the site of another firm from which, the consignor may have bought these. Alternatively, the consignor may also deliver the goods to the transport office of the transporter, if these are not very bulky or heavy. The consignor is responsible for the delivery of goods to the consignee. But the entry of the transporter makes the situation a bit complex. Now, the transporter is responsible for goods (as soon as he leaves the door of the godown of the consignor). But the consignor may not take the responsibility of goods to the extent of their value. Thus, insurance firms enter the picture and insure the goods to be transported at a reasonable price. If the carrier meets with an accident of any type, the insurance firm pays the full amount of these goods to the consignee. The consignor is not paid anything because the goods belonged to the consignee (as the sale was effected). The consignee pays the insurance amount; he is charged by the consignor in the bill in this context. Further, demurrage is also a major issue of concern. Goods reach the godown of the transporter in the destination city but the consignee does not claim these goods for a long period of time. In that event, the transporter charges demurrage from the consignee. It is the cost of keeping the goods in the godown of the transporter. It must be borne by the consignee.

Evaluation and Control : The objectives of a transport activity centre are compared with performances and deviations are noted. Resources are monitored and it is judged whether these are being consumed according to the need of the transport activity/project at hand or not. The efficiency of a transport system can be judged from the following systems:

(a) *Customer Perception Measurement :* Company-sponsored surveys and follow-ups by transport executives in the actual markets would prove to be handy in this context. It is better to ask the customer about the date of delivery of a consignment than to ask the transporter (truck driver) about it. The customer ought to be satisfied, irrespective of the window-dressed answers of the truck driver. Surveys can be conducted either by the executives of the transport organisation or by marketing research executives (appointed by the transport organisation). These can include the study of order cycle time, quality of order fulfilment, time taken to execute the order, problems associated with the actual transport staff (like drivers, loaders, labour, etc), costs incurred by the clients, methods of saving costs etc. This list is not exhaustive.

(b) *Best Practice Benchmarking :* The performance of the transport company is compared with that of the best firm in the field of transport. Various transport policies, practices, procedures and limitations are compared with those of the comparable leaders. Deviations are noted and efforts are made to eliminate or minimise them.

(c) *Customer Satisfaction Measurement :* This technique is used to measure overall customer satisfaction. Thus, it measures the ability of a transport firm to execute a perfect order, which is an order executed at best price, in a minimum possible time-frame, with actual the documentation and under perfect conditions.

Passenger Transport and Transport Management Process: In the parlance of tourism administration, passenger transport is perhaps the most vital element. People would become tourists only if they were to travel from the places of their permanent residence to the places where tourist spots are actually located. Thus, humans would have to be transported, irrespective of the fact whether they are carrying bulky luggage along with them or not. Thus, as soon as we start talking about humans as passengers, the human element enters the canvass of transportation.

We have discussed logistics in this chapter because we want our readers to be clear about the concepts of transport and logistics. However, in the parlance of tourism administration and management, we would like to give more importance to passenger transport. The following steps must be noted with great case.

Aims and Objectives of Tourists Passengers : The tourist or passenger has some objectives to achieve when he plans a tour. His objectives should be understood by the travel agency that he contacts for the purpose of undertaking the tour. Different people have different tour ambitions. Thus, they have different tour programmes and proposals that they share with their tour operators.

A tourist or passenger informs the travel agency about : (a) The destination or destinations to be visited; (b) Expected Date of Departure (EDD); (c) Expected Date of Arrival (EDA); (d) Expected Time of Departure (ETD); (e) Expected Time of Arrival (ETA); (f) Number of days of stay; (g) Class of hotels in which, he intends to stay; and (h) The budget.

This information is given by the tourist/passenger to the executive of the travel agency. The latter gets in touch with the officials of the airline, road-line, cruise operator, etc. He also tries to change the programme of the tourist according to the flight schedules, coach department schedules, railway timetables, etc. He has also to inform the tourist or passenger about the places he would be visiting at the tourist spot. Finally, he would tell him about the modes of transport that would be available at the tourist spot and other facilities that would be availed by him because of the courtesy of the travel agency. Example : The tour executive can offer him free airport-hotel and hotel-airport transfers so that the passenger/tourist does not face any problem related to transportation in a foreign land.

Analysis of Social and Environmental Impact : In this step, the executive needs to understand the general environment of the country in which, he intends to send the passenger/tourist. There are six distinct elements of environment, as follows:

(a) *Tourist :* He is a tourist or passenger. He may or may not use the tour agency or 'the transport system (being organised or looked after by the tour agency) solely for the purpose of tourism.

(b) *Travel Agency :* It gets all the bookings done on behalf of the tourist or passenger. Naturally, transportation is one of the elements of the tour or travel programme. A travel agency works on a professional basis. It not only arranges tickets for the passenger/tourists, but also it makes arrangements for the stay, food (at least breakfast) in hotels, airport transfers, sight seeing and other activities of fun and frolic for the passenger/tourist.

(c) *Home State :* The government influences the rules related to foreign exchange, security aspects, etc. Further, the environment, ecology and climate of the home country also play vital roles if the passenger/tourist is involved in domestic tourism.

(d) *Foreign States :* The embassies issue visas to the passenger/tourist and fix the time periods of his stay in their respective countries. Tourist visas are different from those that are issued for permanent stay. Further, the environment, ecology and climate of the foreign country also play vital roles if the passenger/tourist is involved in foreign tourism.

(e) *Transporter :* The carrier of passengers/tourists is different from the freight carrier in most of the cases. In India, both private and public carriers are available in all the four modes of transport. In airlines., Air India is the national carrier, though passengers may not choose to use its services. In road travel, the TCI is the leader for long and short distance transport.

(f) *Other Agencies :* Insurance firms insure the lives of passengers. Airport authorities charge airport taxes. Road transport authorities charge road tax. Shipping companies and cruise liners also charge taxes according to the laws of their respective lands. All these taxes are governed by organisations like the WTO, PATA, and IATA. Every mode of transport has an apex body in every country that decides such taxes. Quite naturally, these tax regimes would have to conform to international norms. A natural corollary of this fact is that airlines, road transporters and cruise liners cannot charge exorbitant amounts of fare simply because the passenger/tourist does not know about these.

Fulfilment of the Needs of Passenger : The travel agency tells the transporter about the needs of the passenger/tourists. Nowadays, all the bookings are done on-line with the help of a Computerised Reservation System (CRS). This is especially true with respect to airline bookings. But road transport and ship transport bookings can also be done online. If need be, the travel agency, which is a small retailer, can also talk to the large travel organisation that has large number of (bulk) bookings in hotels, airlines, resorts, etc. The seats are finally booked. But these have to be booked according to a fixed tour programme that is called Tour Itinerary in the parlance of tourism administration. Every travel agency decides about the complete programme from day one to the day last of the tour. It includes basic transport modes, hotels, resorts, transfer modes (from hotel to airport and vice versa) and types of food offered. This statement is invariably in a written format; it also describes when the tourist/ passenger would check into a hotel and leave it. Every part of the schedule is deeply interconnected and there is no room for mistakes. Quite naturally, transport systems must also be equally perfect. Even a single weak transport link can spoil the entire show. And if the passenger is in a foreign country, our readers can imagine what the state of affairs can become for him ! That is why, senior executives prefer only professional travel agencies so far as executions of their foreign tours are concerned.

Programme Finalisation

After a lot of toil, the tour itinerary is finally ready. It is modified many times. Many other modes of transport may have to be added depending upon the needs (and may be, whims) of the client. The travel agency or its principal helps the client in the finalisation process. Finally, payments are made and tickets are booked in road coaches, airlines or sea cruises, or in all of these three, depending upon the need of the tourist. Accordingly, hotels are also booked at the spots, which the tourist/passenger intends to visit. The travel agency informs its counterparts in other countries about the tour programme. It sends them E-mail and tells them about the schedule, which also lists the names of passengers, their passport numbers, ages, dates of birth, etc. Tickets are used to get visas. The tourist or passenger is also told to get inoculations, if there is a need to get these. Inoculations must be taken before leaving for some countries. The passenger may have to be immunised against Small Pox, TB, Whooping Cough, Malaria, Diphtheria, etc. Tourists should contact the Civil Surgeons in their respective cities or towns to get more information. Their travel agencies also have lists of physicians who provide inoculations at reasonable costs. A certificate is issued after the inoculation procedure. It tells that the person in question has been immunised against a particular disease for a specified duration of time. It is advisable to get such inoculations from a government hospital.

Execution of Tour and Travel Activities : It is natural that this execution would always include the execution of travel activities as well. That is because tourism and travel cannot be executed in isolation. The tourist or passenger can either travel within the country of' his residence or move out of it. In the former case, he is called Domestic Tourist and in the latter, he is called Foreign Tourist transporter who assists the tourist whenever there is a need to do so (during the journey). The tourist is given a set of documents that confirms that he is eligible to travel by the vehicles of the transporter on fixed dates and timings. These documents could be air tickets, railway tickets, cruise tickets, vouchers of various types receipts or tour itineraries. On the basis of these documents, the transporter allows the tourist to use its vehicles. The travel agent or the representative there of helps the tourist arrive at the place from where, the tourist is supposed to get the next vehicle or transport mode to continue his journey. He also receives the tourist when he arrives from another destination. Foreign tourists are managed that way because they are not aware of the new environments of the foreign countries they enter.

Assessment of Services

During the execution stage, it is not possible to evaluate the services provided by the transporter. The tourist would give his comments during the journey. But his suggestions would be implemented by the senior managers of the transporter only after careful analysis and in-house discussions. The rules and procedures of a transporter cannot be changed overnight. It has also to take due care of international norms and regulations. But the suggestions regarding cleanliness, punctuality, complaints against crew members, delayed flights, loss of baggage, etc. are accepted. Actions are taken immediately so that passengers do not find opportunities to file such complaints again. Control is a continuous process. It is in vogue even during the course of the journey. The top brass studies various aspects of operations of the organisation. It also gets suggestions from its staff from time to time. The suggestions of tourists (actual clients) are also considered. Final decisions, which are likely to affect the working of the transport organisation, are taken only by the top brass. Procedures and rules are normally not changed. Fares and other rates may be revised or reduced according to the policies of the IATA, WTO or DATA and taxes imposed by the governments. But these are matters of routine nature and the transport company is not likely to change its policies and procedures due to these.

Landmarks in the Transport Sector : These landmarks have been discussed in subsequent sections. However, we are giving other important landmarks related to transport in this section. Refer below, this programme is being made for the client (tourist or passenger). Hence, his whims, fancies and preferences are always taken care of while defining the entire programme. Note that the programme has to be given to the transporter well in advance.

Example : Air tickets are booked first of all and then, visas are applied for. Visas cannot be obtained if the travel agency does not show the air ticket of its client to the official of the relevant embassy or high commission. Bookings of airlines can be cancelled within 14 days from the date of booking.

Landmarks* in *the Transport Sector

S. N.	*Major Landmark*	*Date*	*Personality/Firm Responsible for Development or Execution*
1.	Great Eastern ship launched. Its weight was 18,915 tonnes. It had 24 feet screw propeller and 58-ft paddle wheels. Its speed was 18 knots. It was designed by Isambard Kingdom Brunei during 19th century AD.	Nineteenth Century	Isambard Kingdom Brunei (designer engineer)
2.	First airplane		Oliver and Wilbur Wright (inventors)
3.	Grand Trunk Road constructed	1540-1545	Shershah Suri (ruler)
4.	First steamship invented	1775	JC Perrier (France)
5.	Cook transported 570 passengers from Leicester to Loughborough	1841	Thomas Cook
6.	Henry Wells (USA) started as a shipper but became a tourist transporter at a later stage. His firm, Well Fargo, became a well-known firm in the field of tourism and transport. American Express launched a few years later	1841	Henry Wells
7.	Mass excursion started by Thomas Cook. First trip was from Liverpool to Caemaryon. Tourists travelled to Liverpool by train. Then, they took a steamer to Caemaryon.	1845	Thomas Cook
8.	Cook executed a tour to Europe for his clients	1862	Thomas Cook
9.	First turbiane ship called Turbinia developed. In its maiden voyage, it achieved a speed of 34.5 knots	1894	Sir Charles parsons
10.	The best known luxury sea liner was the Titanic. It sank on its maiden voyage in April, 1912. Nearly 1600 persons died, most of them effluent.	16-04-1912	

Contd....

S. N.	Major Landmark	Date	Personality/Firm Responsible for Development or Execution
11.	Igor Sikorsky (1889-1972) built and plotted the first ever successful 4-engine plane	1913	Igor Sikorsky (1889-1972) of Russia
12.	First ever single-rotor helicopter	1939	igor Sikorsky (1889-1972) of Russia
13.	First flight of Imperial Airways from Delhi to Cairo	08-01-1927	Imperial Airways
14.	First Air station of Delhi	1927	
15.	First Flying Club at Delhi	1928	Delhi Flying Club
16.	First full-fledged airport at Delhi (12500 ft) for 747 B aircraft	1939-45	
17.	First ever powered seaplane to make a successful flight (Hydravion)	1910	Fiend Fabre (France)
18.	World's longest land vehicle is the Arctic Snow Train. It has a length of 572 ft (174.3 m)	—	The United States Army
19.	Firs trans-Atlanitc air mail had a bag of 192 letters. It was taken abroad the first non-stop transatlantic flight. The transit from New Found land to Ireland took 16 hours and 12 minutes	1919	Flown by captain John W Alcock and Lieutenant Arthur Whitten Brown
20.	First train from Mumbai to Thane. The total distance was 32 km	1953	The British Government in India
21.	Flight in a solar powered balloon across the English Channel. Air burner was used to lift the balloon and solar panel was used to keep the air warm during the 1.25 hour crossing of the channel	1981	Julian Knot
22.	Fly overs constructed in Delhi to facilitate smooth flow of traffic authorities during the Asian Games	1979-82	The Government of India and local
23.	First joint Indo-Soviet space mission executed. Squadron Leader Rakesh Sharma is the first Indian in space	03-04-1984	Rakesh Sharma

Contd....

S. N.	Major Landmark	Date	Personality/Firm Responsible for Development or Execution
24.	First Indian-American in space	1997	Kalpana Chawla
25.	Exuba, a luxury vehicle designed by Ashok Leyland on the base of a cargo vehicle (of 1912).	2002	Ashok Leyland Ltd.
26.	First private international airport of India constructed	2002	Place: Nedumbassery
27.	Phoenix 1000, an American submarine, US Submarines became the first ever submarine to be gifted. It has been built by US Submarines. It is 213 ft long and has an interior space of 5000 sq m. It has four levels, an exercise room, a kitchen, dining and lounge. It can handle 40 guests at one time for day trips and 16 guests for the night. It can dive up to a depth of 1000 ft and has an on-board docking station for an 8-person mini-submarine that can dive up to a depth of 2000 ft. Two diesel engines provide power to it on the surface and 40 tonnes of 220-V batteries propel it underwater. It carries enough oxygen to keep it under water for 3 weeks. Its cost is US $ 80 million. Suitable only for billionaires.	25-12-2002	
28.	Space Shuttle (Columbia) crashed during its twenty-eighth mission in space. All the 7 crew members dead. These astronauts had completed 80 experiments before evaporating into thin air over Fort Worth (Texas)	01-02-2003	Kalpana Chawla, Rick Husband, Illan Ramon, Michael Anderson, Laurel Clark, William McCool, David Brown

Effects and Essence of Development : We are discussing three types of implications in this section.

Socio-economic Implications of Developments in the Sphere of Transport : The following effects and essence have been observed by experts :

(a) Developed transport networks have led to mass movements from rural areas to urban areas. This migration pattern had become more prominent during the eighties and nineties of the last century. The major metropolises of the country are the coveted destinations of most of the rural youth. Further, rural people prefer to move to cities that are in the immediate vicinity of their respective villages.

(b) Economic development has been facilitated by the road networks in rural areas. Farmers are able to market their agricultural and farm products with ease. Pucca roads are available in many a village of India.

(c) Vast road and rail networks have also led to the development of eco-tourism, farm tourism and heritage tourism. But the government and private entrepreneurs must not be complacent over this trend. There is a lot of potential in the field of tourism after the development of road and rail networks.

(d) Logistics management is easier and better today than it was nearly forty years ago. That is because efficient rail, road and air networks have facilitated the movement of cargo, perishable goods and other materials that are used by various components of the tourism industry.

(e) Inland water transport system has not been fully developed in India. There is a great scope of its development and contribution towards the travel and tourism industry. The responsibility for developing this network lies with the State. That is because a private firm cannot develop waterways. There is a proposal to link the Indian rivers to help such states as are drought-affected most of the times. If this system is developed by keeping the need of the travel and tourism industry, domestic and international tourists would certainly use these facilities. Thus, water management would be coupled with water transport.

(f) Private airlines are making air transport competitive and efficient. These trends are healthy and ought to continue.

(g) Private bus operators and coach services for tourists are available only in major cities. Small cities that have tourism potential must also have such services. Private firms can take the initiative in this context.

(h) Vast road and rail networks have increased employment

levels in cities. Airlines also employ staff to facilitate their businesses.

(i) Intra-city transport networks have been strengthened. But this feature is prominent only in four metropolitan cities and 400 other cities of India. Rural areas of India must have facilities related to tourism and travel. These facilities are available but these are not of high quality.

(j) Inter-modal transport systems in the context of tourism administration have boosted the economies of all the major transport industries, namely, air, road, water and rail transport.

(k) People, especially tourists, are now more keen to comfortable and luxury even if they are on religious tours. They want their family members to travel comfortably. Thus, they do not mind paying extra for such services as were hitherto deemed out of reach, flamboyant and costly by them. Air travel is an example in this context.

(l) Tourists demand full value for the money spent by them in transport systems. They expect railway stations to be clean, coaches to be spick and span, aircraft to be the role models of efficiency and luxury and cruise liners to be synonymous with floating paradise. As many of them do not undertake long tours (for 15 - 20 days) quite often due to their busy schedules, they try to extract the maximum out of their currently planned travel and tour itineraries. (M) Many businessmen couple business with family trips and tours to famous cities or historic spots. This trend has been catching up at a fast pace in India.

Observation of Culture Implications : The following cultural implications have been observed in the context of development of transport networks in India :

(a) People travel to far-off places with ease. They mingle with people of different regions and tribes. These interactions have developed a national spirit that binds the nation as a unique cultural entity (despite the differences in individual cultures and value systems). Example North Indians visit Chennai and enjoy South Indian festivals.

(b) Cultural programmes and festivals also involve people of different races. Even foreigners take pride in witnessing the cultural performances of India. This was made possible because of the provision of facilities related to travel and transport. Example : Indian and foreign tourists visit Goa and attend the famous Goa Carnival during December each year. The parade on December 25 brings several thousand people on the streets of Goa.

(c) Transport networks have increased interest of tourists (domestic and foreign) in various cultural festivals and competitions. They either witness such competitions or are proud to participate in the same.

(d) Many festivals and cultural programmes have become so famous that these have acquired international recognition. This was made possible because of the developments in transport networks. People were able to visit the sites of these festivals and fairs and publicise them through word-of-mouth campaigns. Example: Snake boat races of South India, Kullu Dussehra, Mysore Dussehra, Baisakhi of Punjab, Pongal, Onam, Holi, Lohri and Deepavali are some of the festivals that have been acknowledged as mirrors of Indian culture and art forms. The famous Sun Temple of Konark is the venue of dance festival in December every year. Goan Carnival is also world famous. Dandiya of Gujarat is attended by millions; so is Ganesh Puja in Maharashtra. The Durga Puja festival (in West Bengal) attracts visitors from India and abroad. The holy shrine of Vaishno Devi (near Jammu) can be approached (from Katra) by a helicopter. Indian Airlines is organising flights to Leh, which is the roof of the world. Many other examples can be quoted in this context.

Observation of Environmental Implications : On the environmental front, our position is slightly week. Some of the implications are as follows:

(a) Diesel fuel is used to propel coaches and ordinary buses. Diesel contains sulphur, which, upon combustion, delivers sulphur dioxide. So, our roads are the living examples of "pollution tubes." There is no solution in sight, however.

(b) In Delhi, the local transport system is based on CNG as a fuel. But other cities continue to use diesel and petrol as fuels for their vehicles. So, pollution levels are very high in Kanpur, Mumbai, Kolkata, Chennai, Ahmedabad and other major cities of India.

(c) Pollution creates problems in all parts of the country. Global warming, ecological imbalances and decay of fauna and flora are directly related to movements of human beings. Growing urbanisation leads to creation of new road and rail networks. Jungles are cut and crop fields are trimmed as a result. Wildlife suffers and so does the ecology. The present area of India under forest is only 19 per cent of the total area; it should be 33 per cent of the total area. The government has created biosphere reserves and also, defined norms for wild-life parks. However, other areas are polluted by humans and vehicles alike. Tours and leisure activities of travellers add to the burden to local resources, which include water, air, food, fuel, etc. But economic compulsions force the transporters to carry on their businesses.

(d) Foreign tourists, arrivals in India are less. But domestic tourism activities contribute a lot towards pollution. All the railway routes have not been electrified. Diesel engines create a lot of pollution. These issues ought to be addressed by the Ministry of Railways. A lot of time is needed to electrify even the major railway routes.

(e) Aircraft use aviation fuel, which has a high calorific value. It is also a contributor to the process of global warming. Private airlines have jumped on to the bandwagon of domestic transport. Naturally, they would also add to the already high levels of air pollution.

(f) Noise pollution is on the rise in major cities, thanks to vast transport networks and growing number of vehicles.

System of Tourism and Various Elements : In a tourism transport system, the tourist expresses his desire to visit a place. It can be a domestic or an international destination. He contacts a travel agency so that the latter may be able to help him define a tour programme. He buys a package tour if he is new to the place of visit. If he is well versed with the proposed place of visit, he only buys a ticket for travelling to that place. In that case, he finds the hotel accommodation himself. He also arranges intra-city transport, food, beverages and breakfast at the tourist spot in the city. But nevertheless, he needs a transport mode to take him to the destination of his choice. So, every type of tourist needs suitable transport mode. For this purpose, the travel agency helps him. If he is not buying a package tour, he can just walk into the office of an airline and get the ticket booked for reaching the coveted destination. But if he is buying a package tour, it would be appropriate if he were to interact with a professional travel agency. Transport is not an easy game in the parlance of tourism, especially in the context of international tourism.

The tourist gets the bookings done after contacting the travel agency. He tells them that he intends to be at a tourist spot on a specified date by a specified time. The executive of the travel agency comprehends his needs and then suggests a few alternatives for the journey. These alternatives are, in fact, combinations of inter-modal transport. There can only be basic modes of transport for a tourist. At one time, he can have all these in suitable combinations. He may have to skip some of these modes simply because these may not suit his schedule. Example: he may have to travel by sea most of the time and his tour may involve only one trip by air. Further, he may have to take all the trips (in all the sectors) by air because of shortage of time. Finally, some modes of transport may be too costly for him to afford and so, he may tell the executive of the travel agency to look for a cheaper mode of transport. If he becomes a frequent traveller, he learns about these tricks. But if his tours are far and few, he had better count on the travel executive who knows much more than him in this context.

The tour itinerary is finally made; it is in a written format. In this itinerary, all the dates and timings of departure are mentioned. The names of hotels as well as the number of days of stay in each one of these is also mentioned. Finally, all the modes of transport (along with sharp timings) are mentioned. The below-given table shows an itinerary that is a real case study. This tour was undertaken by the author from November 2 to 10, 2002.

The tour- programme is finally executed. The tourist takes the requisite foreign exchange, passport (with stamps of visas), his personal effects, tickets (of air, rail, cruise ship, cable car or road) and the tour programme. Besides, he also carries some vouchers with him. These vouchers are given to him by the travel agency. These are, in fact, the documentary evidences that he is a bona fide tourist and is eligible to stay in the hotels mentioned in such vouchers. He is also eligible to travel by the modes of transport mentioned in such vouchers. The travel agency contacts the travel agency of the tourist destination (in fact, it sends a copy of that voucher that is relevant to the travel agency of the destination or spot). The latter gets an idea that the tourist having the given passport number is arriving according to a pre-specified schedule. In many cases, the tourist pays in advance to the travel agency in his country. The travel agency of the destination receives its due amount when the travel agency of the tourist sends it the details as well as payments by wire transfer or electronic cash.

Thus, we can conclude that the travel agency, which is located at the destination and is responsible for arranging hotels, excursions and transport of the tourist, gets the money in advance. However, there are exceptions to this rule. In many cases, the travel agency of the origin gives only the voucher to the tourist, but tells him to pay when he arrives at the tourist spot. This procedure is being followed in Bangkok and Kuala Lumpur. Thus, when the tourist arrives at the airport, he pays to the travel agent at the airport itself after showing him the voucher. Then, he is eligible to avail the services of the travel agent of the destination and move into the hotel, as mentioned in the itinerary. The schedules are followed in strict sense of the word. It is obvious that all the concerned travel agents or their executives are aware of the tour programme. They are also responsible for taking the tourists from one place to another, if this has been mentioned in the schedule. However, they are not liable to transport him from one place to another, if the schedule does not mention such activities. Airport-to-hotel transfers and vice versa, morning breakfast, welcome drinks, courtesy luncheons, etc. are a part of the schedule. The tourist is eligible to avail these facilities and/or services because he has already paid for these well in advance.

Tour Itinerary with Details of Transport

Day	Tour Programme
Day 01 (2nd Nov' 02)	**Delhi-Bangkok** Assemble at Indira Gandhi International Airport at 2200 hrs to connect your flight TG 316 for Bangkok on 3rd Nov' 02 at 00:05 Hrs.
Day 02 (3rd Nov' 02)	**Bangkok-Pattaya** Arrive Bangkok, after clearance of your immigration & customs, We will meet you. Transfer by air-conditional coach to Pattaya. On arrival, transfer to Hotel Beverly plaza, Pattaya, Evening is free for shopping. In the evening it is time for famous Night show- "Tiffany" (Optional). Overnight in the hotel
Day 03 (4th Nov' 02)	**Pattaya** After breakfast, we will take you on a tour to Coral Island, a little way off Pattaya. There are three small Islands, well known for their crystal blue water, Coral and other colourful forms of life under the sea, which can be viewed from glass-bottomed boat Evening is free for self exploration. Overnight in the hotel.
Day 04 (5th Nov' 02)	**Pattaya-Bangkok** After breakfast, proceed to Bangkok by an air-conditioned coach. In the afternoon we take you for half-day tour of Bangkok visit the Marble Temple, the Reclining Buddha Temple and the magnificent 5.5-ton solid gold statue of Lord Buddha Overnight in the hotel, Ambassador Main Wing.
Day 05 (6th Nov' 02)	**Bangkok-Singapore** After breakfast, transfers to Airport to catch the flight TG 413 at 11:15 hrs. On 6th Nod 02 for Singapore

Contd...

Day	***Tour Programme***
	Arrive Singapore, transfer to your hotel Tropical. Check into the hotel. Day is free to relax or do your work on your own Overnight at the hotel
Day 06 (7th Nov' 02)	**Singapore** After breakfast, we will take you for a half-day city tour. Evening is free for self-exploration or shopping. Overnight in the hotel
Day 07 (8th Nov' 02)	**Singapore- Kuala Lumpur** After breakfast, day is free for last-minute shopping and transfer to the coach station Arrive in Kuala Lumpur Coach station. Here you will meet our representative for transfer to hotel Malaya. Check into the hotel Overnight in the hotel.
Day 08 (9th Nov' 02)	**Kuala Lumpur (Day trip to Genting Highland)** After breakfast, We will take you for the day trip to Genting Highlands. Visit to Theme Park (optional). Evening back to Kuala Lumpur. Overnight in the hotel.
Day 09 (10th Nov' 02)	**Kuala Lumpur-Delhi** After breakfast, we will take you for a half-day city tour and later on we will transfer you to the airport to connect your flight for Delhi at 1320 hrs. on 10 "I Nov' 02. Arrive in Delhi 22:45 hrs, with the everlasting memories of your trip,

If the tour gives satisfaction and pleasure to the tourist, he comes back with a happy mind. He informs the travel agency of his country that he was pleased to undertake the trip. He gives good word-of-mouth publicity for the travel agency. He goes through it to other tourist spots. But if he is not satisfied by the services of hotels, transporters, spot managers, waiters, restaurant attendants, etc. he does not choose that travel agency again. He contacts another travel agency whom he deems fit for planning another successful tour.

In sum, tourism involves hotel accommodation, transport, fun activities of the tourist, transfers from one place to another and complementary gifts or meals. However, the tourist must be clear about what he is going to get. The travel agency in the destination city or spot must also be clear about such details.

Transport systems are involved in all the stages of the tour. These can be inter-modal systems as well, as is usually the case in international tourism. In the activities related to domestic tourism, a single mode of transport normally suffices, though tourists use different modes of transport within cities or townships. Example: Tourists may arrive at the Sun Temple at Konark by bus. But they may use taxi's and coaches to move around and enjoy the environs of the beach. In international tourism, at least three modes are added to one itinerary, according to our experience. The cable car, air-conditioned coach and air travel can be combined to make the tour cost efficient and rational on the ground of time scale, to quote an example.

8

Promotional Activity

Before the introduction of price mechanism in the world, the goods and services produced were exchanged through simple barter system. The exchanges have always taken place through various means and it is through these exchanges that some sort of markets were evolved. These exchanges, however, have undergone a great change in the past and particularly since the advent of the industrialized societies first in the West and subsequently all over the world. In the early nineteenth century, most of the country's production was conducted in small manufacturing units and on small scale. The market for the goods produced was also small and limited to the areas surrounding the manufacturing unit. Due to limitation of connectivity to other far-off places in the country it was rare that a particular manufacturer's product were sold in other parts of the country.

Another reason for products not finding wider markets was the absence of distribution channels and non-availability of products in sufficient quantities as required by these channels. The means of transport to carry the goods over to distant areas had not yet been evolved. Limited purchasing power as a result of considerable unemployment was yet another factor responsible for smaller and localised markets. Markets for products other than required as necessary for life was limited. Besides, only a fraction of the total population could afford to indulge in purchase of products other than those which were considered to be essential.

Origin and Growth

From the times of simple barters to the present-day complex marketing systems, exchanges of goods have always been taking place. These exchanges, however, have undergone many changes since the advent of the industrialized societies first in the West and subsequently all over the world. In the nineteenth century, most of the production of industrialized countries was conducted in small manufacturing units as the market for the goods was limited to the areas surrounding the manufacturing unit. It was seldom that a manufacturer's product found place in other parts of the country.

There were several factors responsible for limiting the sale of products of the manufacturing units within the local areas. The main cause was the lack of efficient and inexpensive transport systems to move the products to other areas. Another important cause was the absence of system of distribution channels as also non-availability of sufficient quantity of products as required by these channels. The absence of quality products due to lack of competition and the means of transport to carry the products to distant areas were yet other inhibiting factors. Besides, large majority of people during this period had limited purchasing power as a result of considerable unemployment. Market for goods other than the necessities was rather limited. Only a fraction of the population could afford to indulge in purchase of products other than those essential for living.

Huge Production

The post-industrialization period witnessed the induction of mass production of goods. A large number of people now had access to the products. Coupled with increase in purchasing power, as a result of higher employment and better wages, more and more people could buy products. Rapid industrialization placed at the disposal of the consumer a variety of products of improved quality and in abundant quantity from a number of competing manufacturers. More and more manufacturers came in the field as the number of products exceeded the demand. As a result of mass production and competition, the consumers for the first time had a choice to purchase the products from more than one manufacturer.

Consumer choice as a result of competition compelled the manufacturers to give greater consideration to the needs of the consumers. Rapid industrial advancement also witnessed the growth in communication and transport systems. The advent of mechanised transport, first the railways and later road transport, made the physical distribution of products possible over much larger areas. The increasing quantity of production of different manufacturing units found markets in far off places and was distributed by means of railway and road transport systems enabling more and more people to purchase the same. Subsequently, mass communication means like telephones, telegraphs and newspapers greatly helped the manufacturers in disposing their goods and services. All these developments eventually led to the introduction and adoption of a new concept, i.e., the marketing concept by a large number of progressive and forward-looking manufacturing organizations.

Marketing Concept

Marketing has been variously defined through time, by different people. However, the definition which reflects the nature of marketing most adequately is: "Marketing is a human activity directed at satisfying needs and wants through exchange processes." The British Institute of Marketing has formulated the following definition:

Marketing is the management function which organizes and directs all those business activities involved in assessing and converting customer purchasing power into effective demand for a specific product or service and in moving the product or service to the final customer or user so as to achieve the profit target or other objectives set by the company.

In essence, the marketing concept is a customer orientation backed by integrated marketing aimed at generating customer satisfaction. The important aspects of marketing concept are:

Customer Orientation: *The* companies practising this concept think in terms of the benefits they are selling rather than the products.

Dual-core Marketing Job: This implies that the first task of the marketer is to identify the customer's needs in order to guide the development of the suitable products and services and the second task is to motivate all the potential customers, through various means, to purchase these products and services.

Integrated Marketing : The customer orientation alone on the part of the management is not enough. To be effective it must be backed by an appropriate organizational set-up within the company. Integrated marketing represents such a set-up. It signifies the substitution of a single logic for several different logics of the various departments of the company. It implies the responsibility of the marketing department to ensure coordination of various company actions affecting the buyers.

Application of the marketing concept has certain important benefits. First, the management using this concept realise that customer needs are more basic than particular products. This provides a more reliable and enduring base to the operations of such managements. Second, the focus on the customer needs helps the management to spot new product opportunities more speedily. Third, merchandising becomes more effective under this concept. This is because managements view their tasks as that of supplying want satisfaction rather than creating demand for its products among the customers. The physical product is only a part of the satisfactions sought by the buyer because he wants, in addition, conveniences, service and certain other symbolic values. Fourth, the managements are able to create more harmony between their interests and those of the society because the market orientation under this concept means that the managements build their future profits through seeking better ways to satisfy human needs.

Marketing Practical : It is a well-known fact that as long as the inherent sense of curiosity and adventure dwells in the hearts of human beings, the desire to travel in order to see new sights and experience new things, to live under different environments, will always grow. It may be presumed that such being the case, marketing in tourism industry is greatly simplified as part of the process already been completed by the desire for travel in people. The best example would be that a person may or may not choose a tangible product which has been introduced by a manufacturer in the market, solely depending on his ability to afford it or his likes and dislikes. On the other hand, without exception, all human beings will always nurture a desire to travel in order to see places. The question then arises that if the desire is ever present in people to travel and experience' new things, why then would the tourism industry need marketing efforts at all?

Are the marketing problems in tourism so much different from marketing problems in other industries that it is justified to make marketing in tourism a subject for separate and specialized enquiry? To what extent can the concepts and principles, the techniques and methods of marketing which have been applied effectively in other industries be applied to tourism?

Answer to both the above questions can be found by identifying and considering the differences between markets for physical, tangible goods on the one hand and the market for tourism on the other. The marketing concept, as the overriding philosophy of any business undertaking, contrasts with the production orientation. Here the emphasis is on producing goods or services whereafter a sales policy has to be devised to sell what has been produced. In tourism, on the other hand, the product, from a destination viewpoint, is an amalgam of various elements or components, some of which are tangible and some are intangible (services). The only open path for the organization in this case would be to inform itself about the consumer needs, expectations, attitudes of mind, likes and dislikes in order to formulate and constantly develop the tourist supply components or products.

The marketing concept should, therefore, be understood as a reorientation of the business policy and an overhaul of the organization's or enterprise's management concepts and practices. It helps the tourist organization or enterprise to establish a consistent and effective communication system with actual and potential tourists in the selected markets or market, and to get to know their wishes, needs, motivations, likes and dislikes in order to be able to condition the tourist supply accordingly. The marketing concept, therefore, facilitates a breakthrough in the tourist system. Tourism is a very complex industry because of its multifaceted activities which together produce the tourist product' and various sub-sectors that are themselves complete industries, if considered independently (lodging industry, transport industry, etc.). Besides, its complexity lies mostly in the fact that tourists are located in different places having different socio-economic structures, different needs, tastes, attitudes, expectations and behaviour patterns. It is therefore necessary to understand the people's tastes and preferences. The understanding that people are different in the same market helps in satisfying their needs in a better way.

Meaning and Definitions

Tourism marketing could be defined as the systematic and coordinated efforts exerted by tourist enterprises at international, national and local levels to optimise the satisfaction of tourists, groups and individuals, in view of a sustained tourism growth. According to Krippendorf, "Marketing in tourism is to be understood as the systematic and coordinated execution of business policy by tourist undertakings, whether private or state owned, at local, regional, national or international level to achieve the optimal satisfaction of the needs of identifiable consumer groups, and in doing so to achieve an appropriate return."

Tourism Products

A 'product' may be defined as the sum of the physical and psychological satisfactions it provides to the buyer. Marketing, by definition, is the development of a product to meet the needs of the consumer and then employing the techniques of direct sales, publicity and advertising to bring this product to the consumer. Availability of a product is the prerequisite for any organization which indulges in the marketing function. Unless there is a certain 'product,' be it tangible or intangible or a service, marketing is not possible.

In the case of tourism, the product is the country's natural beauty, climate, history, culture and the people. Other aspects of the produce would be the existing facilities necessary for comfortable living such as water supply, electricity, roads, transport communication and other essentials. In other words, the tourist product can be seen as a composite product, as the sum total of country's tourist attractions, transport, accommodation and entertainment which hopefully result in consumer satisfaction. The tourist product can be entirely a man-made one or nature's creation improved upon by man. Each of these components of a tourist product is supplied by individual providers of services like hotel companies, airlines or other suppliers, and is offered directly to the tourist by them. A consumer can combine these individual tourist products through a number of ways. There would be many possible destinations, each with a number of hotels, each to be reached by more than one airline. Thus the potential choice of the consume is very large.

The growing number of tourist destinations have placed at the disposal of a tourist a variety of tourist products in abundant quantity from a large number of competing nations. This eventually has led to the adoption of the new concept, i.e., the marketing concept in tourism by various countries promoting tourism. The important point about modern marketing is that it applies to situations where the choice can be limited to a relatively small number of brands giving the consumer a reasonable choice. The process of selection thus becomes easier. In the field of tourism this process is taking place by the increasing use of package tours. A package tour is a travel plan which includes most elements of a vacation such as transportation, accommodation, sightseeing and entertainment. The tourist product is a composite product, whether it is sold as a package or assembled by the individual tourist himself or his travel agent. The tourist product can therefore be analysed in terms of its attractions, its facilities and its accessibility.

Attractive Ventures

Of the three basic components of a tourist product, attractions are very important. Unless these are there, the tourists will not be motivated to go to a particular place. Attractions are those elements in the tourist product which determine the choice of a particular tourist to visit one particular destination rather than another. The attractions could be cultural, like sites and areas of archaeological interest, historical buildings and monuments or scenic like flora and fauna, beach resorts, mountains, national parks, or events like trade fairs, exhibitions, arts and music festivals, games, etc.

The Dexterity

Facilities are those elements in the tourist product which are a necessary aid to the tourist centre. The facilities complement the attractions. These include accommodation, various types of entertainments, picnic sites, recreation and so on. These are indeed important for every tourist centre.

The Availabilities

Accessibility is another important component in the tourist product. It is a means by which a tourist can reach the area where attractions are located. Tourist attractions of whatever type would be of little importance if their locations are inaccessible by the normal means of transport. If the tourist attractions are located at places where no means of transport can reach, or where there are inadequate transport facilities, these become of little value. The tourist attractions, which are located near to the tourist-generating markets and are linked by a network of efficient transport, receive the maximum number of tourists.

Market for Tourists

Identification of markets like that of the product is crucial for any organization which adopts the marketing concept. In fact, the first step a marketing organization will have to take is to identify its markets. The term 'market' is used in a number of ways. It may be employed to designate the place where the buyer and seller of a good or service meet and between them the exchange transaction takes place. The buyer of goods or services may be the actual buyer or the potential buyer. It may be used in connection with a particular geographical area or in connection with a particular type of service or product. In the context of marketing and promotion, all of the above aspects are relevant, but especially those related to actual and potential buyers, to product and/or service and to geographical location. Another important additional element to be considered is the time factor. Taking into consideration all these elements, the 'market,' therefore, can be defined as "the totality of actual and/or potential buyer of a given product or service in a specified geographical location at a given point in time or during a given period of time."

Fragmentation of the Market

A tourist market may be identified corresponding to each tourist product. The term market may be used to describe the collective actual or potential customers of tourism service or destination. It may apply to the geographical area, country, region or city from which a service or destination draws customers. The identification of tourist market, a segment of the total market, is of crucial importance. With a view to avoid waste, it is essential to reach only that fraction of the total market which is most likely to be attracted. Due to financial constraints, it is not possible for an organization to reach the entire market. Segmentation of the market is therefore made in order to achieve the most efficient use of marketing resources.

Market segmentation is the process of identifying groups of buyers of the total market with different buying desires or requirements. Most markets are too large for an organization to provide all the products and services needed by all the buyers in that market. Some delimitation of the market is therefore necessary to ensure efficiency and also to conserve financial resources of the organizations. This leads organizations to select target markets necessitating market segmentation. Market segmentation has certain obvious advantages in that the organization is (i) better placed to spot and compare marketing opportunities, (ii) makes finer adjustments of the product and marketing appeals possible to cater to the needs of the buyers and (iii) can develop marketing programmes and budgets on the basis of a clearer idea of the response characteristics of specific market segments.

The markets are divided on the basis of several factors. The most commonly used bases of market segmentation include (i) geographic segmentation (the market is divided into different geographic locations such as cities, provinces regions or countries); (ii) demographic segmentation: (on the basis of demographic variables such as age, sex, occupation, income, education, social class, religion, etc.); and (iii) psychographic segmentation (on the basis of psychographic variables which refer to such aspects of an individual as his life-style, personality, buying motives and product knowledge and use). In tourism, market segmentation is very important. The strategy of market segmentation in tourism recognises that few vacation areas are universally acceptable and desired. Therefore, rather than waste promotion resources trying to please all travellers, the best market strategy is to isolate those segments of the entire market which are likely prospects and aim at the promotional efforts specifically to the wants and needs of these selected groups. Thus, one of the early steps in marketing tourism is to divide the present and potential market on the basis of meaningful characteristics and then concentrate promotion, supply and pricing efforts on serving these most prominent sections of the market—the target markets. Usually the market segmentation for tourism is in terms of demographic, geographic, psychographic, social and economic criteria. For example the market for a particular area might be largely archaeologists in their mid-years who have an income of over $80,000 per year and who live in mid-eastern United States, or it might be largely businessmen in the age group of, say, 40-60 years who have an income of over $100,000 per year and who live in southern parts of Germany. In tourism marketing, the total tourism market can be divided into the major segments mentioned above. A further segmentation, however, is possible within each of the above major segments for practical marketing purposes. This includes:

The Vacation Tourist : The vacation or the holiday tourist is the most common and popular tourist. He is immensely affected by changes in price, and is easily influenced by skilled and aggressive marketing effort. This type of tourist is resort oriented (Rome, New York, London, Paris are resorts as much as Venice, Goa, Pattaya, Miami). The vacation tourist market has been regarded as highly seasonal.

The Business Tourist : In recent years the market for business tourist has increased greatly. The choice of destination of a business tourist is generally determined by the nature of his business. The marketing efforts will not influence the choice of the business tourist much. Unlike the case of the vacation tourist, who has proved to be very sensitive to price changes, the demand for business tourism is relatively price inelastic. The demand will tend to be big-city oriented. The visits are of shorter duration and relatively frequent. Trade fairs, conventions, exhibitions, conferences and similar events attract this kind of tourism.

The Common-interest Tourist : This segment comprises visits to relatives and friends, and visits for the purposes of education, pilgrimages, etc. Demand for this type of tourism will be relatively price elastic. The common-interest tourist will not be very readily influenced by the promotional efforts. The average length of his stay will be relatively longer. Because of his friends and relatives, he will not be a significant user of hotel and other such types of accommodation. The visits will not be frequent and expenditure relatively little on his stay as compared with the other two groups.

Important Characteristics

From the ancient times when travel was a prerogative of a select few who travelled in search of adventure to the present-day jet travel, there have been many changes. Travel in ancient times was a simple affair and could be undertaken without utilizing the services of organizations like travel agents or tour operators. As a result, tourism marketing, as we know it today, was not needed then. The types of facilities which were required by the people for travel were provided to them by a handful of suppliers of such services. It was, however, the introduction of mass travel during the twentieth century that services of travel agents and others were needed. Introduction of air travel, especially jet travel expanded the travel, markets necessitating application of marketing techniques. Marketing in the field of tourism made its formal appearance only in the second half of the twentieth century. As the travel business expanded as a result of the introduction of air travel, it became necessary for managers of travel to use techniques of marketing for selling the tourist product.

Marketing helps to create new customers by way of first identifying their needs and then trying to satisfy these. Customer satisfaction becomes a crucial part of travel sales. The first task of the travel marketer is identification of the customer needs in order to guide the development of suitable products and services. The second task is to motivate all the potential customers, through various means, to purchase those products and services. The objective of marketing in tourism can, therefore, be stated to be as attracting and motivating all the potential customers or users of tourist services to a particular destination and not to another.

Tourism marketing, therefore, begins by a detailed assessment of the actual and potential demand and, on this assessment, development of facilities and services for use by customers. Tourist demand can be divided into 'actual' and 'potential'; 'actual' demand represents those who actually travel to a certain tourist destination while 'potential' demand is the number of persons who fulfil the basic elements of travel and are, therefore, in a position to travel. Marketing of tourist product has certain peculiar characteristics. Although the general principles of marketing, which have proved quite effective in the marketing of products of other industries, could be applicable to marketing of tourist product, there are certain differences in approach. These differences are because of the peculiar character of the tourist product. Among the peculiarities of the tourist product are:

Tourism is an Intangible, Non-material Product : Unlike a tangible product, say, a motor car, no transfer of ownership of goods is involved in tourism. Instead, certain facilities, installations, items of equipment are made available for a specified time and for a specified use. For instance, a seat in an aeroplane or a train for a journey from one point to another or a booking in a hotel through a travel agent or services such as information and advice are provided to a customer.

Production and Consumption of Tourist Services are Closely Interrelated : The travel agent or tour operator who sells his product cannot store it. Production can only take place or can only be completed if the customer is actually present. There is a close link between production and consumption of tourist services. Most tourist services cannot be consumed incrementally. In other words, consumption, once begun, cannot be stopped, interrupted or modified at all. As a result, risk and uncertainty for the customer are higher, and his need for reliable pre-purchase information is stronger. The potential customer's decision risk and dependence on accurate information is further increased because he cannot see, inspect, compare, or try out tourist services before deciding to use them.

A Tourist Product is Assembled by Many Producers : The tourist product cannot be provided by a single enterprise. Each of the components of a tourist product is highly specialized and together make the final product. This is not so in the case of other tangible products where one manufacturer produces a total product. In tourism, on the other hand, airline considers 'seats flown' or passenger miles to be product; a hotel produces 'guest nights', a travel agent 'bookings', while a theatre, museum or an archaeological site measures its 'production' in number of visitors. In the tourist's view, however, the product he buys covers the complete experience of his visit to a particular place. In other words, the tourist product is not an airline a rail seat, or a hotel bed or a theatre ticket, but rather an amalgam of many components which together make a complete product. Because of these peculiar characteristics, coordination in marketing efforts is very crucial.

Tourism Demand is Highly Unstable : Tourism demand is influenced by factors such as seasonal, economic, political, etc. Seasonal changes greatly affect the demand. Seasonality means that tourism plant is frequently used for only a limited part of the year and therefore uneconomic. Many tourist areas have short season—often as little as three months. A corollary of this seasonal usage is the seasonal unemployment, which is a serious problem. Some of the developing countries which have recently established tourist industries suffer particularly from seasonality. It also places strains on the transport system and other services. Thus seasonality presents a problem not only in relation to employment but also in relation to investment. On the other hand, political unrest and economic instability caused by currency fluctuations, inflation, etc., greatly affect tourism demand.

Intermediaries Play a Dominant Role : In most industries, manufacturers have predominant control over product design, distribution, promotion and the pricing. On the other hand, in tourism, sales intermediaries like tour operators, travel agents, reservation services and hotel brokers play a dominant role and enjoy superior marketing strength. From the standpoint of tourism marketing, this strong position of travel trade has significant implications. The travel trade determines to a large extent which services will be sold and to whom. The type of services to be offered as well as the pricing policies and promotion strategies to be adopted by tourist enterprises, are, therefore, determined not only by the needs and preferences of the customers but also by those expressed by travel sales intermediaries.

Travel Motivations are Diverse in Nature : It is comparatively simple to determine why people buy a certain make of refrigerator, smoke certain brands of cigarettes, use certain brand of toothpaste or prefer a certain type of packaged food. The subjective and objective reasons, expectations and desires which influence tourists' choice for certain holiday destination, type of accommodation and vacation activities are far less evident. Very often two people make exactly the same choices for entirely different and sometimes even mutually exclusive reasons. Travel motivations, unlike motivations for buying a tangible article like a refrigerator, are heterogeneous—that is, they are composed of diverse elements. Marketing in tourism, therefore, as compared to marketing in other industries, needs a somewhat different approach.

To a considerable extent, tourism marketing depends on various market factors mentioned above. Unlike the normal consumer product or service, the tourist product is marketed at two levels:

(i) The national or regional tourist organization will be engaged in a marketing campaign to persuade the potential tourist to visit the country or region for which it is responsible. In view of the fragmentation of supply, the complementarity of tourist services, the predominance of many small- and medium-sized enterprises and importance of tourism to an economy, the official tourist organizations have important functions in tourism marketing. The official tourist organization will, however, not sell a tourist product directly to customers. It will have two major objectives. In the first place, it will seek to create knowledge of its country in tourist-generating markets and persuade visitors in these markets to visit that country. Secondly, it will seek to create an image of its country's tourist attractions in the best possible manner in tourist-generating countries so that the potential visitors are attracted.

(ii) The various individual firms providing tourist services can market their own components of the total tourist product after the national tourist organizations have launched marketing campaigns to persuade the potential tourist to visit the country or region for which it is responsible.

Management at Work

During the initial days of industrializations, when the supply was short of demand, the emphasis was on sales management rather than market management function. The rapid industrial advancement subsequently placed at the disposal of the consumer a large variety of goods of improved quality and in abundant quantity from a large number of competing manufacturers resulting in supply exceeding demand. This compelled the manufacturers to give greater consideration to the needs of the consumers. This factor eventually led to the adoption of the marketing concept. Marketing concept in the field of tourism comprises the following major functions:

(a) Market research

(b) Product formulation and development

(c) Product distribution

(d) Advertising

(e) Sales promotion

(f) Public relations

Market Research

One of the basic considerations for successful marketing is the need for research. It provides the information base for effective marketing. It relates to providing answers to various questions pertaining to the marketing activities. Market research can be defined as the "systematic collection of information relating to supply and demand for a product or a proposed product in such a way that the information maybe used by the organization to formulate informed decisions about its policies and its objectives." The marketing process, in fact, starts by finding out answers to questions like who are the potential tourists where do they come from, what are their likes and dislikes, etc. In order to formulate any marketing strategy, it is very essential for a national tourist organization and others engaged or marketing a tourist product to know the answers to the following questions:

(i) Who are the persons who engage in tourism and where do they live?

(ii) Who are the potential customers and where do they come from?

(iii) What are their likes and dislikes?

(iv) What are their travel preferences and interests?

(v) What do they buy and where do they stay?

(vi) What mode of transport do they use?

(vii) What are their entertainment preferences?

(viii) What are the trends in competition?

(ix) What type of marketing programmes would be needed?

Market research provides answers to all the above questions. A national tourist organization's promotion efforts without appropriate answers to the above questions will go waste. To make the overall marketing efforts effective and successful, as in the case of manufacturers of consumer products, the national tourist organization in a country has to be totally aware of the international trends in the travel habits, vacation habits and, most important of all, the reasons attributed to the better success of a competing destination. A marketing manager cannot visualise successful marketing strategy without having an up to date knowledge of their markets in general. It is very important to have detailed information on all the aspects of a market. Results of such research will work as guidelines for launching a successful marketing programme.

Market research is a continuous process. There are various methods used to collect the data. Among the great variety of methods used, some seem to be widely resorted to because of their advantages over others. Two broad categories of marketing research techniques are (a) desk research and (b) field research.

Desk Research : Desk research includes the collection and analysis of all available data, statistics and published information on tourist trends and markets. In tourism much of the basic information about tourist trends and markets is available from existing sources. There are a number of international organizations like United Nations, UNESCO, IUOTO, WTO, EC, OECD, IATA, ICAO, etc., which publish certain statistical information. Other data and statistics may be obtained from national tourist organizations, trade associations, carriers, hotel companies, etc. This information proves very useful in helping national tourist organizations to identify their markets and determine the objectives. This published information is of a particular use to those countries which do not possess resources enough to undertake independent market research.

Field Research : Field research, on the other hand, is the research work carried out in the tourist-generating markets itself. The special investigations in the field are to be carried out with a view to know more details of the market situation. Field research includes many methods among which the most common are the sample surveys and motivation research.

Sample surveys could be defined as the study of a given population through only a part or a fraction thereof. Much marketing information is obtained through the use of samples. In this method the population or 'universe' for which information is required is defined; for example, all households in a country might be the universe or population under investigation Then, a statistically valid sample of the population is drawn and information is obtained from the sample. Sampling technique consist of personal interviews of tourists, travel agents, carrier and hotel managers, etc., with the help of prepared questionnaires, by mailing questionnaires or through telephonic contacts.

There are certain advantages of this method. Lower cost is the major reason why data are collected by sampling in place of complete enumerations. The actual obtaining of information from the sample units (i.e., households in this case) is done by way of use of interviews and questionnaires. The questionnaire is administered to the sample population and various data obtained. The sampling place could be anywhere. Interview may take place at homes or offices, at the places of arrival/departure or temporary stay. In many countries there are a number of specialized firms which carry out sample surveys.

The survey investigations can be classified by reference to the kind of information they seek to provide. There are surveys of market behaviour, which record the holiday habits of the population, cross analysed by socio-economic and other characteristics. The trends in holidaymaking over many years may be seen and inferences made about the motives of holidaymakers. Furthermore, surveys maybe undertaken to monitor the conduct of marketing campaigns.

Motivation research, on the other hand, attempts to describe and forecast the motives of the population under investigation by use of techniques originally used in psychology. Assuming that every individual knows what he wants, motivation research is oriented to discover the needs of potential tourists in order to adopt the tourist supply accordingly and thus be able to satisfy them. In other words, motivation research is the investigation into the motives behind travel. It concerns itself to answering the 'why' of human behaviour in contrast to answering the 'how', which is subject to sampling surveys. It analyses rather than describes the attitudes of both actual and potential tourists to travelling in general and to the tourist product offered in particular. Motivation research provides answers to very important questions. Research in the past has shown that people from some countries are traditional good travellers (the French, the Germans, the American and the British), while others have become a nation of travellers only recently (the Japanese). One of the most important techniques used in motivation research is the depth-interview method. The questionnaire to be used for this method needs to be carefully designed. As motivation research aims at discovering the deep, subconscious and even unconscious motives of human beings, an ill-designed questionnaire is likely to reach no deeper than the conscious level where rational factors prevail. Other techniques used are the projective methods like word-association tests, sentence-completion tests and pictorial tests, etc., and observations. These means have been devised to record the reactions of a person and to understand his motives.

Market identification through the method of market research leads to the next logical step, which is to develop a sound tourist marketing strategy. It may, however, be mentioned here that the market research, as a continuous process of investigating market conditions, is just a means to an end which is to develop a marketing strategy. This strategy aims at achieving certain objectives which could be an increase in the tourist traffic as well as increase in the foreign exchange receipts. These should be compatible with the characteristics of the market or markets and with the capacity of the tourist plant and facilities available. Realistic assessment of the market—its size, conditions and trends would therefore be the first step in developing the country's tourist marketing strategy.

Marketing with Mixture

In general marketing, the term 'mix' has gained prominence in the last few decades. Marketing mix means a mixture of elements which interact and complement each other to achieve the targeted results. Marketing mix can also be defined as "The mixture of controllable marketing variables that the organization uses to pursue the desired level of sales in the target market".

Marketing mix is a combination of the marketing variables which any organization uses at a particular time in order to achieve the results. The term 'marketing mix' was first introduced by Professor Neil Bordes in the year 1953. Professor Bordes got the cue from a study of management of marketing costs by Professor James Gulliton who described the marketing executive as a mixer of ingredients. The objective of marketing is to identify, anticipate and satisfy the customer needs in relation to markets. Within the limitations given by the market situation, by the available resources and the general direction provided by the organization's overall aims, there is a broad range of different activities suitable for achieving the organization's goals. The organization or a firm can use a variety of marketing 'instruments' in regard to its products or services, their pricing, their distribution or sale and their promotion. The combination of specific activities is called the marketing mix. Commonly described as the four P's or the four variables, originally used to describe the marketing mix by McCarthy in 1960, these include:

(i) Product
(ii) Price
(iii) Promotion
(iv) Place or distribution

Tourist marketing mix is largely a complex group of several factors intervening to achieve the end- product, which is the increased effectiveness in demand output in relation to supply and marketing investment by tourist enterprises. Marketing mix helps the marketing manager or a firm or an official tourism organization to understand where marketing action can be initiated to improve the acceptability of a tourist product and, at the same time, stimulate the demand. An example of this would be a policy of price reduction of tourist facility or service. This could be substituted either by increasing available facilities and services for the same price or by strengthening promotional activities due to competition and increasing sales output. A policy to combine both reduction of prices and extra facilities or extra advertising campaigns may or may not however achieve desired results.

A tourist enterprise can use a combination of specific activities to achieve the best desired results. An enterprise can decide which of them to use, how, when and where to use and which resources to allocate to them. The various components of the 'mix' may be seen as cooperating with or replacing each other as complements or substitutes. Thus, the tourist marketing mix is largely a complex group of factors intervening to achieve the marketing 'end product', which is increased effectiveness in demand output in relation to supply and marketing investments (input). A balanced mix is necessary to reach this targeted result. The tourist marketing mix can include the following elements:

(i) Product policy,

(ii) Pricing policy,

(iii) Promotion programmes, and

(iv) Channels of distribution and sales.

The use of tour variables in the marketing mix in travel and tourism industry can be described by an example of a well-known luxury train "Palace on Wheels" in India.

The Product

- The characteristics of the product
- Size and facilities offered
- Staff members and their attitudes
- Image, reputation, positioning (upmarket or economical)

The Price

- Normal
- Promoting

- Discounted
- Corporate
- Wholesaler rates
- Seasonal

The Promotion

- Advertising (electronic, press)
- Sales promotion
- Public relations
- Direct mail

The Distribution

- Channels of distribution
- Reservation systems (CRS)
- Intermediaries (travel agents, tour operators)
- Airlines
- Clubs/Associations

The 'marketing mix' helps in the integrated approach to marketing. It helps the marketing manager, whether an individual or a firm or an official tourist organization, to understand where marketing action can be initiated to improve the acceptability of the tourist product and stimulate demand. 'Marketing mix' has both short-term as well as long-term aspects. The short-term aspects relate to meeting the immediate moves of competitors and include aspects like price reduction, aggressive promotion, introduction of a new product in the market, etc. Long-term aspects, on the other hand, are based on longer range plans derived from the study of all kinds of trends like natural, economic, social and technological.

Model Case Study

In the late seventies, the city of New York had a major problem. It had acquired a very bad image, a place where a visitor could be mugged, a woman walking alone in the dark molested or a hotel room burgled. There might have been only two such incidents on an average in a day in a city of twelve million people, but they were prominently splashed in the newspapers and a fear psychosis caught the rest of the Americans who avoided New York. Due to this fear, the number of visitors to New York from other parts of the USA and abroad dwindled, tax revenue declined, hotel occupancies went down and even restaurant sales were adversely affected. Several business corporations started moving out of New York, the largest and the most exciting city in the United States of America. New York is also one of the largest states and the commercial hub of the country. The Broadway Theatre is the city's major tourist attraction. Among the other attractions are mountains and lakes, including the famous Niagara Falls.

The authorities of the New York State decided to do something about it, to change the image of the New York State into a fun place for tourists, removing the ugly image of the city as an unsafe place to live in or to visit. They could not allow the economy of the city to be ruined by some stray incidents here or there. Economists had predicted a loss of thirty thousand to sixty thousand jobs due to this bad image.

The Governor of the State created a new division of Marketing and Advertising which was assigned the creation of a new image to attract visitors. They hired the services of a major advertising agency to conduct research as to what Americans, other than New Yorkers, sought in a vacation and how they perceived New York as a place for their dream vacation. Some thirty thousand Americans were interviewed.

The research revealed that most Americans visited New York State for (a) Broadway Theatre for plays and musicals, and (b) its open country, mountains and lakes.

The advertising professionals then submitted their plan of action—a major advertising campaign—on television highlighting the two attractions. A score of leading Broadway actors and actresses sang a theme song on television commercials around the new slogan: *I Love New York.* The natural beauty of the State along with opportunities for open-air sports were highlighted. The State initially sanctioned five million dollars for this advertising campaign. A variety of publicity material was created for those who would seek information about New York. People were encouraged to call up and seek information, about New York on a toll-free telephone number (which does not cost the caller anything from anywhere in the USA because the owner of a toll-free number foots the bill). The advertising ran for five weeks and the total number of calls received for information exceeded ninety-five thousand.

The campaign was an instant success. Within a year, it was discovered that average hotel occupancy was running at over eighty per cent, tax revenue had increased, new jobs had been created, restaurant sales increased and people started wearing *I Love New York* shirts and buttons on their own. Airlines flying out of New York collaborated to create their own TV commercials around the theme *I Love New York* and a massive promotion of New York started under its own steam in all parts of the USA and Canada, without much outlay on the part of the New York State. New York State also increased its own contribution and intensified its advertising campaign.

Since then, tourism to New York has been on the upswing. No one talks about muggings and molestings anymore though it has not been wiped out—perhaps reduced marginally.

But, the change of New York's image is an example of tourism marketing in creating a new product which consumers could relate to. The product did not exist in the minds of the people—the marketers created it by fulfilling the needs of the customers.

You may as well ask—where is the marketing in it? It is a simple case of selling New York as a tourist city.

There is a difference. You sell a product that you have and do not concern yourself about customer's preferences. The customer may lose interest, your sales may decline and ultimately you may be out of business. Here, the potential travellers were ignoring New York and going to other destinations because of fear. If no timely marketing action had been taken, New York would have fallen on even more bad days.

The same is true of other products. Supposing you were in the business of manufacturing and selling shoes. If you did not worry about the fast-changing fashions and pattern of demand, there might not have been enough buyers to purchase the type of shoes you manufacture. If you want to remain in business, you have to manufacture shoes which buyers want and for that purpose constant research is needed.

Therefore, marketing is an action plan to cater to the needs of the consumer, and 'selling' is to cater to the whims of sellers only.

As we mentioned in the *I Love New York* story, the first and foremost requirement in such an action plan is market research. We must find out from the customers what they like or prefer. In the case of New York, the prospective visitors found their fulfilment in seeing the famous Broadway plays, visiting restaurants and enjoying the scenic beauty of New York State. And, the State offered that package. The new image of New York as a 'fun' place eclipsed the old image of lawlessness in the city. The second stage was preparation of the marketing plan— what to do, how and when to do it and getting approval from the decision-makers.

How to Communicate ? The third stage is communications with the buyers—in this case potential visitors to New York. The decision was to develop advertising commercials for television, based on the I *Love New York* theme and produce publicity material to support the campaign and simultaneously build up an organisation to disseminate the information in response to enquiries. Communications include promotion, advertising and public relations in all its aspects.

How to Monitor ? The fourth and most important stage is monitoring. We have to constantly watch how our campaign is doing. Is it producing results or is it unproductive? If it is producing results and increasing sales, it is fine. Otherwise, we have to devise new strategies. There lies the success of marketing.

This, in sum, is the marketing process. Marketing principles are: research, planning, communications and constant monitoring. In the modern world, a well-thought out marketing plan is essential for success in any business.

The following definition, developed by the British Institute of Management, may explain what marketing is all about:

Marketing is simply customer orientation—looking at your business from the customers point of view.

or

Selling focuses on the needs of the seller, marketing on the needs of the buyer.

Let us take one more example, nearer home—Nepal, an independent kingdom in the Himalayas, was never a popular tourist destination with affluent Indian tourists till someone decided to package it in a way that Indian people could relate to it. Summer is relatively an off-season in Nepal. Most foreign tourists from Europe and America come to Nepal in the winter months, combining Nepal with India. The hotels are, therefore, half-empty in summer. A pioneering travel company called Holiday Nepal, persuaded hotels of different categories in Kathmandu to offer rock-bottom prices for rooms and meals for Indian visitors. Indian Airlines and Royal Nepal Airlines were persuaded to give discounts of thirty per cent on their fares during summer. The Casino in Nepal agreed to offer chips worth Rs 500, free of charge, to each passenger buying the package. The local tour operators joined hands in offering sightseeing at reasonable prices. Thus, all-inclusive tour packages to Nepal, lasting three to four days were advertised from major cities of India at very attractive prices. Knowing that the Indians prefer to travel with family, two children below twelve years of age were allowed free in the hotel room with parents. The package prices were so attractive that thousands of people grabbed it, setting in a new trend for Indians going to Nepal for holidays.

Now, Nepal is a popular tourist destination for Indian visitors—no passports and visas are necessary for Indian citizens to visit Nepal and the Indian rupee is a legal tender in the country, along with Nepalese rupee. In the Nepalese tourist statistics, Indians are the largest group of foreign visitors every year—about forty per cent annually.

Unique Qualities

Although principles of marketing are the same for all products, tourism has some peculiarities. These are summed up as under:

- The tourism product is a combination of products and services. No single entrepreneur can produce it and each segment needs a high degree of specialisation.
- The tourism product cannot be transported; a customer has to reach it to make use of it.
- The tourism product or products cannot be stored for sale at a later date, a hotel room or an airline seat has to be

used everyday or it is a total waste. In case you are dealing in readymade garments, you can store them if you are not getting the right price but it is not so with a tourism product. It has to be used today or it goes waste.

- Any political upheaval, economic instability or natural calamity can immediately hurt the tourism product.

  Therefore, there is a certain amount of urgency in the marketing of tourism. This fact has always to be kept in mind— product must be sold today, even at a loss.

  Tourism marketing process will, therefore, comprise the following:

- Fact-finding, data gathering (Market Research).
- Communications to inform the public (Tourist Promotion).
- Ensuring sale (Distribution Channels).
- Coordination, control and evaluation (Monitoring the total Marketing Plan).

Four "Ps" : While preparing a successful Marketing Plan, we deal with four Variables Called the four "Ps" in marketing jargon. These are:

Product: In tourism, it means attractions, friendliness of the people or tourist resources of a country. In the case of an airline, it means not only the seat in the plane, but also the courtesy, attention, punctuality, quality of food and other services. Similarly, a hotel room means much more than a room.

Price: It implies the optimal rate at which a tourist product could be sold.

Place: Most suitable distribution channels, i.e., the places where the product could be effectively sold.

Promotion: The entire gamut of the communications process required to let customers know about the product.

Every national tourist organisation, airlines, major hotel or hotel chain has a marketing division to organise the above marketing process for success. Small business operations like travel agencies, can develop their own marketing plans without outside help.

Once we collect all the data about the market, the next step is communication—to carry information to all the participants in the chain of distribution and the end user, the consumer. This includes all aspects of promotion: advertising websites, e-mail, public relations, sales brochures, merchandising, sales calls, newsletters, direct mail, etc.

An essential factor in successful marketing is that all promotion must be based on facts and truthful description of the product. Exaggerated descriptions are counter-productive and should be avoided. Our advertising message, brochures, newsletters should all contain information which is credible and true.

Nothing Easy

Marketing is not always as simple as we have explained above, especially for highly expensive products like travel. It needs more detailed examinations. Market segmentation is one of the areas requiring a closer look when it comes to the marketing of holidays.

A holiday overseas or even a holiday within a country, is a relatively expensive product. Everybody cannot afford to buy it. And, if a person can afford it, he may not be able to afford time to enjoy a vacation. His business or employment may not permit him to take off for two to three weeks.

Therefore, those who market the tourism product have to segment their markets. If we were in the business of selling shoes, we could afford to do some adventure marketing as most people need shoes once or twice in a year. But holiday is something which can always be postponed or sacrificed to buy something else more urgently needed by the family, i.e., a car or a television set, etc.

The tourism marketeer, therefore, has to promote his product to a selected segment of population in a country which can afford the price and the citizens also have the time, interest and leisure to enjoy it. Let us take the example of an Indian holiday sold in the USA. It is quite expensive, in the range of US$3,000 to 4,000 for a single person and for a couple, the cost may be US $5,000 to 10,000.

An Indian vacation will, therefore, appeal to only that segment of the population in the USA who are well-off and have leisure, i.e., retired couples or very highly educated, well-paid professionals who are curious about India. The India Tourist Office in the USA will, therefore, try to select only those American magazines for advertising which cater to readers falling into this category. The Tourist Office will also keep contact with travel agencies in the USA which are patronised by the rich, the elderly and the educated professionals. This scrutiny is called market segmentation, focusing marketing on those who have time, money and interest in India. India also attracts young travellers who are educated and curious but with low budget. They find ways to travel to India by making their own arrangements in economy hotels.

Advertising Role

Advertising is defined as a paid public message. In tourism advertising, it is designed to describe an area or a plan. It can be in newspapers, magazines or on radio, television, hoardings, posters, etc. Advertising is the commonest form of promotion reaching the potential travellers.

But advertising cannot be done haphazardly. If your budget is large, you can have the services of an advertising agency which will do the research for you and advise you regarding the selection of media for your message to reach the right kind of people. Advertising agencies have creative writers who write an interesting text for your message and develop headlines for your advertisement. Such people are called copy writers. An advertising agency also has design artists to prepare the design and layout of your advertising message. These are all known as creative people. The services of an advertising agency do not cost much because they get a commission from the media for placing advertisements. This commission is normally fifteen to seventeen per cent, but advertising agencies charge from their clients for preparing designs and layouts.

A good advertising agency can create memorable advertisements for its clients. In 1970, the British Airways (then called BOAC) came up with an advertisement in the USA which offended the members of the British Parliament, but attracted a lot of American visitors to Great Britain. The Advertisement read:

> London Bridge is in Arizona,
>
> Queen Mary is in California,
>
> Come to Britain
>
> While it lasts!

Similarly, the USA celebrated the bi-centennial year of American Independence (from Great Britain) in 1976. The British Airways (then BOAC) came up with an advertisement with an amusing title:

Do come Home All is Forgiven.

In the late sixties, there were anti-American feelings among the Frenchmen and students were shouting anti-American slogans asking the 'Yankees' to go home. The Trans World Airlines, an American carrier, came up with an apt advertising. The title read:

Yankee go Home

with TWA!

It was an instant success!

The tourist product is varied. Advertising, therefore, has to highlight the quality of the product to be marketed, It may be an airline, travel agency services or a hotel. The interests of all these segments of travel services overlap and are often complementary. Therefore, sometimes they join hands to launch joint advertising programmes. For instance, the interests of a national carrier and the NTO are similar. The national carrier needs more passengers, preferably to its home destination which is also the primary function of the NTO. By pooling their resources, they can have more impact.

The Singapore Tourist Promotion Board, the NTO of Singapore and Singapore Airlines often advertise jointly in overseas markets. An example:

Most countries offer discount on goods, Singapore offers discounts on discounts.

Under the text of the advertisement, it is written— Singapore Airlines. But the expenses were shared equally between the two organisations.

Again describing the tropical greenery of Singapore, the advertisement read:

While most countries have a Park in the City, Singapore has a City in the Park.

Thailand (Tourism Authority of Thailand-TAT) has been advertising jointly not only with their national carrier, Thai

International Airways, but also with hotels and other organisations interested in jointly promoting tourism to Thailand.

Visit the World's Most Exotic Country

Flying the World's Most Exotic Airline.

(Tourism Authority of Thailand with Thai International).

Discover Asia's Most Exotic Country With a Touch of Hyatt.

(TAT with Hyatt Hotels)

Where on Earth

Will you find a herd of Elephants?

In a Rose Garden.

(TAT with Rose Garden Resort Hotel)

In such joint advertising, the TAT shared the expenses, on equal basis with the participating company.

India too has been advertising extensively in overseas markets, but seldom jointly with hotels and the national carrier. It is true that hotels, national airlines and the Department of Tourism all promote India in their own way. If, however, they could join hands with the Department of Tourism in special cases, their money could go much further.

Here are some good examples of advertising done by the Department of Tourism, the Government of India, in foreign markets:

India

It is not just another country

It is another World.

To persuade the price-conscious people to realise that India is not out of their reach, the Government of India's Tourist Office in London released an advertisement with the title:

Out of This World Not Out of Your Reach INDIA £740.
(Prices have now gone up.)

The text offered a one-week packaged tour to India including return air fare, accommodation in the best of hotels. An attractive proposition—£ 740—is an affordable amount even for an office worker or a sales girl in the UK.

How to establish Public Relations ? : While advertising is a paid-public message, public relations seek to communicate with the potential buyers of travel through publicity secured free of charge. But the Public Relations Manager has to be ingenious and smart to know what the press is interested in. For instance, all important travel happenings are news for consumers as well as the Travel Trade Press. If two new hotels have been added to the city of Delhi, a press release on this subject will be of interest to the Travel Trade Press in the USA or Japan. Even the photographs of the new hotels could be used. Similarly, a new and faster train to Agra or a new airlines service to Srinagar are news items of interest to the Travel Trade Press. If visas for tourists to India are liberalised, the information is of interest even to the general consumers and press as well. But, the text must be attractively written in the press release.

Another popular way of getting more or less free publicity for a destination is to invite good travel writers to your country on what is called familiarisation tours. On their return, they write their impressions in their respective papers. This is one of the most effective methods of tourism promotion because the readers tend to believe these reports more than the tall claims made in a paid advertisement. Writers from some financially sound major newspapers do not accept Government hospitality, for instance, the *New York Times* or *Los Angeles Times.* In such cases, a clever public relations man can offer non-monetary assistance which is appreciated. For instance, an intelligent guide to escort the writer or to help him in making appointments with the right type of people will go a long way to win the goodwill of the writer.

In tourism, travel agents' familiarisation trips to a destination are also an important way of public relations with the travel agents. Travel agents who sell tours must know their product well and there is no better way to let them know the product than experience the product and have a taste of it. Therefore, NTA and national carriers, collaborate to organise such familiarisation tours for travel agents. Often, the travel agents' group tours are hosted jointly by the two organisations. Sometimes, subsidised familiarisation trips are also offered to the members of travel agency industry. But the objective is the same.

Other forms of public relations in tourism are special press releases, feature stories with pictures, newsletters, screening of touristic films, audio-visuals of a destination, an airlines or a hotel's participation in travel exhibitions and fairs, etc.

The sky is the limit in the area of public relations but the following basic principles must be kept in mind by the man in-charge of public relations affairs.

Honesty : The first rule of good public relations is to be candid and honest. Any attempt at an exaggerated portrayal of your product is likely to hurt you in the long run.

Imagination : Cheap tricks to get attention are unproductive. They often arouse suspicion. The gains are temporary.

Consistency : The core of public relations is consistency in approach—sympathetic listening and effective communications.

Distinctiveness : The uniqueness of your tourist product and services has to be stressed—how it is better than competing products.

Interest : Good public relation depends upon winning not only attention but also the sympathetic understanding and cooperation of the consumers. Consumer satisfaction is the key to success. In other words, honesty pays in all public relation activities.

Printed Literature : Advertising and public relation activities are supported by printed literature—brochures, pamphlets, posters. The printed literature in tourism promotion must be of outstanding quality to attract attention. Remember, tourism product is generally bought by the affluent members of a society, and they prefer the best.

The qualities of any good tourist literature are clarity and brevity, information that people want and finally creativity in the text and distinctiveness.

Sales Calls : Trained salesmen, very familiar with the product, must call on travel agents, corporate offices and other potential clients.

Telephone Sales : The telephone is an important instrument of effective marketing. Those who respond to enquiries on the telephone must be experienced, well-informed and motivated sales persons. Information given in a pleasant way helps clinch a sale.

Postal Enquiries : Postal enquiries received in the office in response to advertising, e-mail, or on their own, must be replied to immediately, preferably with a personal letter. It creates trust in the prospective traveller.

Delay in response results in loss of interest. Remember, they have other options.

Use of mailing agencies for response to personal enquires is not favoured. They have their own priorities and often the replies are delayed. For holiday planning any delay is fatal.

Kerala Model : Of the many States of India promoting their destinations, Kerala stands out above others. You look at the print media, large advertisements stare at you declaring Kerala as "God's Own Country". You open a TV channel—a slick advertisement shows you promoting Kerala's greenery, backwaters, ayurvedic packages, the sea, cuisine and peace—describing it as Water Colours of God. The hype created by this all-round promotion is supported by excellently produced literature, generally associated with destinations abroad. The marketing campaign has been proceeded by product development and the tiny State can now boast of at least four resort properties operated by Taj Group of hotels—joint ventures between the Taj Group and the State Tourism Department. The Oberoi Group—another luxury chain of hotels has an investment plan of Rs 100 crore to invest in hotel development in Kerala.

Till 1995, Kerala promoted its tourism in a low-key, like most other States of India with a modest budget. Kerala as an exciting tourist destination was really rediscovered by some foreign magazines. National Geographic Traveller—a prestigious travel magazine of the USA, listed in its issue, dated October 1999, fifty destinations of a lifetime in the world and identified Kerala as one of them along with Taj Mahal in Agra. The identification was done after tremendous research by some of the finest travel writers and experts. Following are some extracts from this article written by Bill Mckibben. "Kerala is a very easy place to simply sit back and enjoy. The name means the 'land of coconuts', and the palms shade nearly the entire state from tropical sun; many call the beach at Kovalam the best in India; visitors can spend a day riding small ferries through the backwater lagoons or watching elephants cavort in the wildlife sanctuaries; the spicy food may be the best vegetarian food on the planet."

"But for me the real reason to visit Kerala, which lies at the southwestern tip of the subcontinent, is for intellectual adventure: Kerala is a bizarred anomaly among developing nations, a place that offers real hope for the future of the Third World. Consider this small State in India, though not much bigger than Maryland, has a population as big as California and per capita income of US$300. But, its infant mortality is low, its literacy is among the highest on Earth and its birth-rate below America's and falling faster. Kerala's citizens live nearly as long as Americans or Europeans. Though mostly a land of paddy covered plains, statistically Kerala stands out as the Mount Everest of social development; there is truly no place like it."

Time Magazine of the USA followed it up with another article in its issue dated 10 April, 2000. Titled 'Afloat and Afloat—Kerala is Worth A Journey'—it raves about the ayurvedic treatment. About the holiday ambience, the article says, "Despite its growing popularity, Kerala has all the charm of a backwater—the name actually given to it for its network of canals, lakes and small rivers. You will find none of the sleek resort hotels that congregate around the beaches of Southeast Asia. And, none of the hassle and aggression that tourists frequently suffer in North India. South India is different, as if an invisible line had been drawn across the country below Goa and its hordes of tourists and ravers."

With this beautiful product, if you add a pro-active Department, tourism is bound to prosper. Here business and Government have worked more seamlessly than perhaps any other place in India—to play up the virtues and erasing negative aspects. K. K. Krishan Kumar, the Managing Director of the Taj Group of Hotels described the Kerala Tourism as the most pro-active. No wonder the tourists are growing every year—from one lakh, forty-two thousand, nine hundred and seventy-two foreigners in 1995 to over two lakhs in 2000—of twelve per cent per annum compared to the overall growth of only one per cent for the whole of India. They come by charters and also by cruise ships. The domestic tourism too has expanded from thirty-nine lakhs in 1995 to over fifty-two lakhs in 2000. Many of them are pilgrims. Earnings from tourism have increased four-fold since 1995 to Rs 500 crore. Average expenditure of foreign tourists is Rs 2326 and Rs 709 for Indians. The complexion of inbound tourism from abroad is tilting from the backpackers to affluent groups. The new tourist does not mind shelling out Rs 3000 for a night's stay— despite the fact that Kerala does not offer the type of night life other destinations like Las Vegas and Hong Kong do. Even the former Prime Minister Atal Bihari Vajpayee came to Kerala for a holiday and spent ten days, so did the French Education Minister and the cricketer, Anil Kumble. Kerala has become very popular with the honeymooners. *India Today*, which carried a cover story on Kerala Tourism in its issue, dated 10 January, 2001, reported about a resort in Munnar where its reporter counted twenty out of forty-three rooms occupied by honeymooning couples from Gujarat and Maharashtra. After his holiday in Kerala, the then Prime Minister said, "Nature's silent beauty provides a perfect setting here for contemplation."

How did They Market : Before starting the actual marketing, Kerala Tourism has been busy developing infrastructure to meet the flow of new tourists from India and abroad. It included an intensive backwater development. Houseboat terminals in major backwater nodes; tourism activities in the different popular areas; development of Kovalam waterways for houseboat operations; development of budget accommodation, way-side facilities, thrust on development of tourism, roads; illumination of historical buildings, etc.

The marketing followed—Kerala has been trying to focus the attention of the world to the State as a number one destination in India. Promotional budget was enhanced from only Rs 150 lakhs in 1995 to Rs 600 lakhs in 2000 - 2001. Better than Rajasthan which is a progressive State in terms of tourism promotion.

In the current promotions, the authorities changed the focus from print media to electronic media—TV channels. Services of a very senior cinematographer from Mumbai were hired to do some promotional advertising films. He worked for twenty days, with a crew of hundred in twenty different locations in peak monsoons. The result was a minute-long ad film—and a series of ten and thirty-second spots—Water Colours of God—a quality of international standards film. It cost Rs 70 lakhs and an equal amount was spent on airing it on some of the select channels.

The CD-Rom Kerala also gives an exhaustive information on God's Own Country.

Simultaneously, Kerala Tourism's website, www.keralatourism.org was developed. It is considered to be one of the best and the largest in the country. It is updated every week with new video and music clips which can be downloaded.

All information has been computerised and a comprehensive database developed. With a network of dissemination centres set up in the country.

Kerala Tourism actively participates in Trade Fairs and Exhibitions in India and aborad. It organised, for the first time for a State—A Buyer Sellers Meet—with two hundred buyers from overseas. It also organised Road Shows in major markets for Kerala tourism like Ahmedabad and Mumbai. A ten day familiarisation tour for promotion of ayurvedic rejuvenation holidays is organised every year, exclusively for travel agents and travel writers to promote ayurveda tourism. To remove the impression that Kerala is only for seasonal tourism, markets like the Gulf have been identified for promoting monsoon tourism coupled with ayurvedic treatment. Similarly, it is promoted in the domestic markets with brochures in different languages.

Kerala Government claims to be a facilitator only in the matter of tourism—trying to attract investors in this field and making it easy for them. A Tourism Investment Cell has been formed a guide investors. No wonder Kerala is a new success story of tourism in India.

Summary : Like all products, tourism needs marketing. In fact, marketing for tourism is more important than for manufactured products, because tourism products are highly perishable. A seat in the plane or a room in the hotel not used today is a total waste. There is an element of urgency in the marketing of tourism.

The tourism product is an intangible product. It cannot be

stored for future use and it cannot be moved to be shown to the consumer. The consumer has to come to it to feel it.

Marketing is different from sales. Selling caters to the whims of the manufacturer while marketing looks after the needs of the consumers. If we do not take into consideration the changing preferences of consumers, we may be out of business very soon. Therefore, a successful businessman always has his written marketing plans. To prepare a marketing plan, we need to take the following steps:

- *Research:* To find out where our customers are, where they live, what they do and what their likes and dislikes are.
- *Preparation of a Marketing Plan:* On the basis of the above research.
- *Developing communication channels:* To let the potential customers know about our product. It is also called promotion or publicity.
- *Regular monitoring and evaluation of sales results:* If the plan is not working, we must change the strategy.

In this connection, remember also the four 'Ps' of marketing: a) Product, b) Price, c) Place, and d) Promotion.

In order to market any tourism product, we have to package and develop the product in relation to the needs of the customers; For instance, if the prospective visitors to India are not interested in India's cultural heritage and prefer mountains or sea resorts, we have to focus our marketing efforts on these attractions of India.

In order to get the best from our marketing plans, we have to segment the market further. If we are marketing India tours costing US$3,000-4,000 per person in the USA, we have to identify the people who can afford this price and also have time to take a tour to India which may last two to three weeks. Therefore, a good marketeer will select only those magazines for advertising which reach that segment of population and approach only those travel agents who have that kind of clients. The principal means of market communications are:

- Advertising or paid commercial messages.

- Public relations—ways and means through which we can get free publicity or attention to our product, i.e., developing websites, press releases, news items of interest to general public, sponsoring familiarisation tours of travel writers and travel agents to the host destination, participation in travel exhibitions and sales calls on travel agents, etc.

The supporting measures for a marketing plan are well-produced travel brochures relating to the product, whether it is a destination, airline or a hotel. Visual presentation of the product are essentially special tourist commentaries.

Two things are important in both advertising and public relations: consistency and honesty. If we exaggerate the attractions of our tourist product, it can harm our business in the long run. Again, our message must be consistent and repeated time and again. By frequently changing our message, we miss the attention of the readers.

9

Practical Application

A major contributing factor in growth of air travel holiday tourism has been the development of the 'inclusive tour', a method of packaging a holiday. This has been the result of a dramatic growth of tourist traffic to the Mediterranean countries from Europe in the last thirty years. The idea of buying a package of travel, accommodation and perhaps some ancillary services such as entertainment, etc., became an establishment in Western Europe in the 1960s. Essentially, an 'inclusive tour' is a package of transport and accommodation and perhaps some other services, which is sold as a single holiday for an all inclusive price. This inclusive price is usually significantly lower than could be obtained by conventional methods of booking transport and accommodation separately from individual hotel and transport tariffs. The principal feature of the inclusive tour is that the tourist may buy for a single price a holiday which is cheaper than would be possible for the holiday maker if he brought the components of his holiday separately and directly from individual hotels and from transport companies or from a retail travel agent.

Tour Operation

The chief functionary or the principal in this system is the "tour operator". It is the tour operator who buys aircraft seats and hotel beds and certain other facilities such as surface transport or entertainment and makes up the package. Historically, the tour operator has mostly emerged from retail travel agency. However, today a clear distinction must be made between a tour operator and a travel agent. The latter, the retail travel agent, undertakes to sell the travel services of his principal, i.e., airline companies and other transport undertakings, hotel groups, shipping lines and the provision of such ancillary services as traveller's cheques, insurance, etc.

The tour operator is a manufacturer of a tourism product unlike the travel agent who is the retailer of the tourism products. He plans, organises and sells tours. The tour operator makes all the necessary arrangements—transport, accommodation, sight-seeing, insurance, entertainment and other matters and sells this 'package' for an all inclusive price. A package tour is designed to fit a particular group of travellers. There may be special interest tours, i.e., trekking, wildlife tours, etc., and can be escorted. An escorted tour normally includes transportation, meals, sight-seeing, accommodation, guide services, etc. It is the "escort" or the "group leader" who is responsible for maintaining the schedule of the tour and for looking after all the arrangements.

Packages of Tour

Group Inclusive Tour (GIT) : This is the most popular form of tour in this category where people travel in groups of 15 or more persons. These tours are available for any destination. The terms and conditions for group inclusive tours are laid down by IATA. The escort for such groups normally travels free as the airline provides him with free passage and accommodation. The Foreign Inclusive Tour (FIT), on the other hand, is an unescorted package tour. The FIT tours are comparatively more flexible. The traveller can buy a pre-determined package with arrangements for sight-seeing, hotels and certain meals, where necessary. He does not tour with a group. He can make his own arrangements and programmes according to his liking. The inclusive tour is one of the several devices which enable tourists to enjoy the lower price.

The Group Inclusive Tour (GIT) programme consists of a series of integrated travel services. Each of the travel services like seat in a aircraft, a hotel room, etc., is purchased by a tour operator in bulk and resold to his retailers or customers directly as part of a package at an all-inclusive price. The product commonly referred to as a 'package tour are single destination holidays'. In other words, a customer would buy a package holiday from a tour operator or a wholesaler to any single destination, for instance, a tour operator in a particular country will sell a package at a particular price for a cultural holiday in India, a beach holiday in Bali, a wildlife adventure trip in Kenya or a shopping holiday in Singapore, etc. However, some packages comprise two or more destinations. In fact, lately, twin destination packages have become quite popular as with little additional price one can visit more than one country. These tours are quite common and popular in Europe.

Merits of Price

The success of a package tours is the result of the fact that the operator, by purchasing his principal services in bulk rather than individually is able to negotiate lower prices. This lower price of the package tour or inclusive tour is made possible by obtaining the air travel and the hotel accommodation in bulk. As tour operating today has become a highly competitive business its success mainly depends upon the operator maintaining the lowest possible prices while continuing to give to its customers a 'value for money'.

Because of the bulk purchase, tour operators are able to procure substantial discounts from carriers, hoteliers, etc., and offer their package deals at much lower rates. The profits of the tour operator and the success of his operations, however, depend a great deal on the achieving of very high load factors for the aircraft and high occupancy rates for the hotel. In this way unit costs can be maintained sufficiently low to enable the tour operator to offer his package at a price which is often lower than the cheapest available fare alone. A breakthrough in the business of tour operation came when airlines recognised that tour operation could fill the empty seats, and introduced special fares for use exclusively by tour operators for combining into an inclusive tour.

The tour operator has thus emerged as the key manufacturer of the tourist product. The product is the inclusive tour, packaged, standardised and mass produced. The tour operator may sell this product directly to the public or through the channels of the retail travel agencies. It can be marketed successfully in the tourist-generating countries to a mass market just because it is standardised, packaged and quality controlled.

The product is, therefore, susceptible to the similar marketing techniques that are applied to the marketing of consumer goods.

Package Tour Marketing (Discounts) : In a competitive world market situation, where there is a choice of several alternate holiday destinations, a tour operator has to make a careful decision regarding promoting and marketing a particular package. After considering various alternatives, a tour operator has to narrow down the choice to few potential destinations. A realistic appraisal of the potential of the selected destinations is to be made.

Selection of a potential destination by a tour operator is to be based on several factors; some of these factors include the:

(i) number of tourists which the area presently attracts;

(ii) growth rate in tourist arrivals in these areas;

(iii) share of the competing companies;

(iv) estimate of the total share of the market which the company could expect to gain in the next few years of operation;

(v) availability of suitable and convenient connections to a destination;

(vi) negotiations with principals like the airlines and hotels; and

(vii) negotiations with local handling agents at the destinations, etc.

Tour Pamphlet

Once all the above factors have been considered, a tour operator would then package a tour and incorporate it in a brochure known as "tour brochure". A brochure is a document bound in the form of a booklet. It is a voluminous publication with special emphasis on the quality of a paper, the graphic design of the cover and the layout of pages. The tour operators brochure is the most vital marketing tool for selling his product. Since tourism is an intangible product which cannot be pretested by the prospective consumer prior to the purchase, the brochure becomes the important channel of informing a customer about the product and also motivating him to buy the product.

The brochure contains a comprehensive and detailed information about a destination including cruises, bus tours, safaris, charter vacations, etc., with colour photographs regarding all the destinations which a company is promoting. Detailed information about hotels, weather conditions, frontier formalities, etc., is also given. The price of various tours is invariably mentioned along with the dates when tours take place. Many tour operators take great care with production of their brochures. There are, however, no travel industry standards or guidelines or the production of brochures. Established tour operating companies take great care while designing their tour brochures. The following are some important areas which need to be taken care of while getting the tour brochure printed:

(i) Quality of paper
(ii) Layout
(iii) Quality of printing
(iv) Photography
(v) Detailed itineraries
(vi) Special features
(vii) Weather conditions
(viii) Maps of areas
(ix) Tour conditions
(x) Hotel information
(xi) Terms and conditions of tour.

Several large tour operating companies get their brochures designed and printed in their own advertising departments. Some get the brochures printed in conjunction with the design studio of their advertising agency, who in turn negotiate with the printer to obtain the best quotation and ensure that the print deadlines are adhered to. Adhering to the print deadline is extremely important as the company has to introduce the brochure at a predetermined date, coinciding in most cases with travel trade and consumer holiday fairs. The introduction of a brochure at these events both to travel trade and consumer is crucial for marketing a package.

Elements of a Tour Brochure : Two different versions of a tour brochure printed by two different companies are shown in the following pages. Brochure-I is printed by one of the leading tour operating companies having a worldwide network of its branches. A four-colour brochure printed on glazed art paper contains various programmes in the form of packages which the company is promoting through its brochure. However, only a few programmes of the company concerning India/Nepal have been shown to give to the reader an idea as to how these are packaged.

In the brochure, several programmes have been offered for their clients. These have been appropriately titled to motivate the client. For instance, Programme-titled 'Indian Experience' is a nine-day classical tour covering Delhi-Agra-Jaipur-Delhi. From day one which is a departure day from USA to India till the ninth day with departure from India to USA, each of the days' details have been worked out. The client can also take extension of one week's holidays to Goa to relax on a beach or go to look for a tiger at one of the several game parks. Most of the tour operators offer extension programmes beyond the planned itineraries. A client has initially to pay a printed price for a basic programme and an additional price in case he takes an extension. The brochure gives both departure and return dates of the programme.

Programme-II entitled "Splendours of the North" covers two weeks' programme covering in addition to Delhi-Agra-Jaipur, places like Varanasi, Gwalior and Udaipur. Programme III is a special programme of 18 days entitled "Forts and Palaces". This programme has been specially put together for those clients who have interest in arts and architecture covering forts and palaces. Programme-IV is twin destination programme covering both India and Nepal. A 22-day programme takes a client first to Nepal and then to India. Titled as "Classical Journey" it covers places associated with religion, culture, legends and mysteries. Travelling at a leisurely pace a tourist can absorb the splendid sights and saviour the unique flavour in both Nepal and India. Programme-V is again a special interest programme for those interested in nature and wildlife. An 18-day programme takes a client through rich tropical jungles, extensive grasslands, temperate forests of India which are reserves of wildlife and some of the world's most stunning national parks. Programme-VI is a 19-day programme to South India entitled "Southern Trader" covering golden beaches and temples in the region.

Programme-VII is a 17-day tour entitled "Culinary Feast" covering both North and South India and tailor made for those who have interest in Indian cuisine. Similarly Programme-VIII again is a twin destination programme covering India and the Maldives. An special interest programme of 16 days covers the finest beaches in the Southern coast as also the Maldives. The programme in India covers some of the famous trade routes discovered by the Arabs, Greek, Roman, Portuguese, Dutch, French and British traders. A sample of the brochure may be seen in the following pages.

Experience of India

Programme-I

9 Days: Delhi-Agra-Jaipur-Delhi

Day I & 2. Depart from USA: Fly from your departure city in the USA to India.

Day 3. *Delhi.* Arrive in Delhi and transfer to the hotel. The rest of the morning is at leisure. In the afternoon there will be a brief tour of the sights of New Delhi. You will see its many monuments and buildings designed by Lutyens, including India Gate and the President's house.

Day 4. To Agra: In the morning you will visit the sights of Old Delhi, the Red Fort, the Jama Masjid—India's largest mosque—and the Chandni Chowk bazaar. Early in the afternoon you will set off for Agra arriving in time for dinner, and stay at the hotel for 2 nights.

Day 5. Agra: The morning will begin with a visit to Agra Fort, a massive complex with exquisite marble work, a testament to the power of successive Mughal emperors. You will then be taken to the incomparable Taj Mahal, seen as a magnificent expression of Emperor Shah Jahan's undying love. In the afternoon there will be a visit to the tomb of Itimad-ud-Daulah, known to be the forerunner of the Taj Mahal, and later you may wish to return to the Taj Mahal to see it in the soft light of the setting sun.

Day 6. To Jaipur: You drive to Jaipur via Fatehpur Sikri, the once prosperous capital of the Mughal empire. Built by Emperor Akbar, Fatehpur Sikri remains in near perfect condition, as a reminder of the architectural wealth and power of one of India's most famous empires. You will stay at the hotel.

Day 7. Jaipur: In the morning you visit Amber where the ascent to the ancient capital is made by gaily caparisoned elephants. The fort has a variety of places within its winding 20- kilometer walls, including the unusual Chamber of Mirrors. En route to Amber you will see the Palace of the Winds in the morning sun. The afternoon tour allows time to explore the City Palace, still home of Jaipur's royal family, and the site of the Jantar Mantar or astrological observatory where India's impressive scientific heritage can be appreciated.

Day 8. To Delhi: You leave the romantic 'Pink City' of Jaipur, departing from the golden deserts of Rajasthan to the imperial grandeur of Delhi. You return to the hotel where a room has been reserved for you until the departure for the airport late in the night.

Day 9. To USA: Early morning flight from Delhi to USA.

Note: You may want to spend an additional week relaxing on one of India's most famous beaches in Goa or go in search of the elusive tiger at one of India's game reserves.

OUT		RTN	
14	Jan	6	Jan.
28	Jan	20	Jan.
3	Feb	11	Feb.
17	Feb	25	Feb.
3	Mar	11	Mar.
17	Mar.	25	Mar.
31	Mar.	8	Apr.
8	Apr.	22	Apr.
5	May	13	May
11	Aug.	19	Aug.
8	Sep.	16	Sep.

Contd...

OUT		RTN	
22	Sep.	30	Sep.
6	Oct.	14	Oct.
20	Oct.	28	Oct.
3	Nov.	11	Nov.
17	Nov.	25	Nov.
8	Dec.	16	Dec.
22.	Dec.	30	Dec.

Programme-II

Splendours of the North 25 *Days.* ***Delhi-Varanasi-Agra-Gwalior-Jaipur-Udaipur-Delhi***

Day 1 &2. Depart from USA: Fly from your departure city in the USA to India.

Day 3. Arrive in Delhi: Arrive in Delhi and transfer to the hotel for 2 nights. Afternoon free to rest after your flight.

Day 4. Delhi: Visit New Delhi, the capital city and a 'Jewel in the Crown' with its buildings—many of which were designed by Sir Edwin Lutyens—the Qutub Minar and Emperor Humayun's tomb. The historic capital of the Mughal and British rulers is a fascinating blend of the old and the new. In the afternoon see the famous Red Fort—once the most opulent fort of the Mughal Empire—the Jama Masjid, Raj Ghat and Old Delhi's bazaar.

Day 5. To Varanasi: Fly to Varanasi, the holiest of Hindu cities situated on the sacred River Ganges and a centre of philosophy and religion. Just outside the city is Sarnath, where Buddha preached his first sermon. Visit the Sarnath museum where the ancient Sarnath monastery's treasures are displayed. Stay at the hotel for 1 night.

Day 6. To Agra: Early morning boat ride along the 'ghats', the steps which lead down to the river, to see the gathered faithful, ritually cleansing themselves of their sins. In the afternoon, fly to Agra, once the capital of the Mughal empire and the home of the Taj Mahal. Transfer to the hotel for 3 nights.

Day 7. Agra: Morning visit to the Taj Mahal, Shah Jahan's monument of eternal love to his wife Mumtaz Mahal. Also visit the massive complex of Agra Fort with its many palaces. In the afternoon, visit the tomb of Itimad-ud-Daulah or the tomb of the great, emperor, Akbar, at Sikandra. A second visit to the Taj Mahal in the soft light of the setting sun is also well worthwhile.

Day 8. Gwalior: Gwalior is known for its massive fort built atop sheer cliffs rising out of the plains. Within the walls the Jain statues, Rajput palaces, 9th century Hindu temples and a Victorian school. Travel to Gwalior by train and, on arrival, drive to the royal guest house, for lunch. After lunch, sightseeing will commence, followed by return to Agra.

Day 9. To Jaipur: Transfer by road to Jaipur, stopping en route at Fatehpur Sikri, the deserted red sandstone city which Akbar built as his capital in the 16th century and abandoned just 15 years later. In Jaipur, stay for 3 nights at the hotel.

Day 10. Jaipur: Jaipur is known as the 'Pink City' for its many pink-coloured sandstone buildings in the walled city. See the City Palace, the Jantar Mantar observatory and the 'Palace of the Winds'. In earlier times, the ladies of the court would stand behind the sandstone screen to see and not be seen. The afternoon is at leisure.

Day 11. Jaipur: The highlight of morning is a ride on elephant back to the ancient capital of Amber, perched on a hill and surrounded by a 20-kilometere-long wall. In the afternoon visit the colourful and friendly bazaars of Jaipur.

Day 12. To Udaipur: The princely state of Mewar is known for its lakes, palaces and gardens. Fly to Udaipur and stay at the hotel for 2 nights. En route to the hotel you visit the vast City Palace. In the afternoon visit private royal gardens and other sites of interest.

Day 13. Udaipur: The full day is at leisure. Optional excursions are available to the nearby hilltop forts and temples.

Day 14. To Delhi: Morning you fly back to Delhi, bidding farewell to the magical city of Udaipur. A room has been reserved at the hotel up until the time of your departure for the airport late night. The afternoon is free for final shopping.

Day 15. To USA: Early morning flight to the USA

OUT		RTN	
7	Jan.	21	Jan.
21	Jan.	4	Feb.
.28	Jan.	11	Feb.
11	Feb.	25	Feb.
25	Mar.	8	Apr.
11	Mar.	25	Mar.
8	Apr.	22	Apr.
22	Apr.	6	May.
19	Aug.	2	Sep
2	Sep.	16	Sep.
9	Sep.	23	Sep.
23	Sep.	7	Oct.
7	Oct.	21	Oct.
14	Oct.	28	Oct.
21	Oct.	4	Nov.
4	Nov.	18	Nov.
11	Nov.	25	Nov.
25.	Nov.	9	Dec.
16	Dec.	30	Dec.

Programme-III

Forts & Palaces 28 *Days:* ***Delhi-Agra-Jaipur-Khimsar-Jaisalmer-Jodhpur-Udaipur-Delhi***

Day 1 & 2. Depart from USA: Fly from your departure city in the USA to India.

Day 3. Arrive in Delhi: Arrive in Delhi and transfer to the hotel for 2 nights. The rest of the afternoon is at leisure.

Day 4. Delhi: In the morning, visit the sights of New Delhi, the city built by the British with its many monuments and buildings designed by Lutyens. You will see the India Gate, the President's house as well as the Pre-Mughal monuments and the tomb of Emperor Humayun. In the afternoon, visit the sights of Old Delhi, the living legacy of the Mughals. Visit the Red Fort, the Jama Masjid—India's largest mosque — Raj Ghat and the Chandni Chowk bazaar.

Day 5. To Agra: Early morning, board one of India's most modern trains, the Shatabdi Express, to Agra. Stay at the hotel for a night. After breakfast visit the vast Agra Fort. The afternoon is free and you may wish to visit the tomb of Itimad-ud-Daulah, often referred to as 'Baby Taj'. Visit the Taj Mahal, the marble memorial of an emperor's undying love to see it in the most perfect of lights, the light of the setting sun in the late afternoon.

Day 6. To Jaipur: Drive to the land of the Rajputs and its capital, Jaipur. Spend 2 nights at the hotel. En route visit Emperor Akbar's deserted capital city of Fatehpur Sikri, built in 1571, abandoned 15 years later and which has remained unchanged for over 400 years.

Day 7. To Jaipur: After breakfast, visit Amber Fort, pausing en route to see the 'Palace of the Winds', Hawa Mahal. Arriving at Amber, ascend to the fort on an elephant and visit the myriad marble palaces. After lunch, visit the City Palace and the Jantar Mantar astronomical observatory.

Day 8. To Khimsar: Morning visit to the small village of Khimsar. Afternoon free. (Accommodation will most likely be in picturesque Rajasthani tents.)

Day 9. Khimsar: Arrive at the medieval desert town of Nagpur, with a fine 11th century fort and a mosque built by the great Mughal emperor, Akbar. Return in the afternoon.

Day 10. To Jaisalmer: Following the sun, drive west into the heart of the Thar desert to Jaisalmer, a perfect example of a walled, desert city. Spend 2 nights at the hotel.

Day 11. Jaisalmer: Morning walk to the hilltop fort, through the maze of narrow streets dotted with Jain temples and havelis (ornately decorated mansions). After lunch an excursion to the sand-dunes at Sam and the opportunity to take a short camel ride.

Day 12. To Jodhpur: Drive east, to the edge of the desert before arriving at the ancient and imposing fort city of Jodhpur. Spend 2 nights at the hotel.

Day 13. Jodhpur: A morning tour of this ancient desert city takes you to the magnificent Meherangarh Fort, with its many palaces which serve as a constant reminder of the city's glorious past and the doomed romantic chivalry of the Rajput warriors. The afternoon is free.

Day 14. To Udaipur: Continue your journey south to the oasis city of Udaipur. En route, visit the Jain temples of Ranakpur and have a light lunch at Castle. Continuing on through the Aravali Hills, arrive at the Lake Palace in time for dinner and spend 3 nights here.

Day 15. Udaipur: A short tour of Jagdish Temple and the City Palace. The afternoon is free to relax in your luxurious surroundings or perhaps take a short cruise on Lake Pichola.

OUT		RTN	
12	Jan.	29	Jan.
26	Jan.	12	Feb.
9	Feb.	26	Feb.
23	Feb.	12	Mar.
9	Mar.	26	Mar.
23	Mar.	9	Apr.
7	Sep.	24	Apr.
21	Sep.	8	Oct.
5	Oct.	22	Oct.
19	Oct.	5	Nov.
2	Nov.	19	Nov.
16	Nov.	3	Dec.
30	Nov.	17	Dec.
21	Dec.	17	Jan.

Day 16. Udaipur Leisure for optional sightseeing in the area.

Day 17. To Delhi: Morning flight to Delhi. A room will be at your disposal at the hotel until you depart for the airport at late night.

Day 18. To USA: Early morning flight from Delhi to the USA.

The Outing

Programme-IV

22 Days: ***Delhi-Kathmandu-Temple Tiger-Varanasi-Khajuraho- Agra-Jaipur-Udaipur-Aurangabad-Mumbai***

Day 1 & 2. Depart from USA: Fly from your departure city in the USA to India.

Day 3. Arrive Delhi : Arrive in Delhi. After immigration clearance and baggage collection you will be met by a representative and transferred to the Hotel for 2 nights. The historic capital of the Mughal and British rulers is a fascinating blend of the old and the new. In the afternoon, see the famous Red Fort, the Jama Masjid and Old Delhi's bazaar. In the evening meet your fellow North American travellers at a cocktail reception.

Day 4. Delhi-Kathmandu: The sights of New Delhi include the buildings of the British Raj, many designed by Sir Edwin Lutyens. Morning visit to the Qutub Minar and Emperor Humayun's tomb. In the evening board a 2-hour flight to the Mountain Kingdom of Nepal. Upon arrival transfer to the hotel.

Day 5. Royal Chitwan Park Temple Tiger: In the morning visit to Pashupatinath which is dedicated to the Lord Shiva and continue to the airport for a short flight south to Bharatpur. From the airport, drive through the traditional Tharu villages before crossing the Narayani River by boat and arriving at Temple Tiger, your jungle home for the next 2 nights. In the late afternoon go on your first game viewing.

Day 6. Temple Tiger: The full day is spent in the pursuit of Chitwan's wildlife, both on elephant back and by jeep. Here you will look for the Indian rhinoceros and the Bengal Tiger in addition to hundreds of species of birds and smaller mammals.

Day 7. To Kathmandu: In the morning fly back to Kathmandu hotel. In the afternoon, explore the streets of Kathmandu, full of wooden pagodas, temples and Buddhist stupas. See Durbar Square and the Swayambhunath shrine. In the evening you meet the British members of your group at a special welcome dinner.

Day 8. Kathmandu: Early morning drive to the picturesque little village of Nagarkot to see the sunrise over Everest and the Himalayas. Return via Bhadgaon, one of the three ancient capitals of Nepal. See the five-storeyed Nyatapola Pagoda, the Golden Gate and the Palace of Fifty five windows. The afternoon is free.

Day 9. To Varanasi : Fly to Varanasi, the holiest of Hindu cities, situated on the sacred River Ganges. Transfer to the hotel for a night.

Day 10. To Khajuraho: Early morning boat ride along the 'ghats', the stone steps which lead down to the river, to see the gathered faithful, ritually cleansing themselves of their sins. After breakfast at your hotel, visit the important Buddhist centres of Sarnath before your flight to Khajuraho in the afternoon. Stay at the hotel for a night.

Day 11. To Agra: Morning visit to the Chandela dynasty temples, famous for their spectacular sculpture and erotic carvings. In the afternoon fly to Agra. Transfer to the hotel for 2 nights.

Day 12. Agra: Morning visit to the Taj Mahal—Shah Jahan's monument of eternal love—and Agra Fort with its many palaces and halls. In the afternoon there is an optional visit either to the tomb of Itirnad-ud-Daulah or to Emperor Akbar's tomb at Sikandra.

Day 13. To Jaipur: Transfer by road to Jaipur, stopping en route at Fatehpur Sikri, the deserted red sandstone city which Akbar built as his capital in the 16th century. In Jaipur stay at the hotel for 2 nights.

Day 14. Jaipur: Morning drive out to the ancient capital, and magnificent fort at Amber on elephant back. After lunch explore Jaipur itself which is known as the 'Pink City'. See the City Palace, the Jantar Mantar observatory and the 'Palace of the Winds'.

Day 15. To Udaipur: Early morning fly to Udaipur. Stay at the hotel for 3 nights. En route to the hotel visit the vast City Palace. Afternoon, visit the private royal gardens.

Day 16. Udaipur: At leisure. Optional excursions available to the nearby hilltop forts and temples such as Chittorgarh or Eklingi.

Day 17. Udaipur: Drive out to visit the Jain temple at Ranakpur, one of the most impressive Jain temples in India. Return in the evening.

Day 18. To Aurangabad: Fly to Aurangabad, the most southerly and the last of the Mughal capitals. In the afternoon visit the Ellora cave temples, rock-hewn shrines of Hindu, Jain and Buddhist art. Stay at the hotel for 2 nights.

Day 19. Aurangabad: The Ajanta caves were discovered by a British Army patrol in the 19th century. The Buddhist sculptures and frescoes representing everyday secular and religious life are a thousand years old.

Day 20. To Mumbai: Fly to Mumbai, the wealthiest and one of the most cosmopolitan of Indian cities. Transfer to hotel until the time of departure.

Day 21. Mumbai: Visit the sights of Mumbai: the Gateway of India, the Prince of Wales Museum, Marine Drive and Malabar Hill. Afternoon free to explore, relax, shop.

Day 22. To USA: Early morning flight from Mumbai to the USA.

OUT		RTN	
8	Jan.	29	Jan.
22	Jan.	12	Feb.
5	Feb.	26	Feb.
19	Mar.	9	Apr.
2	Apr.	23	Apr.
10	Mar.	1	Oct.
24	Sep.	15	Oct.
8	Oct.	29	Oct.
22	Oct.	12	Nov.
5	Nov.	26	Nov.
19	Nov.	10	Dec.
17	Dec.	7	Jan.

Jungle Odyssey

Programme-V

18 Days: ***Delhi-Corbett-Ranthambore-Bharatpur-Agra-Bandhavgarh-Khajuraho-Delhi***

Day 1 & 2, Depart from USA: Fly from your USA departure city to India.

Day 3. Delhi: Arrive in Delhi and transfer to the hotel for a night.

Day 4. To Corbett National Park: After breakfast, set off into the foothills of the Himalaya and Corbett National Park. Spend 4 nights at the luxurious Tiger Tops Corbett Lodge. The park is set in the undulating Shiwalik foothills of the Himalayas with the Ramganga river flowing through it. Thickly forested, it provides cover for a vast amount of diverse game.

Days 5,6 & 7: Game viewing in Corbett the next three days are dedicated to bird-watching and sighting animals, both in and outside the park. In this region, together with the elephant, leopard, hog deer and gharial, to name but a few animals, there is an extraordinary array of birdlife with over 520 known species.

Day 8. To Delhi: Drive back to Delhi, across the rich farmland of the Gangetic plain. Stay overnight at the hotel.

Day 9. To Ranthambore: An early morning flight brings you to Jaipur from where you continue to Ranthambore by road. Formerly the private hunting grounds of the Maharajas of Jaipur, this park has always boasted an abundance of many species of game, including tiger, leopard, marsh crocodile, jungle cats and sloth bear. Spend 2 nights at the Lodge. Evening game drive.

Day 10. Ranthambore: Early morning and evening game drives, exploring the area by jeep and beginning your search for the elusive tiger and its prey. After the morning game drive, visit the ancient fort in the heart of the park.

Day 11. To Bharatpur: Early morning drive to Bharatpur and spend 2 nights at the Bharatpur Forest Lodge/Saras Lodge. Evening bird-watching down in the wetlands.

Day 12. Bharatpur: Bharatpur is one of the finest bird sanctuaries in Asia with a huge variety of birds, both migratory and resident, including duck, storks, waders and birds of prey. Early morning watching birds of prey. During daytime, relax at your lodge before returning to watch the birds coming in to roost later in the afternoon.

Day 13. To Agra: Leisurely start for the incomparable ancient capital of Agra. En route visit the exquisitely preserved city of Fatehpur Sikri. This deserted red sandstone city was built by Mughal emperor Akbar in the 16th century. Arrive in Agra and spend a night at the hotel. In the soft light of the setting sun visit the world's greatest monument to love, the Taj Mahal, built by Shah Jahan as a memorial to his beloved wife, Mumtaz.

Day 14, To Bandhavgarh : A morning flight brings you to Khajuraho from where you continue your journey through Madhya Pradesh by road to Bandhavgarh National Park. Spend 3 nights at the Bandhavgarh Jungle Camp.

Days 15 &16. Game viewing in Bandhavgarh : Bandhavgarh was formerly the Rewa Maharaja's hunting preserve and was declared a national park in 1968. Incorporated in 1994 into Project Tiger, it has long been famous for its health and stable tiger population. Other animals found here include the jungle cat, leopard, deer, gaur, various species of monkeys and a wide variety of birds. Over half the area is covered by sal forest and towards the north there are large stretches of bamboo and grassland. Two days will be spent game viewing in the early mornings and evenings with the daytime being free for further explorations.

Day 17. To Khajuraho / Delhi: Drive to Khajuraho where, time permitting, you explore the decorative and unique temples for which the town is famous. After lunch, fly to Delhi and transfer to the hotel where a room will be at your disposal until your departure for the airport late at night.

Southern Traders

Programme-VI

19 *Days:* ***Mumbai-Hyderabad-Bangalore-Mysore-Madras-Madurai-Thekkady-Cochin-Goa-Mumbai***

Day 1&2. Depart from USA: Fly from your departure city in the USA to India.

Day 3. *Mumbai:* Arrive in Mumbai where you stay at the hotel. In the afternoon you explore this bustling metropolis, India's commercial capital. See the Marine Drive, Malabar Hill and the Gateway of India.

Day 4. To Hyderabad: Travel to Elephanta Island by motor launch, visiting its 7th century rock-cut temples. The afternoon is free to explore Mumbai, before your evening flight to Hyderabad where you will stay at the hotel on Banjara Hill for 2 nights.

Day 5. Hyderabad: Hyderabad became famous as the capital of the fabulously wealthy Nizam of Hyderabad. Visit the impressive and strategically placed Golconda Fort. Also visit the Charminar Gate and the thriving Mecca Masjid. Hyderabad's market was reputed to be the finest in India and it retains much of its old charm.

Day 6. To Bangalore: Early morning, fly south to Bangalore and check in at the hotel. Known as the Garden City, Bangalore is situated at 1,000 metres above sea level. It is famous for its botanical gardens, race track, polo fields and distinctive style of architecture. Afternoon is free to explore on your own.

Day 7. To Mysore: Drive from Bangalore to Mysore, stopping at Srirangapatnam, where the legendary warrior Tipu Sultan built a summer palace. In Mysore, visit the Maharajah's Palace, Chamundi Hill and the Statue of Nandi, the sacred bull of Shiva. Stay at the hotel.

Day 8. To Chennai: Morning for leisure before taking the Shatabdi Express to Madras, arriving in the evening. Madras was the chief British settlement under Clive and provided the base for British expansion in India. It has soaring Gothic monuments along the palm-fringed esplanade. Stay at the hotel for 3 nights.

Day 9. Chennai: This will be spent exploring some of India's oldest monuments which are situated here: Fort St. George built in 1653 and the garrison church of St. Mary's which is the oldest Anglican church in India. The afternoon is for leisure.

Day 10. Chennai: Drive south to Kanchipuram, one of the seven sacred cities of India. It has a spectacular temple complex with many *gopurams* cupolas. After lunch at the hotel drive down to the famous shore temples at Mahabalipuram which date from the 7th century and were the work of the sculptors of the Pallava dynasty.

Day 11. To Madurai: Fly to the temple town of Madurai, stay at the hotel for one night.

Day 12. To Thekkady: Morning tour of this famous town which boasts of the magnificent Meenakshi Temple, remaining today a 'living' temple. Afternoon drive to Thekkady which is located in the cool of the Cardamom Hills, a beautiful area of tranquil winding roads, tea gardens, rubber estates and plantations growing pepper and coffee. Stay 2 nights at the village in Thekkady.

Day 13. Thekkady: An excursion to Periyar Wildlife Reserve, famous for its herds of wild elephant and spectacular birdlife.

Day 14. To Cochin: Morning drive via Kottayam for lunch at Vembanad Lake. After lunch travel to Alleppey by boat along the famous 'backwaters'. These are a series of lagoons and waterways surrounded by a profusion of tropical vegetation. They cover thousands of acres adjacent to the Kerala coast where riverside village life can be observed all along the route. On arrival in Alleppey you will be met and driven to Cochin where you stay at the hotel on Willingdon Island for 2 nights.

Day 15. Cochin: Known as the 'Venice of the East', Cochin is a town characterised by its colonial influences and many canals. Morning visit to the Portuguese church of St. Francis, the Jewish Synagogue of 1568 and the Matancherry Palace, built by the Portuguese and renovated by the Dutch. In the late afternoon, cruise on the Pathira Manal along South India's most beautiful water route and watch the sunset from on board. Dinner will be served on board and you return to the hotel later in the evening.

Day 16. To Goa: A Portuguese colony until 1961, Goa is an oasis of palm-fringed beaches, whitewashed churches and Mediterranean style houses. You arrive in the morning by plane from Cochin and transfer to the hotel.

Day 17. Goa: A morning excursion brings you to Old Goa, the former capital of the State, where you visit the Se Cathedral in the abandoned city. The afternoon is free to relax on Goa's famous beaches.

Day 18. To Mumbai: After a morning leisure, an early afternoon flight to Mumbai, where a room will be at your disposal at the hotel until departure for the airport late at night.

Day 19. To USA: Early morning flight from Mumbai to the USA.

Note: This tour offers an ideal opportunity to extend your stay in Goa.

Flights from Madras to Madurai can Vary from last minute changes at certain times of the year and it may be that you travel from Madras to Madurai by air-conditioned train.

OUT		RTN	
12	Jan.	30	Jan.
26	Jan.	13	Feb.
9	Feb.	27	Feb.
23	Feb.	13	Mar.
9	Mar.	27	Mar.
23	Mar.	10	Apr.
5	Oct.	23	Oct.
19	Oct.	6	Nov.
2	Nov.	20	Nov.
16	Nov.	4	Dec.
30	Nov.	18	Dec.
21	Dec.	8	Jan.

Culinary Feast

Programme-VII

17 Days: ***Delhi-Lucknow-Calcutta-Hyderabad-Mumbai-Goa-Mumbai***

Day 1&2. Depart from USA: Fly from your departure city in USA to India.

Day 3. Delhi: Arrive in Delhi and transfer to the hotel for 2 nights. Afternoon for leisure.

Day 4. Delhi: Morning visit to New Delhi, the capital city and a 'Jewel in the Crown' with its British imperial buildings, many of which were designed by Sir Edwin Lutyens, the Qutub Minar and Emperor Humayun's tomb. In the afternoon see the famous Red Fort, once the most opulent fort of the Mughal Empire, the Jama Masjid, Raj Ghat, Old Delhi's bazaars and the thriving spice market. Dinner will be at the open-air Hauz Khas Village.

Day 5. To Lucknow: Morning excursion to a private residence for demonstration of authentic Mughlai cooking, followed by lunch with your host. Late afternoon flight to Lucknow where you spend 2 nights at the hotel. Lucknowi delicacies for dinner at a special restaurant.

Day 6. Lucknow: Visit the elegant city. Visit the great Bara Imambara, Hussainabad Imambara with its golden dome and the Residency, the centrepiece of one of the most dramatic sieges of all time. Finish with a visit to the marketplaces which are the pulse and nerve centre of city life, selling an enormous array of delicious local foods. Special Avadhi dinner.

Day 7. To Calcutta: Morning cooking demonstration and afternoon for leisure before you take an evening flight to Calcutta. Spend 2 nights at the hotel.

Day 8. Calcutta: Early morning visit to the flower market by Howrah bridge followed by a visit to what is considered to be one of India's finest botanical gardens, set amid lakes and lawns, sprawled along the west bank of the Hooghly. Travel to the gardens in the traditional way, by ferry. Evening drinks will be hosted at the much renowned Tollygune Club followed by a traditional Bengali dinner at the hotel.

Day 9. To Hyderabad: Morning tour of this remarkable city, visiting the Victoria Memorial. Afternoon flight to Hyderabad where you spend 2 nights at the hotel.

Day 10. Hyderabad: Hyderabad became famous as the capital of the fabulously wealthy Nizam of Hyderabad. Visit the impressive and strategically placed Golconda Fort, Charminar gate, the thriving Mecca Masjid and the market which was reputed to be the finest in India. Return to Golconda Fort in the evening for a stunning light-

and-sound show on the ramparts followed by a special Hyderabadi dinner where you will sample some of the many specialities of the city's cuisine.

Day 11. To Mumbai: Morning flight to Mumbai where you spend 2 nights at the hotel. In the afternoon explore this bustling metropolis. See the Marine Drive, Malabar Hill and the Gateway of India. In the afternoon a demonstration of Indian cooking will be organised by the legendary chefs of the grand hotel.

Day 12. Mumbai: Morning visit to Crawford Market and the Punjabi Family Curry and Spice markets. Afternoon for leisure. Dinner will be hosted at a private home with a typical tempting, local cuisine.

Day 13. To Goa: Late morning flight to Goa where you spend 3 nights at the hotel. Evening cocktails at Sunset Point followed by a poolside barbecue, serving local and seafood specialities.

Day 14. Goa: A Portuguese colony until 1961, the city of Old Goa still retains strong Portuguese influences which you explore today, including the Se Cathedral. Later visit a local fenni (Goan wine) production site and farmers market in Mapusa. Dinner will be at Casa Portuguese on Baga Beach with a specially prepared local menu.

Day 15. Goa: Full day for leisure, relaxing on Goa's exquisite beaches followed by a cooking demonstration in a private home where a typical Goani dinner will be served.

Day 16. To Mumbai: Return to Mumbai where a room will be at your disposal at the hotel until the time of your departure for the airport late at night.

Day 17. To USA: Early morning flight from Mumbai to USA.

OUT		RTN	
4	Feb	20	Feb
4	Mar	20	Mar
14	Oct	30	Oct
18	Nov	4	Dec

West and East

Programme-VIII

16 Days: ***Mumbai-Goa-Cochin-Trivandrum the Maldives***

Day 1 &2. Depart from USA: Fly from your departure city in the USA to India.

Day 3. Mumbai/Goa: Arrive in Mumbai and transfer to the hotel for relaxation before an afternoon flight to Goa. Spend 4 nights at the hotel.

Day 4. Goa: Morning for leisure, relaxing on Goa's famous beaches. Afternoon, introduction to the Malabar Coast with a walk around the hotel's own Portuguese fort remains.

Day 5. Goa: Morning cruise up the Mandovi River to Old Goa for a look around the Cathedral of St. Catherine da Se, and many other churches, convents and basilicas surviving amidst the ruins of this grand 16th century Portuguese city. Lunch at a typical Goan restaurant with an opportunity to stroll around the present capital, Panaji. En route to the hotel, visit an Old Goan mansion.

Day 6. Goa: Morning visit to the wetlands, up river, to see the crocodiles and a good variety of local and migratory birds. Afternoon for leisure.

Day 7. To Cochin: Early morning flight to Cochin, the Venice of the East and stay 3 nights at the hotel on Wilingdon Island. Afternoon, introduction to Kerala and its spice traders followed by a sunset cruise to the mouth of the harbour.

Day 8. Cochin: Morning visit to Matanchery to see India's oldest synagogue, Jew town and the Dutch Palace, followed by visits to India's first European church, St. Francis' Church at Fort Cochin and a fine merchant's home. Afternoon for leisure before visiting a private home in Ernakulum (Cochin's twin city) to see a demonstration of some of Kerala's magnificent dance and martial arts traditions and ayurvedic exercises and cures. Dinner will be served at the private residence.

Day 9. Cochin: Morning drive down to Alleppey for a cruise through the backwaters of Kerala, along canals bordered by mango trees, villages, paddy fields, where life is lived both beside and on the water. Lunch on the shores of Vembanad Lake, before returning to Alleppey where you visit a small coir factory before returning to Cochin.

Day 10. To Trivandrum : Morning drive south through lush Kerala to Trivandrum, the hilly and spacious capital of Kerala, arriving in time to visit the Napier Museum in the Botanical Gardens and see the Padmanabhaswamy Temple (closed for entry to non-Hindus). Stay a night in Kovalam at the hotel.

Day 11. To the Maldives : Early morning flight to Male, the capital of the Maldives, a chain of 1,200 low coral atolls straddling the equator and of which only 9 are larger than two square miles. Stroll around this main atoll to see Hukuru Miskiiy (The Friday Mosque) before taking the boat to Emboodhu Finolhu Island Resort on Male's south atoll for 4 nights.

Day 12. The Maldives : Morning, introduction to the Maldives both above and beneath the sea. Afternoon for leisure.

Day 13. The Maldives : Day of leisure, relaxing on some of the finest beaches the world has to offer, enjoying the tranquillity of the island, resting in hammocks, swimming or snorkeling.

Day 14. The Maldives: Take a cruise out to sea to visit some of the neighbouring atolls, enjoying a picnic lunch and a magical sunset as you return to your island retreat.

Day 15. To Male : Morning for leisure. Afternoon return by boat to Male in time to catch your return flight to the USA which departs very early the next morning.

Day 16. To USA : Early morning flight to the USA.

OUT		RTN	
26	Jan	10	Feb
30	Mar	14	Apr
5	Oct	20	Oct
16	Nov	1	Dec

Reservation Form of Passengers : Please read the Booking Conditions and Traveller's Advice carefully. Complete this form in BLOCK LETTERS and mail with deposit of $300 per person and/ or full payment if within eight weeks of travel.

Passenger's Last Name	First Name	Mr./Mrs. Ms./Miss	Date of Birth	Pass-Port No.	Nationality	Place of Issue	Date of Issue

Emergency Contact Name and Number

Special Requirement Please note here any other requirements or arrangements which differ from the basic tour. Every effort the Basic tour. Every effort will be made to secure the arrangements requested, but success cannot be guaranteed.	Would you like us to book your international flights ☐ Yes ☐ No If yes, please indicate class of service ☐ Economy ☐ Business ☐ First Number of Passengers ☐ Suite ☐ Twin ☐ Single.................. ☐ Tour Name .... ☐ Departure Date............................... ☐ How did you hear about us : ☐ Name of Newspaper......................... ☐ Name of Magazine...........................
Important Notes	
CHANGES : Any alterations made to the booking will be charged $50 per alteration VISAS : Please note that visas are required for travel to India, Nepal and Bhutan.	☐ Tourist Office ☐ Name of Guide book ☐ Name of Travel Agent ☐ Travelled with us before (Year) ☐ Other...

In signing this reservation form, I/we accept the Conditions as set forth in the brochure on behalf of all those listed above. I/we all declare that I/we have been offered trip cancellation/baggage insurance and that I/we will not hold travel agent nor its agents responsible for any expenses incurred.

Travel/Agency Stamp/ Client Address	Signed............................... Date....................................

A tour operating company, in addition to printing programmes, also gives details about package prices, booking conditions and an information sheet for the advice of the clients. The information sheet is an important document for the client as it gives important details about flights, domestic travel, transfers, surface transport, visa and health requirements of a destination. This practical information comes very handy for a tourist. All this information can be part of a tour brochure or can be printed separately as in the case of company whose programmes have been discussed. This separate printed form which is also a Passenger Reservation Form for booking a programme is distributed together with the brochure. An example of the same is as follows:

Booking Conditions

Booking Procedures : Once you have chosen your holiday, please read the conditions of travel as your booking is subject to the terms listed below. A contract is entered into once your signed booking form and deposit is received by your travel agent or us and we accept and confirm the booking.

Payment : An appropriate deposit for each tour chosen will be your only obligation until eight weeks prior to departure. The balance of the tour cost must be paid eight weeks before you travel. If the final balance is not received on time we reserve the right to treat the booking as cancelled by you and to levy cancellation charges. If you book your tour within eight weeks of departure, the full amount of the tour must be paid at the time of booking.

Insurance Advice : You will be automatically billed for and enrolled in our travel insurance programme. Should you not require this insurance you must indicate so at time of booking. After receipt of your booking you will be sent a complete brochure on your coverage.

Alterations by a Client : If you request any amendments to your travel arrangements once we have confirmed a booking, telex charges and other expenses will be payable by you together with an amendment fee of $50 per alteration. If, after the commencement of your tour, you request for any amendment to your arrangements or accommodation we will do our best to implement it, but we cannot guarantee that it will be possible. In the event of such an amendment being made, you will be liable for any cancellation/ retention charges that may be levied for the previously booked service and for any costs incurred by us or our agents in attempting to secure any revised arrangement.

Cancellation by a Client : Should you wish to cancel your tour, you must notify in writing. Such notification only will be deemed to have been given on receipt of your letter, since we can only act on receipt. Please state the reason for cancellation as you may be covered by your insurance policy. If notification of cancellation is received more than six weeks before departure you will only lose your deposit. For notification received within six weeks of departure, cancellation charges are as follows:

Day before departure	Total tour cost lost
42 to 29	25%
28 to 16	75%
15 to 1	85%
Day of Departure	100%

Cancellations received on Fridays for tour departures that weekend (Saturday, Sunday and Monday) will be treated as no-shows.

We cannot give any allowance or refund for meals, rooms, excursions, etc., not taken when these are included in the price of the tour and no refund can be made on lost, mislaid or destroyed travel tickets or vouchers.

Cancellations by Tour Operator : All holidays in our brochure are based on group airfares and hotel rates involving a given minimum number of passengers. If this minimum is not reached we reserve the right to cancel the departure and offer an alternative date, or the same date with a supplementary charge, or at your option, a refund of all sums paid by you. Such cancellation will not take place after the date at which the final balance becomes due. We may be obliged to cancel your tour due to circumstances beyond our control. These may be for reasons of *force majeure* (cancellations of international and domestic scheduled services, technical problems with transportation, closure of airports, war—whether declared or not—threat of war, riots, civil disturbances, strikes, disasters, terrorist activities of threat of such, alteration of international and domestic scheduled services). In such cases we shall inform agents and direct clients without delay and shall offer clients, the choice of an alternative holiday of comparable standard, if available, or a prompt and full refund of all monies paid.

Alterations made to the Scheduled Programme : Our holidays are planned several months in advance and changes may be unavoidable due to circumstances amounting to *force majeure* or similar reasons beyond our control, delays in departures on travel arrangements caused by technical problems, weather conditions, overbooking or closure of a hotel, strikes, riots, decisions by state governments or tourist organisations altering the itinerary, the duration of time spent in a city or even omitting a city or part of the itinerary due to the local situation. In such cases we will offer comparable alternative arrangements or at your option make a full refund of all money paid by you. If any of the circumstances listed above occur during the course of the tour, we reserve the right to alter the scheduled itinerary accordingly and no compensation will be paid. If your tour must be curtailed due to circumstances amounting to *force majeure,* reparation costs will be met out of unused accommodation costs. No compensation will be made out of accommodation costs. We will make every reasonable effort to provide you with the booked tour arrangements but minor changes may occur. If they are significant we shall, if it is possible, before your departure, inform you or your travel agent. Again, we will offer comparable alternative arrangements or at your option make a full refund of all monies paid, by where such our control you will be entitled booked tour arrangements but minor changes may occur. If they are significant we shall, if it is possible, before your departure, inform you or your travel agent. Again, we will offer comparable alternative arrangements or at your option make a full refund of all monies paid, by where such changes are within our control you will be entitled to a commensurate compensation in accordance with the notice and gravity of the changes.

Price : Tour prices are based on US dollars. They are subject to variation if there are increases due to governmental action, exchange rates, increases in scheduled airfare or increases in fuel surcharges. Any increase in the original tour price will be notified to you at least eight weeks before departure. If you make your booking within eight weeks of departure the surcharge will be included in your voice. The company will absorb an amount equivalent to 2 per cent of the holiday price. Any surcharge will not exceed 10 per cent of the listed tour price. If you settle the final balance by the due date we will absorb any price increases after that due date. In return for this commitment, we are unable to make any refund or reduce any other costs should the value of the US dollar improve against the currencies used.

Visas and Clients Responsibilities : US citizens require a passport with at least 6 months validity from the date of entry. Visas are required and we will furnish the relevant details after receipt of your booking deposit and confirmation of your booking. (Please see the Traveller's Advice on this form for more details.) Non-US citizens should consult with the appropriate Consulates and Embassies. It is the responsibility of the individual traveller to secure the proper documentation prior to joining the tour.

Tour Operators' Responsibilities : We do not own or operate any of the accommodation or transport or other facilities used in connection with our holidays. We, therefore, cannot accept liability for negligence of the staff of these organisations. We do accept responsibility for failure to exercise reasonable care on the part of our employees. The information contained in this brochure has been complied with all reasonable care and is accurate to the best of our knowledge and is given in good faith.

When you travel with an airline the Conditions of Carriage of that airline will apply. These conditions are the subject of International Agreements and may limit or exclude liability. Your travel agent can advise you of these conditions.

It may be necessary to recast the holiday because of lack of participants. You will be contacted eight weeks prior to your departure date and advised that a supplementary size applies. If all group members accept the increased cost the tour will operate as scheduled. However, if the supplement is not accepted by you then you will be entitled to a full refund of all money paid or a transfer to another tour.

The company makes arrangements with airlines, hotels and other independent parties to provide you with the travel services you purchase. These parties are independent suppliers over whom we have no direct control. The company is not liable in the event of any failure by any person or company to render any transportation, accommodation or other travel service to be provided on the journeys, or for expenses incurred due to delays caused by weather, strikes, war, civil disturbances, natural disasters, flight delays, government actions, mechanical failures or any acts of God.

We cannot assume any responsibility for flight delays, cancellations or missed connections and are not liable for any expenses or consequences resulting therefrom and such expenses shall be borne by the client.

The participant waives any claim against the company for any damage to, or loss of, property, or inquiry to, or death of, due to any act, or negligence of any airlines, surface transportation companies, hotels or any person rendering any of the services or accommodations included. We cannot be held responsible for any claim, losses, damages for delay of baggage or other properties, inconvenience, loss of enjoyment, upset and disappointment, distress or frustrations, whether physical or mental, resulting from the act or omission of any party providing services. We do take all reasonable steps to insure the organisations providing services maintain standards which are acceptable within the norm in each locality.

In the event of a service being withdrawn by any of our suppliers, we shall have no responsibility beyond refunding all monies paid by the participant.

All services are subject to the laws of the countries in which these services are rendered.

What Your Tour Price Includes

(1) Economy class on inter-tour flights.

(2) Standard class on rail, road and other transportation as described in our brochure.

(3) In-flight meals and/or refreshments according to flight timings.

(4) 44 lbs or 20 kg baggage allowance, or as specified on your air tickets.

(5) Transfers between the appropriate overseas airports/stations/ports and your hotels according to each itinerary unless otherwise stated.

(6) Twin-sharing standard room accommodation with private bath or shower and toilet in each room where available.

(7) Excursions and tours where specifically detailed.

(8) Meals as described.

(9) Services of a leader/tutor/guest lecturer.

(10) Gratuities for services included on the itinerary.

Your Tour Price Excludes

(1) International airfare.

(2) The cost of personal items such as laundry, drinks with meals or otherwise, incidental, etc.

(3) Airport security charges if levied by any airport to cover the cost of security arrangements.

(4) Airport taxes.

(5) Optional excursions.

(6) Cost of visas and passports where necessary.

(7) Transport between your home and home airport/port/station.

(8) Gratuities for services provided on a personal basis.

(9) Meals other than those specified.

(10) The single supplement payable on all bookings where only one person is travelling.

Extending Further

India-Pakistan-Nepal-Tibet-Bhutan-Sri Lanka-Israel-Jordan-Syria.

Tour Prices

Tour prices do not include international airfares.

INDIA

Indian Experience — Exp — 9 days

Twin	Single
Share	Supplement
$795	$285
Meal Basis	Room and Breakfast

Splendours of the North — Nor — 15 days

Twin	Single
Share	Supplement
$ 2385	$ 865

Meal Basis Breakfast and Dinner

(a la carte where available)

Classical Journey to India and Nepal—CL—21 days

Twin	Single
Share	Supplement
$4185	$1325
Meal Basis	Breakfast and Dinner

(a la carte where available)

Forts and Palaces—FPR—18 days

Twin	Single
Share	Supplement
$ 2795	$ 865
Meal Basis	Breakfast and Dinner

(a la carte where available)

Southern Trader—SOT—19 days

Twin	Single
Share	Supplement
$ 2985	$ 965

The Nature and Scope of Tour Operations

Meal Basis Breakfast and Dinner

(a la carte where available)

Jungle Odyssey—-JOD—18 days

Twin Share	Single Supplement
$3785	$825

Meal Basis Full Board in Campus

Breakfast and Dinner

(a la carte where available)

Train to Calcutta—CCU—14 days

Twin Share	Single Supplement
$ 2145	$ 735

Meal Basis Breakfast and Dinner

(a la carte where available)

Royal Nepal—NEP—14 days

Twin Share	Single Supplement
$ 2425	$ 715

Meal Basis Full Board in Campus/Trek

Room and Breakfast Elsewhere

...and Beyond

The Spirit of Tibet—TIB—16 days

Twin Share	Single Supplement
$ 4275	$ 835

Meal Basis Full Board in Tibet

Room and Breakfast Elsewhere

Bhutan: A Walk in the Hidden Kingdom-BHU—l7 days

Twin	Single
Share	Supplement
$4425	$1085
Meal Basis	Full Board in Bhutan
Room and Breakfast in Delhi	

*Sri Lanka—The Enchanted Isle—SRI—*15 *days*

Twin	Single
Share	Supplement
$ 1625	$ 625
Meal Basis	Breakfast and Dinner
(a la carte where available)	

...revisited

A Culinary Feast—CUL—16 days

Twin	Single
Share	Supplement
$ 3965	$ 985
Meal Basis	Breakfast and Dinner
(a la carte where available)	

East Meets West—EMW—16 days

Twin	Single
Share	Supplement
$ 3865	$ 965
Meal Basis	Breakfast and Dinner
(a la carte where available)	

Middle East

Highlights of Israel—HOI—9 days

(Prices exclude International Air fares)

Twin	Single
Share	Supplement
Low Season	$1365-$485
High Season	$1745-$485
Meal Basis	Breakfast only

The Ancient Lands-

(Prices exclude International Air from UK)

Twin Share	Single Supplement
Low Season	$ 2655-$ 865
High Season	$2695-$ 895
Meal Basis	Breakfast and Dinner

Splendours of the Near East—SNE—13 days

(Prices exclude International Air from UK)

Twin Share	Single Supplement
Low Season	$ 2495 $ 695
High Season	$ 2695 $ 855
Meal Basis	Breakfast and Dinner

Tour Extension

Syria Extension—6 days

Twin Share	Single Supplement
$ 1485	$ 755
Meal Basis	Breakfast and Dinner

High Season—March to December

Low Season—January and December.

10

Official Patronage

The role of the state in tourism is undeniable. In this chapter, we use the term 'State' in its widest meaning, including all bodies exercising public authority—government, ministries and departments, semi-government organisations, central, regional and local authorities.

The role of the state depends on a variety of factors such as:

- the degree of economic development in a country.
- the elements and type of economy.
- the structure of its public administration.
- the institutions of cooperation between the public and the private sectors.
- the priorities of a government on various economic and political issues.

Clearly, there is no single model of government structure to deal with matters pertaining to tourism. Nevertheless, it is accepted that there are certain areas where the government has responsibility. To list a few of these:

1. To establish the framework within which tourism's public and private sectors will operate.

2. To provide necessary legislation, regulations, controls which will be applicable to tourism. It includes protection of the environments and the cultural heritage.
3. To construct infrastructure—land, sea, air transport facilities and communications.
4. To develop human resources with appropriate training for tourism industry.
5. To develop a tourism policy with concrete plans. It may include:
   (a) Evaluating the tourism wealth and assets of the country, natural and cultural and their protection.
   (b) Identifying categories of competitive tourist products with comparative advantages.
   (c) Identifying the needs for development of the infrastructure and superstructure which could affect tourism development.
   (d) Developing programmes for financing of tourism activities in the public and private sectors.

To undertake the above responsibilities, there is obviously need for a government organisation. That organisation is often described as National Tourism Administration (NTA).

The administration could take the form of a separate ministry, a department in a large ministry or a semi-governmental organisation or any other form of a public body exercising public authority.

This National Tourism Administration should be the appropriate body where initiatives for action plans should be taken, the inter-departmental cooperation and coordination should be assured as well as the cooperation with regional and local authorities and public and private sector partnership should be encouraged.

Marketing and promotion should or need not be part of an NTA's responsibility, depending on government decision. It is also the government which decides the role that the private sector will play.

Whatever shape it takes, a National Tourism Administration is unavoidable to coordinate tourism-related activities.

Role of State

Most governments are involved in activities relating to travel and tourism—either at the planning and development stage or later. When tourism is well-established, there is need for collection of taxes from the visitors or from those who provide services to the visitors. Simultaneously, governments get involved in tourism promotion and marketing because it is in their own interest to make sure that the base of tourism expands internationally and domestically. Money has no colour for people who sell tourism. It does not matter whether the money comes from domestic travellers or from international travellers. There is hardly any ministry of the government which does not interface with tourism. The Ministry of Finance is there to provide funds; the Transport Ministry to build roads; the Home Ministry to look after the safety of visitors; the External Affairs to issue visas and the Ministry of Health to take precautions that no visitor with contagious diseases enters the country. Even the Ministry of Agriculture is involved to ensure that undesirable plants or pests do not find their way into the country through visitors. So, the government or government organisations are everywhere from the time the tourist enters a country till he leaves for home. But one ministry of the government is more directly involved than others—the Ministry of Tourism, if the country has one or, the Department/National Tourism Administration (NTA) which has been entrusted with the responsibility of looking after the affairs of tourism.

The United Nations Conference on International Travel and Tourism held in 1963, underlined the need for a National Tourism Organisation (NTA) in the following words:

> "The conference considers that it is incumbent on government to stimulate and coordinate national tourist activities and is convinced that this task can, in the main, be carried out through the medium of national tourist organisations."

The Administration

A recent report by WTO has attempted to point the locus and responsibilities of ministries/government departments in-charge of tourism and travel in 117 countries. Of the total, 37 countries had units (ministries/departments), that were solely responsible for tourism, and another 38 countries had units responsible for tourism and other activities, such as transport, communication, culture, information, wildlife, environment, etc. For the remaining 42 countries, responsibility of tourism was located under another ministry or department such as economy, trade, industry, small business, transport or communications.

In 1974, the French introduced a new variation. They appointed a Secretary (Minister) of Tourism within the Quality of Life Ministry. In the mid-eighties, President Mitterrand replaced it by a Ministry of Free Time—Tourism comes under this ministry.

It is, therefore, not surprising that the role and place of National Tourism Administrations vary widely from country to country. There is virtually no agreement whether the NTA should be a department, or an authority within the government, or an autonomous board or totally a private organisation. At least, six of the world's National Tourism Administrations are in private hands and a dozen more are semi-government.

Today, society is very much an organisational society. Tourism is no exception to it. Virtually, every country has some national body responsible for tourism. The basic characteristics of these organisations have been discussed by World Tourism Organisation in an inventory of National Tourism Administrations (NTAs) published in 1979.

The WTO prefers to describe them as National Tourism Administrations (NTAs) instead of using the traditional term National Tourism Organisations (NTOs). The new concept of tourism management at national level has moved from the traditional concept of National Tourism Organisation being a Central Publicity Body to the newer ideal of National Tourism Administration which sees promotion and marketing as one of its many functions.

The other functions reported in the survey of the NTAs were:

1. Research, statistics and planning.
2. Inventory of tourist resources and measures for their protection.
3. Development of tourist facilities.

4. Manpower development.
5. Regulation of tourist enterprises and travel.
6. Facilitation of travel.
7. International cooperation in travel.

Marketing and promotion are still very important functions of a National Tourism Administration.

The general destination promotion by a National Tourism Administration benefits all sections of the tourist industry. A majority of the NTAs bear all expenses of tourism promotion and marketing, except in some cases where the travel industry chips in from 5 to 10 per cent depending on the health of the travel industry in a country. The system does not work well because some members of the travel industry refuse to pay anything. In India, Britain and Italy, the industry makes little contribution towards the funding of their National Tourism Administrations.

Why Government Fund Tourism Promotion?

On the relationale for providing public supported National Tourist Administrations, Jeffries noted the following in favour of government-funding of the British Tourist Authority (BTA): The argument for government underpinning must be based on the recognition on the one hand that the whole economy benefits and on the other that taxation system represents the only practical way of collecting at least some of the necessary funding without which the whole exercise would certainly collapse.

Where such finding has not been forthcoming, the National Tourist Promotion comes to a virtual collapse. In such cases, the national airlines only try to sell the destination in their own interest.

In practice, the National Tourist Office is the most powerful motivator for the destination. It concentrates on the national base. Other big promoters, such as carriers, have many destinations to promote and do not have the credibility in the public mind of the official government backed service. The National Tourism Administrations have little control over the facilities and services that the private sector travel industry are selling. Few National Tourist Offices sell a tourist product and even fewer own it.

Middleton elaborates, "A large number of businesses generate a wide range of tourist products, most of which are beyond the marketing influence of NTO with regard to volume, design, price and promotion decision."

An NTA may be in a position to influence the product but, it certainly has no control over it. Even in countries where an NTA may own hotels or transportation, its influence is limited to providing leadership and guidance.

Aims and Objectives

The National Tourism Administrations (NTAs) are created to serve national objectives and goals determined by a government.

In general, most Tourism Administrations would have the following goals:

1. To increase international tourism to earn more foreign exchange for the country.
2. Economic development leading to more employment.
3. Increasing national Income—tax revenue.
4. Projecting the right image of the country abroad.
5. Promoting friendship with countries of the world.
6. Preservation of the nation's cultural heritage.

Domestic Roles

1. National integration of the country.
2. Redistribution of income through tourism for balanced economic development.
3. Protection of the rights of an individual to leisure.
4. Preservation of regional and ethnic traditions.
5. Creating awareness in the nation for the protection of environment.
6. Creating respect for the heritage of a country.

   (If necessary, more goals can be added to this general list.)

Manila Declaration on Domestic Tourism : Although international tourism is considered irnportant for economic development of a country, governments increasingly are taking more interest in the promotion of domestic tourism. The Manila Declaration adopted by the World Tourism Conference in 1980 is indicative of the growing interests of the governments in domestic tourism.

Domestic tourism comprises over 80 per cent of the world's tourist movements.

The following are some extracts from the Manila Declaration which underlines the importance of domestic tourism:

> Within each country, domestic tourism contributes to an improved balance of the national economy through a redistribution of the national income. Domestic tourism also heightens the awareness of common interest and contributes to the development of activities favourable to the general economy of the country.... The development of tourism from abroad should be accompanied by a similar effort to expand domestic tourism.

The economic returns of tourism, however real and significant they may be, do not and cannot constitute the only criterion for the decision of the states to encourage this activity. The right to holiday, the opportunity for the citizen to get to know his own environment, a deeper awareness of his own national identity and the solidarity that links him to his compatriots, the sense of belonging to a culture and to a people are all major reasons for stimulating the individual's participation in domestic and international tourism.

Official Policy

Most governments, specially those which are members of the World Tourism Organisation, subscribe to the view that tourism is good for their people and should be supported. But, not many have developed policies which are mandated by their legislatures and implemented effectively. The status of the National Tourism Administrations (NTAs), therefore, remains ambiguous in several countries. Tourism is a new phenomenon and often, the bureaucrats who head the National Tourism Administrations do not have adequate background and experience of this highly sophisticated industry. In India, for instance, Directors General have changed during 20 years very frequently. None of them had any previous experience of travel industry when they joined. No wonder, therefore, the Government of India has no tourism policy approved and mandated by its Parliament. It takes years to learn the basics of tourism. By that time, tourism chiefs are transferred to another ministry.

At times, the goals of the National Tourism Administration and other departments/ministries in the same government come in conflict. In 1980, India's Ministry of Tourism set a target of 3 million tourist arrivals by 1990. But, its sister ministry, Civil Aviation, severally restricted the entry of new foreign carriers. There was little possibility to achieve the target of 3 million visitors in ten years without increasing the seat capacity on international and domestic carriers. The seat capacity of the national carrier, Air India, remained stagnant for 10 years. So, India hardly reached one million arrivals by 1990, two million short. Another new example: The Ministry of External Affairs suddenly raised the visa fee for visitors to India from US $ 5 per person to US $ 50 without consulting the Ministry of Tourism, resulting in a drop in arrivals. Subsequently, the fee was reduced by the Ministry of External Affairs to a uniform US $ 5 for all countries of the world. But the damage was done. It is ironic to see the Ministry of Tourism advertising abroad a warm welcome from the friendly people of India while customs officials under the Ministry of Finance start an aggressive campaign of searching all incoming visitors. These conflicts are not confined to India alone. It happens elsewhere too because coordination among the bureaucrats is uncommon except in very small countries.

More successful tourist countries have National Tourism Policies mandated by their Parliaments. Among them are Canada, Mexico, United Kingdom, Ireland, France, Japan, Spain and USA. All of them have listed similar goals. To quote the objectives of the tourism policy of Japan, "To support growth of domestic and international tourism, contribute to international friendship, development of economy and reduction in regional economic and social differences."

France has the following to say in its tourism policy, "Expand overall tourism demand, stimulate development of employment and income in rural areas, support tourism opportunities for medium and low income segments of population."

Functions of National Tourism Administrations (NTAs) : Despite ambiguity of the role and status of NTAs in the government hierarchy, the function of National Tourism Administrations are similar. The two broad functions are (a) development of tourist product of the country, (b) promotion and marketing of tourist product.

In India, the National Tourism Organisation is the Department of Tourism (DOT) which works under the overall control of the Ministry of Tourism—a separate ministry dealing only with tourism matters. At times, tourism and civil aviation are both under the charge of the same minister. But, the two ministries have distinct identities. The India Tourism Development Corporation (ITDC), a public sector organisation, works under the control of the Ministry of Tourism. ITDC acts as the implementation wing of the Department of Tourism. For instance, if the Department of Tourism wants certain tourism developments to take place in an area where the private sector is shy to go, ITDC is entrusted with the job. In the new environment of liberalisation, the role of ITDC is declining.

Broadly, the activities of National Tourist Administration can be placed under the following heads:

Promotion

1. Establishment of overseas offices.
2. Advertising.
3. Public relations.
4. Production of promotional material.
5. Participation in travel fairs and exhibitions.
6. Familiarisation tours of travel agents/ travel writers.
7. Organisation of sales seminars for travel industry.

Research and Statistics

1. Collecting tourism and travel statistics.
2. Research on tourism.
3. Tourism marketing surveys.

Vocational Training

1. Operating training schools for tourism and hotel management.

2. Developing courses for training and production of course books.
3. Developing specialised programmes.

Planning and Investment

1. Physical planning at national level.
2. Economic planning.
3. Developing social aims.
4. Area development.
5. Financing of tourism infrastructure
6. Financing of tourism accommodation.

General Administration

1. Management of personnel.
2. Maintenance of accounts.
3. Supplies to offices.
4. Legal affairs.

Coordination : Since tourism involves cooperative working of different departments of the government and the suppliers of the tourism facilities in the private sector, the need for coordination is paramount. Some of these functions may be listed as under:

1. Coordination with the government department dealing with activities having an impact on tourism.
2. Coordination with the regional, state and local tourist organisations within the country.
3. Coordination with hotels, airlines, ground transporters, travel agencies.
4. Providing advisory services to different segments of the travel industry.
5. Coordination with professional trade organisations.

The aim of a National Tourism Administrations is to mobilise the tourism resources of a country with the help of professional organisations. The National Tourist Administrations also act as catalysts of all tourism activities and endeavours in a country and give tourist enterprises a sense of direction.

The Comparison

It may be interesting to describe the organisation and working of some of the National Tourism Administrations of leading tourist countries of the world. France, for instance, has the oldest tourist organisation which was set up as early as 1910 (New Zealand claims to have opened its first tourist office in 1902). Having changed its name and functions several times, the French National Tourist Organisation now consists of General Commissariat for Tourism (Commissariat General de Tourism). The NTA is part of the Ministry of Free Time.

In Spain, an Under-Secretariat of Tourism was created in 1962 in the Ministry of Information and Tourism. It performs the functions of Directorate General of Tourism which was in existence before 1962. The organisation assists the Minister in formulating a tourism policy, preparation of tourism plans, etc. The tourist organisations of France and Spain are powerful executive bodies and exercise strong control as coordinators.

In Italy, the tourism development role is vested in the Director General of Tourism within the Ministry of Tourism, Entertainment and Sports. Its main functions are licensing of providers of tourist services, administration of loans, etc. The Italian State Tourist Office (ISTO) has the responsibility of promotion of tourism abroad. Financed largely by the State, it is more or less an autonomous organisation governed by its own council.

In Germany, promotion abroad is the function of the German National Tourist Organisation (Deutsche Zentrale fur Tourismus). The federal government provides most of the funds. Another organisation called the German Tourist Federation (Deutsche Fremteverkehrband) has the responsibility of internal promotion and development. It is composed of tourist organisations of the regions and cities which finance its activities.

In Switzerland, the pattern is the same as in Germany. The Swiss National Tourist Organisation looks after the overseas promotion and the Tourist Federation takes care of domestic tourism matters.

In Britain, which has been promoting tourism for over 60 years, both promotion and development are in the hands of British Tourist

Authority (BTA)—a statutory body created by an Act of Parliament in 1969, working under the overall control of Department of Trade. Besides the British Tourist Authority, there are, in the United Kingdom, four separate Tourist Boards for England, Scotland, Wales and Northern Ireland which work in close cooperation with BTA and its twenty overseas offices to promote tourism to Great Britain.

The United States was one of the latecomers in this field. The US government left the promotional part to the private sector. However, on June 29,1961, the United States Travel Service was set up by an Act of the Congress as part of the Department of Commerce. This Act gave USTS authority to advise and promote travel to the United States and facilitate travel wherever possible. Its main function is to increase the number of visitors to the United States. Renamed US Travel and Tourism Administration (USTTA), it is now headed by an Under-Secretary of State (equivalent to a Minister in India). It has seven overseas offices called the United States Travel Service,

USTTA has a very small budget of only US $ 14.6 million. In the mid-eighties, President Reagan had decided to abolish USTTA but somehow it escaped the axe.

The Reagan administration officials believed that the private sector could safeguard America's share in the world tourism market better than a bureaucratic agency. In fact, they did not deem tourism promotion an appropriate programme to be funded by the government as it benefited only specified segments of society. What President Reagan did not do, President Clinton has done. President Clinton has decided to axe the USTTA and from 1996, it was disbanded.

The control of tourism matters at central level in Japan is in the hands of the Department of Tourism, Ministry of Transport. A tourist organisation was set up in Japan as early as in 1930. The Department of Tourism, in its present form, is part of the Secretariat to the Ministry for Transport. The department has three divisions—planning, tourist promotion and tourist facilities. For purposes of coordination there is an interministerial liaison council on tourism, consisting of representatives of ministries and agencies having direct or indirect impact on tourism. The Council is chaired by the

Director General of the Prime Minister's Office and consists of sixteen Vice-Ministers (equivalent to Secretaries to the Government of India).

The Japan National Tourist Organisation (JNTO) works under the supervision of the Department of Tourism for promotion of tourism from foreign countries. It is financed primarily by the central government, though about ten per cent of the budget is contributed by enterprises connected with tourism—Japan National Railways, Japan Airlines, Japan Hotel Association and Japan Travel Agents Association, etc. JNTO has sixteen overseas offices. The president of JNTO is normally an experienced, retired civil servant.

Tourism Administrations in South-East Asia India was the first country to promote tourism in a systematic fashion in the South-East Asian region. India's close neighbour, Nepal, has a separate Ministry of Tourism and Civil Aviation. Tourism is the country's top foreign exchange earner. The Department of Tourism exercises jurisdiction only in respect of policy, regulatory and promotional matters, but the travel industry, except the national carrier, is in the hands of the private sector. Royal Nepal Airlines is government-owned. Nepal has no overseas tourist offices.

In Pakistan, tourism is part of a composite Ministry of Culture, Archaeology, Sports and Tourism. The ministry has a separate Tourism Division which formulates national plans and policies on tourism and exercises regulatory functions. Besides, Pakistan has a powerful public sector body called Pakistan Tourism Development Corporation (PTDC). The organisation undertakes promotional, developmental and commercial activities in tourism. It packages and sells tours, runs hotels, restaurants as well as tourist information offices. Pakistan has no overseas office. However, there is a strong private sector in the travel industry of Pakistan which competes with the public sector.

In Bangladesh, tourism affairs are dealt with by the Ministry of Communication, Aviation and Tourism. On the pattern of Pakistan, Bangladesh has set up a Tourism Development Corporation which is called Bangladesh Parjatan. This is, in fact, the National Tourism Administration of the country and runs some hotels, sells tours and provides information to visitors through its tourist offices. The

Corporation does not enjoy monopoly in tourism activities. There are many hotels and travel agencies in the private sector. Tourism, as yet, is a peripheral activity in Bangladesh.

In Sri Lanka, the Ceylon Tourist Board (CTB) — the National Tourism Administration—is headed by a full-time chairman. Presently the overall control is in the hands of Ministry of Tourism, Aviation and Media which lays down policies. The Ceylon Tourist Board executes the policies determined by the government, runs tourist offices in and outside the country, and undertakes promotional, developmental and regulatory functions. In addition, government-owned Sri Lanka Hotels Corporation runs hotels in the public sector. Air Lanka is the national carrier and is owned by the government.

CTB is an effective marketing organisation. In spite of law and order problems in the country, arrivals in Sri Lanka were about 4,00,000 in 1995. The Republic of Maldives — a relative newcomer in the field of tourism — has set up a separate Department of Tourism under a Director General who reports to the President's office. It is a small country of two thousand sparsely populated or uninhabited islands. Tourist arrivals in 1996 were 300,000 more than the total population of the Maldives.

Singapore has a Tourist Promotion Board (STPB) headed by a non-official chairman. Other members of the Board are also successful professionals and businessmen.

The Board acts like a private sector company and responds promptly to the changing demands of the visitors. Its financial needs are met adequately by three per cent hotel tax in the country. The money received from this tax is allocated to the Singapore Tourist Promotion Board to meet promotional and other expenses. It is a dynamic organisation and Singapore has now about 7 million visitors in 1996.

The official National Tourist Administrations in Hong Kong is called Hong Kong Tourist Association (HKTA). Like Singapore, they have a Board of Directors and the budgetary requirements are met by a five per cent tax on hotels and restaurants.

Hong Kong, now under the British, will revert to China on July 1,1997. HKTA may not remain the same.

Thailand is yet another developing country which has done very well in tourism, initially because of a sizable number of American forces in East Asia who came to Thailand for rest and recreation, and now on the strength of its own tourist attractions and effective marketing. Thailand is liberal in respect of entertainment and night life. It, therefore, draws tourists not only from far off countries like USA and Australia but also from its Asian neighbours. Together, visitors from Japan, Hong Kong and the ASEAN countries constitute more than half of Thailand's inbound tourism. Over 200,000 Indians visit Thailand annually, despite visa restriction.

The number of foreign visitors to Thailand was 7 million in 1996, compared to 2.1 million in 1983 and only 6,00,000 in 1978.

The Tourist Authority of Thailand (TAT) is the National Tourism Administration of the country. A statutory body, it is an active marketing organisation. A case study of its success during the Visit Thailand Year 1987 has been included in this chapter.

TAT functions directly under the office of the Prime Minister which shows the importance which the government attaches to tourism development. The Administration has over 600 employees all over the country and in its overseas offices.

The national carrier—Thai Airways International—is equally successful and is actively involved in promotion of inbound tourism jointly with TAT.

The following chart compares some National Tourist Administrations and their budgets (1995):

Top Tourism Promotion Budgets (IN US$000)

Rank	*Country*	*1994*	*1995*	*% change*
1.	Australia	75,811	87,949	16.01
2.	United Kingdom	77,885	78,710	1.06
3.	Spain	77,457	78,647	1.54
4.	France	62,729	72,928	16.26
5.	Singapore	49,695	53,595	7.85
6.	Thailand	42,907	51,198	19.33

Contd...

Rank	*Country*	*1994*	*1995*	*% change*
7.	Netherlands	43,800	49,700	13.47
8.	Austria	45,694	47,254	3.41
9.	Ireland	41.830	37,811	-9.61
10.	Portugal	34,904	37,271	6.78

Source: World Tourism Organization (WTO) (Latest Available Figure)

Budgets of NTA : All governments allocate sizeable budgets to their National Tourism Administrations. But, the biggest expense of any tourism destination is on advertising and promotion. National governments worldwide spent US $ 1.4 billion in 1993 to sell their respective countries to the travelling public, according to a survey released by the World Tourism Organisation in 1994.

Spain, the world's number three tourism destination, ranks as the biggest spender on tourism promotion with US$85 million in 1992, followed by Australia US $ 77 million and France with US $ 69 million. The United States and Germany are at the other end of the scale, spending only US $ 12 and US $ 16 million respectively. US Government has stopped spending any money on tourism promotion from 1996.

However, the most startling conclusion of this study is that promotional spending bears little relation to the number of tourist arrivals, the number of overnight stays or tourism earnings. It is, therefore, clear that there is a serious lack of accepted guidelines for tourism marketing, according to Enzo Pad, WTO Chief of Statistics and market research, and the author of this report.

WTO has conducted this survey to enable its member countries to start monitoring the effectiveness of this expenditure. The amount spent on promotion per tourist varies greatly from country to country. Bermuda, for example, spends US $ 37.65 per tourist, Spain US $ 2.15, France US $ 1.21 and the US just 28 cents.

Countries generally target their promotional budgets on the world's largest tourism generating markets—USA, Germany, Great Britain, France, Italy, Japan, Canada, Belgium and Switzerland.

Spending is sometimes misdirected. Italy, for instance, spent 16 per cent of its promotional budget in USA while American visitors represented only two per cent of its total tourist arrivals. Similarly, Greece spent 14 per cent of its promotional budget in the USA with only 2 per cent of arrivals.

Some countries are undervalued by NTAs. Germany, for instance, represents 15 per cent of arrivals in Spain, but Spain spends only 2 per cent of its promotional budget in Germany.

The following two charts show how countries spend their tourism budgets, especially their promotional and advertising budget. Australia, for instance, spends 11.3 cents out of every tourist dollar earned from tourism—the highest percentage in the world.

National Tourist Offices Outside the Country : The national tourist offices abroad are only an extension of the country's National Tourism Administration. These offices contribute to the success to tourism business. In majority of cases, national tourist offices overseas are manned by nationals of the home country assisted by locally recruited personnel. Occasionally, some small countries find it more economical to run their tourist information services through local public relation agencies. A few countries use their diplomatic missions overseas for providing tourist information, instead of having separate tourist offices. Examples: Nepal and Pakistan.

The objective of a national tourist office overseas is to communicate with the local travel trade and potential consumers (travellers) regarding the desirability of travelling to their national destination. In the past, their role was essentially informational—dissemination and distribution of tourist literature of their country and servicing enquiries from the general public. Tourist offices reacted to the existing demand instead of creating a new demand for the country's tourist product. The role has undergone a major change under competitive market conditions. Tourist offices overseas are now engaged in marketing campaigns in cooperation with the local travel trade. They conduct research on the preferences and needs of travellers in markets where the offices are located and send feedback home to package their tourist product accordingly.

The marketing activities of the tourist offices overseas can be divided into two parts: (a) trade-oriented, and (b) consumer-oriented. The campaign with the travel trade consists of a series of public relations activities outlined below:

Tour with Familiar Objective

Tourist offices overseas sponsor visits of groups of travel agents from their respective areas on familiarisation and educational tours. These tours are often organised in cooperation with the national carrier of the country or any other international carrier interested in the area. Normally, the National Tourism Administration of the host country picks up the tab for hospitality or shares it with the carrier, depending on applicable IATA regulations. Similarly, hospitality is extended to travel writers, TV and film producers, journalists, opinion-makers, etc. This is one of the most effective methods of creating the right image of a country. Any article written by a writer who has seen a place and who is respected for his writings in his country is more effective than numerous paid advertisements.

Sales Seminars

Overseas tourist offices organise training workshops or sales seminars for the travel trade of the country where they operate. In these seminars, information is imparted to local travel trade through audio-visual presentations, literature and talks. The objective is to increase sales through better information.

Sales Calls

The tourist office call on travel agencies and airlines executives to advise them about holiday possibilities in their country and the profitability of selling tours to their destination. They also carry samples of tourist literature and sales aids which they give to travel agents, free of cost.

Mailing Directly

In order to keep travel agents informed and well-stocked with literature, tourist offices undertake direct mailing of tourist literature. This helps agents to service their clients better.

The Newsletters

Since it is not possible to call on all travel agents, a good tourist office issues a newsletter regularly to travel agents/travel press giving all that is new and important in travel to their country. In this way, they can communicate directly with the people who sell travel and who also are in a position to mould opinion in favour of their destination. The activities listed above—the list can be more exhaustive— are directed towards informing the travel trade about the quality of a country's tourist product and creating a demand for it. On the consumer side, for the man who travels, the tourist office provides the following services:

Knowing about Services

A tourist wishing to go to a destination writes to a tourist office or calls at the office to get information. Besides, there are numerous telephone inquiries in response to its advertising. A tourist office is required to service these inquiries with printed material, brochures, etc. People who telephone often give their address. The tourist office mails tourist literature to such addresses free of cost.

Display through Window

A tourist office not only puts up displays in its own windows or in its office, but also keeps readymade display units to be put up at travel agencies' airlines windows at various locations'. These displays are often moved from one location to another. For this purpose, a tourist office hires the service of a display specialist who performs this function regularly on the basis of an agreed fee.

Fairs and Exhibitions

A tourist office tries to make use of any opportunity to participate in local exhibitions, fairs, promotion through departmental stores, special weeks, etc. This activity is undertaken to interest the general public in the destination.

Endorsing Weeks

Tourist offices cooperate with local clubs, cultural organisations, hotels, universities, etc., to organise promotional evenings, weeks and food festivals for their country. Here, film shows and talks are arranged, displays of handicrafts and folk dances are organised. Fashion shows can be a part of such programmes. National weeks are generally organised in cooperation with local hotels. A Hilton Hotel in New York may organise a French food festival in collaboration with the tourist office of France, or a Sheraton in San Francisco may cooperate with the Indian tourist office to celebrate an India week which may include Indian food, Indian entertainment and display of Indian handicrafts, etc. Such weeks are organised by tourist offices all over the world. This promotion is possible if there is sufficient interest in a country. A hotel would not cooperate with the national tourist office if the country to be promoted is not popular or not well known to the local population.

The Publicity

An important function of the tourist office is to generate demand for its country's tourist product through advertising in consumer and travel trade media. The effectiveness of this depends on the size of the budget. Through a well-organised and effective advertising campaign, a tourist office can generate thousands of inquiries from the general public for tourist literature.

Media and Public Relations

While advertising may be useful, its effectiveness will be limited if people do not have a good image of a country's tourist product. No amount of paid advertising can be effective till a concerted public relation campaign is organised through the local press to promote the image of the country as an interesting holiday destination.

The Government of India Tourist Office, Tokyo, conducted a limited sample survey through its advertising agency in 1969, asking about five hundred highly educated Japanese representing various professions to describe in one word what came to their mind when they thought of India. Most respondents gave their answer in the following order: heat, poverty, cow, hunger, Hindu, Buddha, Ashoka, the Ganges, Gandhi. The Himalayas came last.

It will, therefore, be seen that there was hardly anything in the survey to show the existence of a positive image of India as a holiday destination. At that time, traffic from Japan to India was about five thousand, mostly business visitors. The only alternative was to launch an extensive public relations campaign with the press and other media. It was discovered that journalists on the staff of major newspapers had never had the opportunity to visit India. Although Japanese people were generally well disposed towards India, their knowledge of India was sketchy. The tourist office decided to sponsor several media tours to India. About four hundred media representatives were sent to visit India on familiarisation tours within the next three years. Advertising in the consumer press was stopped because it was felt it would be ineffective. The focus on media changed the image of Indian for the better and traffic increased 300 per cent in 3 years.

Tourist offices sponsor or assist the visits of travel writers and newspaper editors to their country. Besides, they service the local media through regular press releases and personal interviews with the press. TV stations are supplied films to be screened in their regular programmes. Sometimes, tourist officers manage to be interviewed. Public relations efforts, to a great extent, depend upon the personality, education and dynamism of the representative of a National Tourist Administration in a country. A tourist officer lacking dynamism is a disaster and liability.

Aids for Sale

Among the sales aids used by the tourist offices are: travel folders, brochures, city maps, hotel or accommodation guides, films, posters, readymade display kits, handicrafts of the country, musical records and tapes and travel manuals.

Why Have Tourist Offices Overseas? : It is often asked why a country should have tourist offices abroad since the job of a tourist office could be performed by direct mailing from the home country or through its diplomatic mission in the country. But marketing from the home country is not only expensive but also ineffective. Tourism marketing requires the physical presence of a tourism man in the generating region. Prospective visitors need information and assurance that they will have no problem while they are on a holiday at the destination. Tour operators who sell holidays want to be in touch with the man from the country where they are sending their clients for information and clarification of doubts which their clients may have. The cost of doing all this from a distant home-base office would work out very high. It is in this context that we find there are more than 75 tourist offices, each in London and Frankfurt and 80 in New York. The size of tourist office is determined by the government on the basis of potential of each market.

In several major cities of the world, foreign tourist offices have their own associations and they normally meet once a month to discuss their problems and sometimes work out joint promotions. Although each tourist officer promotes travel to his own country, there is a healthy competition among them. They are all convinced that by generating a desire to travel, they are preparing the ground for travel ultimately to their own national destinations. At one time when the author of this book was posted in Japan, the best spokesman of India's tourist attractions was the Director of the Italian National Tourist Office in Tokyo, who had developed a great fondness for India. Similarly, a renowned columnist of the largest Japanese newspaper, genuinely in love with India, was willing to speak about the wisdom and philosophy of India at any meeting sponsored by Indian Tourist Office—free of cost.

As to the idea of an overseas mission doing tourism marketing for a country, it has been found by experience that it is not productive enough. Diplomats, including the information attaches of embassies, are not trained marketing people who can sell the tourist product of a country. Tourism needs training of a different kind, requiring persistent follow-up on sales leads and close relationships with a vast spectrum of the travel industry. Besides, a mission may be located in the state capital, while the prime tourist markets may be elsewhere in the country. For instance, Washington, the capital of USA, is not a major tourist market but New York, Chicago and Los Angeles are. Similarly, Bonn was till recently the capital of the Federal Republic of Germany but its tourist markets are Frankfurt, Hamburg or Berlin. Canberra is the capital of Australia, but tourist markets are in Sydney, Melbourne or Perth. Addressing a WTO seminar on promotion of tourism product in New Delhi, F. Marvin Plake, former executive vice-president, PATA said:

As of 1977, not a single tourist office represented by a diplomatic establishment scored in the top thirty-five in USA and only one represented by an airline scored any ranking....

The reason that figure thirty-five appears is purely because the remainder, ninety-nine, simply did not scratch the surface.

The presence of tourist offices in potential markets of a country does help in the generation of new traffic. Tour-operators and wholesalers can be persuaded to launch new programmes with small incentives from the National Tourist Offices. The closure of overseas tourist office of a country may not affect traffic in the first year, but in the following years, the effect is substantial.

The absence of professionalism among the staff of overseas tourist offices, especially of developing countries, has been cited as a major disadvantage. Mr. William Hewas Jr, publisher of PATA Travel News commented:

Most NTOs (a) do not know their markets; (b) they do not have experienced, competent marketing personnel. Only a very small portion of their budget is used for trade advertising which is an important area of promotion. The major costs of overseas tourist offices are on personnel and activities which are not cost-effective. A small country, for instance, may spend $ 100,000 for a cocktail party to entertain two hundred PATA delegates. Imagine the results if this amount had been spent on trade advertising.

11

Tips for Tourists

The company believes that a good holiday is based not on luck but on judgement. We have, therefore, compiled the following traveller's service to outline the nature of travel in the Indian sub-continent and to help you prepare for your holiday. Our unrivaled experience has shown that sometimes minor problems can occur. While our ground staff are always on hand to rectify such an occurrence we do request that you have a patient and broad approach to travelling in the subcontinent.

International Aircrafts

International flights to and from India, Pakistan, Nepal, Sri Lanka and Bhutan are not included in the tour cost as outlined on the Tour Prices sheet. We would be pleased to assist you in making international flight bookings from your departure city in North America to the arrival city for the tour that you have booked.

The departure dates listed on the brochure indicate the date that you would leave North America to arrive at your destination city in time to join the first organised programme on your tour. Unless otherwise indicated we have pre-booked the hotel for immediate check-in should your flight arrive early in the morning. Should your flight connections bring you to the arrival city earlier than listed on the itinerary we would be pleased to make additional hotel bookings as required.

Travelling Inland

All flights within the country or countries visited as part of the tour are included in your tour price. Group reservations are made in economy class and all tickets will be handled by your Tour Director. We regret that we are unable to accept seating requests for internal flights as the domestic airlines generally assign seating only at time of check-in. Additional information on baggage allowance and security regulations will be included in your documents sent to you at the time of booking.

The Transfers

Airport/hotel transfers are included in the cost of your tour for your arrival and departure into and out of the country featured on your tour. You will be met at the airport by a company representative after clearing both immigration and customs and transferred in a private car to your hotel. If you have booked your own international flights you must advise us of your arrival and departure details and any subsequent change to these details so that we may be able to meet you upon your arrival.

Road Journey

Most cars used are of local construction, and while they may appear to be antique they are comfortable and ideally suited to the local road conditions, with spare parts readily available. Coaches are also principally locally made and while not of the standard of an American touring coach they are comfortable and well maintained. All of our coaches are air-conditioned with the exception of coaches from some Southern Indian cities where they are not available.

Train Journey

On the tours that feature travel by train we always try to reserve first class air-conditioned carriages, but these cannot always be reserved ahead of time and do not exist on all routes. Please contact our tour consultants to discuss the facilities available on the route you would like.

Pre-requisites for Visa : US citizens require a passport with at least 6 months of validity from the date of entry into the country/ countries included on your tour. Visas are required for entry into India, Nepal, Tibet, Bhutan, Jordan and Syria. At this time US citizens do not require visas for entry into Sri Lanka, Pakistan and Israel.

At the time that you make your booking we will mail you a visa kit outlining the visa requirements necessary for the tour that you are booked on. This visa kit will include visa forms and an information sheet outlining the visa requirements and procedures. All of the visa handling is done through our visa service.

Please note that the above information and service is valid only for US citizens.

Measures for Health

At the time of printing, the countries featured in our tours do not have any compulsory inoculation requirements for entry with the exception of those travellers having been to a country infected with yellow fever within five days of their arrival. However, it is generally recommended that travellers to India have current tetanus inoculations, and gamma globulin injections to protect against hepatitis. If you are travelling in South India or in other jungle areas malaria precautions are advised. For further medical information we advise you to contact your local physician. If you require any special medication we advise carrying an ample supply. Additionally you should carry diarrhoea antidotes and upset stomach medication. Sun lotions, lip balms and sun glasses are highly recommended.

Recommendations and advice on food and drink within the country/countries visited will be supplied at the time of booking. In all countries it is highly recommended to drink only bottled mineral water or other bottled beverages. These are commonly available in all the hotels that you will be staying at.

It is not necessary to purchase local currency prior to your arrival in India or another country featured on your tour. Foreign exchange counters at the hotels provide the same official rate of exchange as the banks or the airports. It is, therefore, not necessary or recommended to purchase local currency at the airport. However, it is recommended to purchase small denominations for use as tips or for small purchases. All major credit cards are accepted at the city hotels you will be staying at. Smaller hotels and wildlife park lodging accept cash in local currency only.

Airport Departure Taxes : The cost of our tours does not include airport departure taxes. It is, therefore, necessary for you to pay these locally and in local currency. Foreign currency is not accepted. The taxes vary in each country and will be advised to you before your departure from the USA. These taxes are subject to change and if they do your tour leader or our ground staff will advise you on site.

Tipping : Tipping for porterage and all specified sightseeing is included. Tipping is not included for services in addition to these such as meals not included, optional sightseeing, etc. In addition, some members of the groups may want to collectively tip the bus driver or local guide. This is not required and is completely at your discretion. Please ask your tour leader any question you may have about this. Our Tour Directors do not accept tips.

Cuisine : In the city hotels, restaurants serve Continental as well as Indian and Oriental cuisine. In the more remote areas and smaller hotels and places the food is basic and mainly Indian. We suggest that in these areas you request vegetarian food since this tends to reduce the risk of stomach upsets. The hotels that we use are keenly aware of the Western visitor's reaction to Indian food and they take great care in the area of hygiene. While health problems can occur, these are usually minor and often result in the change of diet and time zones.

Insurance : We realise that no one likes to consider the unexpected problems that interrupt holiday plans. Unfortunately, difficulties occasionally do arise, despite the most careful planning. So, to offer you peace of mind the company offers a comprehensive Passenger Protection Programme exclusively for our passengers.

The Passenger Protection Programme is not just cancellation insurance. Yes, it does provide reimbursement for penalties that may be assessed due to cancellation for covered reasons, but it also provides much more. For example, the programme offers medical expense reimbursement for covered accidents overseas, especially important because Medicare, and many private insurance policies, restrict coverage of medical expenses incurred abroad. We strongly recommend that all passengers participate in the Passenger Protection Programme. A full description of coverage will be sent to you or your travel agent automatically with your invoice. For your convenience the cost of the programme is automatically added to your invoice and may be purchased with your initial deposit or prior to final payment but cannot be added at a later date.

This is only a brief description of the plan. For full terms, conditions, exclusions and pre-existing limitations, refer to the description of coverage which should be reviewed thoroughly before purchasing.

Travel Insurance Coverage

Trip Cancellation/Interruption	*Total Tour Cost*
Baggage/Personal Effects	$ 1,000
Accident Medical Expense	$ 3,000
In-Hospital Idemnity (Sickness Only)	$ 3,000
Emergency evacuation	$ 2,0000
Worldwide Emergency Assistance	24 Hours
Travel Insurance Rates	
Tour up to $ 2,000	$99
Tours between $ 2,000 and $ 3,500	$169
Tours between $ 3,501 and $ 5,000	$259
Tours between $ 5,001 and $ 6,000	$299
Tours between $ 6,001 and $ 7,500	$359

Brochure II has a different presentation form while all other elements remain the same. In this brochure most of the programmes are multi-destinational. A client has a choice of more than one destination in a particular region. The tour operator promoting these programmes specialises in East Asia. Although the basic programmes cover India, the tour operator however does not take his clients there first. Tour No. 1 entitled 'Asian Highlights' is a 20 days trip starting in USA and covers Hong Kong, India, Nepal and Thailand. A client returns home from Bangkok. In this programme, the client also has a choice of an extension in India and the orient as per his requirements.

Tour No. 2 is a 15-18 days tour covering India and Nepal. Tour No. 3 is entitled "Magnificent India and Nepal" and covers both these destinations in 18 days. Tour No. 4 is again a twin destination tour entitled "Essence of India and Nepal" and is of 12 days duration with possible extensions.

Unlike in Brochure No. 1, the price of the tours, departure dates and terms and conditions of the tour form part of the main brochure. No separate sheet is printed as in the case of Brochure I. The brochure is printed in four colours using glazed art paper. Use of colour pictures in the brochure is another important element which projects the destination. Each of the programmes shows a colour representation of an important monument, event or an activity covering the itinerary. The following pages show the sample of the brochure discussed above.

Asian Highlights

Tour No. 1

"To world's best honeymoon... what better place to start a marriage than the Taj Mahal?"

Day 1,

Movement of Tourists

Today our Asian Highlights itinerary begins as we board our flight to Hong Kong.

Day 2,

Hong Kong : Upon arrival in the evening, you will by staff and transferred to your hotel. Mandarin Oriental

Day 3,

Hong Kong : Tour of Hong Kong Island begins with a panoramic ride up Victoria Peak on the venerable Peak Tram. Then you will visit Stanley Market on the south side of the island, take a *sampan* ride through the Tanka fishing community in Aberdeen, and sample *dim sum* at lunch. At the, a welcome dinner party is hosted by Mandarin Oriental. Breakfast, Lunch, Dinner.

Day 4,

Hong Kong-Delhi : The day is at leisure for shopping or exploring on your own before you transfer to the airport for your evening flight to India's capital, Delhi.

Day 5,

Delhi : Full-day sightseeing tour of Old and New Delhi includes visits to Raj Ghat—memorial to Mahatma Gandhi; the Red Fort—a Mughal masterpiece built by Shah Jahan; the bustling silver markets of Chandni Chowk and Jama Masjid. Continue sightseeing with a drive past the Diplomatic Enclave and visits to the Qutub Minar and Humayun's tomb, then continue down Raj Path past the Secretariat buildings, the Presidential Palace and Parliament.

Day 6,

Delhi-Udaipur : Morning flight to Udaipur. Stay at the hotel. Day ends with a sunset cruise on the lake.

Day 7,

Udaipur : Morning sightseeing in the city, visiting the opulent City Palace and the beautiful Sahelion Ki Badi, "Garden of Friends". Return to hotel to relax in peaceful surroundings.

Day 8,

Udaipur-Jaipur : Visit the Bahai Temple and Crafts Museum this morning, then fly to another once royal city, Jaipur, in the afternoon.

Day 9,

Jaipur : Jaipur was the capital of Rajasthan province, "the abode of rajas", and everywhere you see the monuments of its Mughal rulers. Trip to the strategically located Amber Fort outside town on elephant back, and inside the walls of the citadel, wander among buildings famous for their intricate mirrored inlays: the Hall of Mirrors, Kali's Temple and lattice-windowed palaces. City sightseeing in the afternoon shows the City Palace, home to an impressive collection of artwork, jewels, textiles and arms; Jantar Mantar; and the Hawa Mahal, or Palace of Winds, a tall facade of almost one thousand windows, behind which royal ladies once took the air in privacy.

Day 10,

Jaipur-Agra : Morning drive to Agra, sightseeing en route at Fatehpur Sikri, a hilltop ghost fortress and site of the mausoleum of Salim Chisti, a medieval Muslim saint. Continue on to Agra, renowned as the home of the Taj Mahal, which we view in the light of the setting sun.

Day 11,

Agra : The Taj Mahal was built by Mughal Emperor Shah Jahan in memory of his wife, and the flawless execution and exquisite workmanship of this architectural wonder are an inspiring memorial to love. After visit to Taj, visit the Agra Fort, built on the city's River Yamuna by Mughal Emperor Akbar the Great, and the tomb of Itimad-ud-Daulah.

Day 12,

Agra-Varanasi : The rise early this morning to watch the sunrise turn the marble of the Taj Mahal to a soft glowing amber. You will at leisure until our afternoon flight to Varanasi, for centuries one of India's most revered cities and still a centre for philosophy and religion.

Day 13,

Varanasi-Kathmandu (Nepal) : A dawn boat trip take you along the bathing ghats on the holy river Ganges to witness 2,000-year-old rites of prayer and devotion. Then a short drive bring you to the buried city of Sarnath, where Buddha preached his first sermon. Many treasures of Buddhist art, have been found in the ruins of Sarnath's ancient monastery, and you will visit the museum where they are displayed. In afternoon you will fly north, far into the range of the Himalayas. Your destination is Kathmandu, a Nepalese kingdom ruled by Hindus but with deep, ancient Buddhist roots. Famous as a trade centre since medieval days, Kathmandu is still an important market town.

Day 14,

Kathmandu : (Time and weather permitting, a scenic flight over the Himalayas may be an option today; information will be available upon arrival.) Visit to Durbar Square, the House of the Living Goddess, and the Old Royal Palace. Afterwards, we tour Swayambhunath, the oldest Buddhist shrine in Nepal, before enjoying dinner and a cultural performance this evening.

Day 15,

Kathmandu-Tiger Tops-Chitwan National Park : You will left the mountain-ringed Kathmandu on a short flight to Nepal's Chitwan National Park. Here, after settling into your comfortable rooms at the famous Tiger Tops Jungle Lodge, you will set out to explore the park. The transport here is ideally suited to the rough terrain—you can travel on elephant back, in search of the one-homed rhino and other unique species. This evening we enjoy an entertaining wildlife lecture, illustrated by slides, and an excellent dinner at our lodge.

Day 16,

Chitwan National Park : An early start in order to make the most of your second day in this fascinating wildlife sanctuary. In addition to tiger, Chitwan's tall grass jungles are best known for the one-horned rhino, chital (spotted deer), wild boar, monkey and leopard.

Day 17,

Chitwan-Kathmandu : Transfer to the airport for return flight to Kathmandu.

Day 18,

Kathmandu-Bangkok-Thailand : Morning visit to Patan, founded in A.D. 250 with a stop at the Tibetan Refugee Centre to see the carpet weavers at work. Later day you will fly to Thailand where, upon arrival in Bangkok this evening, you will be transferred to your hotel.

Day 19,

Bangkok : Planted squarely on the banks of the Chao Phraya River and threaded with a seemingly endless system of narrow canals, Bangkok's waters are her highways. Like the Thais, you can use the city's waterways to your best advantage. Same morning you can tour the Grand Palace by private boat before visiting the

Emerald Buddha Temple. Your afternoon is for leisure; on your own, you may wish to see the remarkable collection of Oriental antiques. In night you can enjoy Thai cuisine at your farewell cocktail and dinner party at Sala Rim Naam.

Day 20,

Bangkok-USA or Canada : Asian Highlights itinerary ends, boarding the flight back to the USA or Canada.

Tour No. 2

Magnificent India and Nepal

Day 1,

USA or Canada-London : Magnificent India and Nepal itinerary begins today when you will board your flight to London.

Day 2,

London-Delhi : Upon arrival in London, you will escort to our day-rooms near the airport. Later we return to the airport to catch our flight to Delhi.

Day 3,

Delhi-India : You will arrive at Delhi in morning, with the rest of the day at leisure to rest and unpack before you begin tomorrow's explorations of India's capital city. On the same evening you will attend a briefing followed by a welcome dinner.

Day 4,

Delhi : This day you will be on the sightsee in Delhi. In Old Delhi you will stop at Rajghat, Delhi's monument to Mahatma Gandhi, and visit the Red Fort citadel. Other points of interest include the Jama Masjid and the bustling market-place of Chandni Chowk, where silver merchants ply their trade. You may continue in New Delhi, driving by the Presidential Palace and Parliament House, then stopping to see the Qutub Minar, Humayun's tomb, India Gate and memorials to India's modern leaders.

Day 5,

Delhi-Udaipur : In morning you can leave Delhi, flying on to Udaipur, a serene desert city on the shores of Lake Pichola. We end the day with a sunset cruise on the lake.

Day 6,

Udaipur : While sightseeing in the city, visiting the opulent City Palace and the beautiful Sahelion Ki Badi, "Garden of Friends". Then you may return to your hotel where you can relax in your peaceful surroundings.

Day 7,

Udaipur-Jaipur : We arrive in this princely city and check in at our hotel, once the grand palace of the Maharaja of Jaipur and still retaining its former grandeur. In afternoon you may tour Jaipur, visiting the Maharaja's City Palace; the Jantar Mantar or Royal Observatory; the Ram Niwas Gardens; and the Hawa Mahal or Palace of the Winds, an intricate facade of pink sandstone designed to allow court ladies to take the air without exposing themselves to the stares of commoners. In the night can enjoy the crisp desert air while sipping a cool drink on the palace lawns.

Day 8,

Jaipur : In morning you can take an elephant ride to the fabled Amber Fort and Palaces, overlooking the city, where you will see the deservedly famous Hall of Mirrors and the best views of the valley as seem from the Royal apartments. The rest of the day is at your leisure.

Day 9,

Jaipur-Agra : The morning's journey to Agra takes you through rural India for an insight into the village and countryside life. You will stop at Fatehpur Sikri, built by Emperor Akbar as his capital and abandoned after just a few years when the water supply was exhausted. In Agra, renowned as the home of the Taj Mahal, you can first visit this magnificent monument at sunset, to watch the beautiful white marble turn slowly to a soft, rosy pink.

Day 10,

Agra : The Taj Mahal was built by Mughal Emperor Shah Jahan in memory of his wife, and its flawless execution and exquisite workmanship are an inspiring memorial to love. This morning, you may re-visit the Taj Mahal and also the imposing Agra Fort, built of red sandstone and marble. Later, you can see the enchanting Itimad-ud-Daulah, nicknamed the "Baby Taj."

Day 11,

Agra-Varanasi : With start early in the day to see the first golden rays of the sun warm the marble of Agra's most famous monument, the Taj Mahal. In afternoon you can fly to Varanasi, the holiest and oldest living city in India. For the devout Hindu, Varanasi must be visited at least once in a lifetime to wash away one's sins.

Day 12,

Varanasi-Kathmandu (Nepal) : Early in the morning you can take a boat ride, pass the bathing ghats on the river Ganges, where thousands of Hindus perform morning-rites of prayer. After breakfast you may continue with an excursion to Sarnath, where Buddha delivered his first sermon; you may also visit Sarnath's temple and the Archaeological Museum, full of Buddhist art treasures.

Day 13,

Kathmandu : (Time and weather permitting, a scenic flight over the Himalayas may be an option; information will be available upon arrival.) In morning you can tour the city, a bustling trade centre since medieval times. You can also visit Durbar Square; the Kumari Devi or House of the Living Goddess, the Royal Palace; and Swayambhunath, the oldest Buddhist stupa (shrine) in Nepal. You can drive this afternoon to Bhaktapur, a 9th century fortified town. At the night you will meet for a special cultural performance and farewell dinner.

Kathmandu-Delhi : For travellers concluding their tour, the remainder of the day is free for independent pursuits. *Kathmandu-Tiger Tops-Chitwan National Park, (Extension)* Travellers who have chosen the Tiger Tops option take a short flight from Kathmandu to Nepal's Chitwan National Park, where explorations begin immediately with an afternoon game drive on elephant-back.

Day 15,

Delhi-USA or Canada : Travellers who have not chosen to extend their trip are transferred to the airport early this morning to board a flight home. *Chitwan National Park (Extension)*

Travellers on the Tiger Tops extension spend the morning on elephant-back amidst Chitwan's tall grass jungles, in search of rhinos and the elusive Royal Bengal Tiger. Boat rides, nature walks and a visit to the nearby crocodile farm also provide fresh insights into the natural world.

Day 16,

Chitwan-Kathmandu : In the morning Tiger Tops travellers are transferred to the airport to board a flight back to Kathmandu. The remaining day is at our leisure.

Day 17,

Kathmandu-Delhi : Then you fly to Delhi today where you will are free to relax, do some last minute shopping or further explore the city.

Extend Your Trip

We can help you plan your own extension in India or the Orient, "tailor-made" as you require.

Essence of India and Nepal

Twenty-one Days

Departure Limited to 20 Passengers

Tour Cost Per Person

Land Arrangements	
Double occupancy	$ 5290.00
Single supplement	$ 1650.00
Internal Airfare	$ 580.00
Air Supplement from New York	$ 1499.00

Airfares via Pacific are available.

2003 Tour Dates (Depart from USA or Canada)

Depart	*Return*	*Depart*	*Return*	*Depart*	*Return*
Jan 03	Jan 23	Feb 28	Mar 19	Oct 23	Nov 12
Jan 17	Feb 06	Mar 13	Apr 02	Nov 06	Nov 26
Jan 31	Feb 20	Sep 18	Oct 08	Nov 20	Dec 10
Feb 14	Mar 05	Oct 09	Oct 29	Dec 18	Jan 07

2004 Tour Dates (New dates and prices may apply)

Depart	Return	Depart	Return	Depart	Return
Jan 08	Jan 28	Feb 05	Feb 25	Mar 05	Mar 25
Jan 22	Feb 11	Mar 11	Mar 19	Mar 19	Apr 08

Your land arrangements include:

Hotel accommodations as indicated in the itinerary or similar. Meals as indicated in the itinerary a la carte where-ever possible. Domestic bottled water with group meals.

All group transfers when arriving and departing on scheduled dates.

All sightseeing as shown, including entrance fees.

Service of a professional escort.

All gratuities except to your escort.

Handling of two bags per person.

Airport departure taxes.

Not included are personal expenses such as laundry; personal insurance; excess baggage fees; communication charges; cost of obtaining passport or visas; meals, beverages or sightseeing not included in the itinerary; any airfares.

Essence of India and Nepal

Day 1,

USA or Canada-London : A leader of a group touring from Canada to London writes his experience as follows :

Our programme begins when we board our flight to London.

Day 2,

London : Upon arrival in London, we transfer to our day-rooms to relax until the departure of our flight to Mumbai.

Day 3,

Mumbai, India : We land in bustling Mumbai this morning and transfer to our hotel. We are at leisure until an introductory briefing, followed by welcome drinks and dinner.

Day 4,

Mumbai : This morning we cruise through Mumbai Harbour and visit the cave temples on Elephanta Island. In the afternoon, we visit the Mani Bhawan, Gandhi's Mumbai residence; see the Gateway of India and stop at the Hanging Gardens.

Day 5,

Mumbai-Aurangabad : We fly east to Aurangabad, our base for excursions to two nearby sites of great significance: Ellora and Ajanta. This afternoon we travel to the spectacular Ellora Caves, with their 34 rock-cut temples dedicated to Buddhist, Jain and the Hindu gods.

Day 6,

Aurangabad : We travel about sixty miles from the city for a full day's tour of the monolithic Ajanta Caves, dating back to the 2nd century B.C.

Day 7,

Aurangabad- Udaipur

This morning we fly to Udaipur, where we stay at the Lake Palace Hotel, located in the middle of Lake Pichola; here we are joined by travellers on Asian Highlights tour. Our day ends with a sunset cruise on the lake.

Day 8,

Udaipur : This morning we sightsee in the city visiting the opulent City Palace and the beautiful Sahelion Ki Badi, "Garden of Friends". We return to our hotel to relax in peaceful surroundings.

Day 9,

Udaipur-Jaipur : Jaipur, the 'Pink City', is our destination this morning. After lunch, we begin our introduction to this capital of Rajasthan, "abode of rajahs". The City Palace is still the residence of the Jaipur family, and the City Palace Museum displays paintings carpets, jewellery and arms. We also see the Hawa Mahal, "Palace of the Winds".

Day 10,

Jaipur : Outside Jaipur is the strategically-placed Amber Fort. We look down on the city from the fort, as her Rajput rulers once did, from the back of a gaily-painted elephant. Our elephant takes us up the hill, where we can wander on foot among the impressive Hall of Mirrors, Kali's temple and the lattice-windowed palaces. The rest of the day is free to explore or relax.

Day 11,

Jaipur-Agra : Today we drive to Agra, visiting Fatehpur Sikri and the exquisite mother-of-pearl mausoleum of the Muslim saint, Salim Chisti en route. We arrive in Agra in time to see the sunset over the magnificent Taj Mahal, turning its filigreed marble to a glowing rosy pink.

Day 12,

Agra : Our morning tour begins with a detailed introduction of the Taj Mahal, long-fabled Wonder of the World. Today we also see the Agra Fort and visit the charming Itimad-ud-Daulah, known as the "Baby Taj".

Rules and Regulations : Tour prices quoted in this brochure are valid up to December 31, 1996 and include transfer, baggage handling, accommodations, hotel taxes, meals, sightseeing, entrance fees, gratuities and escort services as indicated in each itinerary.

Not Included in Quoted Tour Price : Costs of obtaining passports; visas unless otherwise specified in individual itinerary; excess baggage charges; travel insurance; personal expenses such as laundry; room service in excess of your meal allotment; gratuities and transportation to/from restaurants for a la carte meals; gratuities to escort, staff and crew of Eastern & Oriental Express, Road to Mandalay or Yanzi Princess; communication charges; meals, beverages or sightseeing; not included in the itinerary any airfares.

Luggage : Tour prices include the handling of two pieces of baggage per person. Baggage and personal effect are at owner's risk throughout the tour. Check with the airline for baggage restrictions applicable to your international flights.

Passport and Visas : Valid passport are required for travel to the destinations in this brochure; check with your travel agent or ask the latest requirements and assistance.

Registration : A deposit of $ 500 per person is required at the time you book, at which time you will receive your invoice and pre-tour documentation. The reminder of the price of your trip is due 60 days prior to your departure date. If your reservation is made within 60 days of departure, the entire price of the trip must be paid at the time of confirmation. When your reservation is initiated within 30 days of your departure, a non-refundable "rush booking" fee of $ 50 per booking will be charged.

Cancellations : Cancellations received up to 60 days prior to departure, $100 per person cancellation fee per tour or extension; 59-45 days, 10 per cent of tour price; 44-15 days, 20 per cent of tour price; 14 days or less 100 per cent of tour price.

Claims and Refunds : All claims for days missed while on tour should be made in writing within 30 days of the termination of the tour. This claim should be accompanied by a statement from the Tour Operating Company verifying the claim. Refunds are based on the actual costs of service involved and not on a per claim basis. Refunds will not be made for unused sightseeing trips or meals. The company will not accept any liability for any claims which are not received within 30 days of the termination of your tour.

Arrangements : Quoted tour prices include planning, handling and operational charges, and are based on the current rates of exchange and tariffs as of July, 1995. In the event of a marked change in foreign exchange rates, fuel costs or tariff rates, tour costs are subject to revision.

Responsibility : The company purchases transportation, hotel accommodation, restaurant services and other services from various independent suppliers that are not subject to its control. The Company, cannot, therefore, be liable for any personal injury or property damage, which may occur due to (1) any act of Commission of such a supplier or (2) defects in or failures of any aircraft, vessel, automotive vehicle or other means of transportation that is not under its control. The company reserves the right to adjust US dollar prices without notice, to reflect fluctuation(s) in the Foreign Exchange Markets. The Company also reserves the right to withdraw a tour or any part of it, to make such alternations in the itinerary as deems necessary or desirable, to refuse to accept or to retain as a member of the tour any person at any time, and to pass on to tour members any expenditures or losses caused by delays or events beyond its control.

Transportation by Air : We will arrange the best priced airfare available in the classes category you request at the time of your booking. Sample air prices are shown in this brochure. Should you cancel or change your air reservation before or after your departure, cancellation penalties may apply.

Airlines concerned are not to be held responsible for any act, omission or event during the time passengers are not on board their planes or conveyances. These tours may use the services of any IATA carrier. The passage contract in use by these companies when issued shall constitute the sole contract between the companies and the purchaser of these tours and/or passage.

Elements in a Tour Brochure : The description of the tour brochure of the two companies shows how different elements of a programme are carefully planned to include all necessary information to make a holiday comfortable. The necessary elements of a good programme in a brochure can be divided into two parts, e.g. (i) 'pre-visit' and (ii) 'on arrival'. Pre-visit details would include the following:

(a) destination information

(b) price of a tour

(c) departure dates

(d) hotel information

(e) visa requirements

(f) health requirements

(g) insurance advice

"On arrival" details would include the following:

(i) transfers

(ii) day to day itinerary

(iii) guide service
(iv) entertainment/cultural programmes
(v) shopping
(vi) currency exchange
(vii) emergency services
(viii) cuisine
(ix) customs to be observed
(x) airport departure taxes

All the elements in a programme of a big tour operator are tailor-made to suit particular interest and need of a client. A tour operator, after carefully considering various alternatives available and based on the market research packages, offers different programmes for including in his tour brochure.

Network of Distribution : The tour operator has thus emerged as the true manufacturer of the inclusive tour product packaged, standardised and quality controlled. The inclusive tour product can be marketed successfully by a tour operator in the tourist generating countries to a mass market, either directly or through travel agents. A large majority of tour operators sell their tour packages through a network of several hundred agents who are the members of the Association of Travel Agents in a particular country. For instance, if a tour operator happens to be USA based he would sell his product through ASTA, (American Society of Travel Agents) in UK, through ABTA (Association of British Travel Agents) in Australia, through AFTA (Australian Federation of Travel Agents) etc. A large percentage of tour packages are marketed in this manner.

Some tour operators resort to a direct selling or selling through a network of their own branches. For instance, in Switzerland, the largest tour operating company 'KUONI' sells its product through 85 of their own Kuoni retail sales offices as also through 765 appointed retail agents who are the members of FASV, the Swiss association of travel agents. Thomas Cook is well known as a travel retailer of its own product in addition to being a major tour operator of package tours. Most of their package tours are sold through an extensive network of their own retail sales offices.

Direct sale of the holiday packages is however resorted to by large tour operating companies having retail sales agencies of their own within a destination where these are located or in other neighbouring destinations. On the other hand, small tour operating companies not having retail sales outside will either concentrate entirely on selling their product or will support a select few travel agencies in important locations spread over the country. However, unlike sales of a tour operator programmes through travel agencies, direct selling involves higher fixed costs in advertising, direct mail promotion and similar other aspects. Direct selling also requires strong and efficient administrative back-up to deal swiftly with consumer and trade enquiries and sales.

Agreements of Sales : A tour operator who decides to sell his tours through a network of travel agents, has to enter into some form of an agreement with them. A formal agreement with the travel agents they appoint is to be drawn up to facilitate the agents to sell the services on behalf of a tour operator. The agreements *inter alia* specify the various terms and conditions of sale including issues like quantum of commission to be paid to the agents. It also specifies if the travel agent is to be a cash or credit agency as also the dates by which the operator is likely to settle his accounts. Another important condition of the agreement relates to a sale price of a tour. Most tour operators impose on an agent the condition in the agreements that their tours shall not be sold at a lower price than that published in the brochure.

Brochure Marketing : Printing of a tour brochure is very expensive. A brochure is a voluminous publication with special emphasis on the quality of paper, the reproduction of illustrations, graphic design of the cover and the layout of the pages. In order to be an attractive sales tool, it has to be printed on glazed art paper in four colours. Special emphasis is laid on the quality of papers and printing, as its main objective is to inform the prospective tourist about the attractions and facilities of a programme being promoted by a tour operator.

Considering all the above aspects, a tour operator has to spend considerable amount of money on printing of a tour brochure. Some of the tour brochures of large companies contain several programmes running into several hundred pages.

Each of the individual programme in a brochure is to be marketed to realise a sale of that programme. Several programmes contained in a brochure are to be marketed both by the tour operator and the agents at a destination to achieve actual bookings for a particular programme. Marketing and promotion of a particular programme in a tour brochure involves several elements starting first with the distribution of a brochure to travel agents located throughout the country. In case a tour operator had retail sales offices of his own, the brochure is also to be distributed to them. The quantity will depend on the size of the agency as also its location. It will also depend on the volume of business generated by the agent during the past few years.

Launching a press campaign is another important element in promoting a holiday programme printed in a brochure. A special advertising campaign is necessary to be launched in selected consumer newspapers in the generating market featuring tour programmes. The selection of the consumer newspapers should be based on factors like the area to be covered, the type of audience to be reached, the appeals to be used, etc. The consumer newspapers are selected because of their wider reach.

Window display campaign is another important and effective way of promoting a tour programme of a brochure. Specially prepared window display materials featuring tour programmes of a company for a particular destination can be used in retail sales office locations. The visual appeal of displays motivates a prospective tourist to enter the office and ask for more details. Simultaneous launching of a press campaign and window display campaign gives added advantage in that it registers a message about a destination more forcefully.

Trade education is another important element in promoting the sale of a holiday package. The sales staff of a tour operating company should be given orientation concerning the tour programme they are to promote through their outlets. This could be handled by planning experts of the tour operating company. A similar trade education programme can be organised for retail agents. All appointed retail sales agencies should be involved in this programme.

Press and public relations activities of the company promoting a programme play a vital role. A large tour operating company has a separate press and public relation department which create special press releases on their various tour programmes. The text of these press releases is given to select consumer newspapers throughout the country. To sum up, the various methods which a tour operator needs to use for pushing a programme through his tour brochure include:

(i) distribution channels for brochure;

(ii) launching press campaign for promoting tour programmes;

(iii) launching window display campaign (in organising trade education seminars/workshops for sales staff); and

(iv) creating special press releases for selected consumer newspaper.

Bibliography

Alastair, M. Morrison : *Hospitality and Travel Marketing,* Delemar, New York, 1989.

Aldous, T. : *Battle for the Environment,* Collins, London, 1972.

Alfred Joh : *Tourism Development,* Star Publication, Sydney, 2003.

Anand, M.M. : *Tourism and Hotel Industry in India,* Prentice-Hall of India, New Delhi, 1976.

Anderson, N. : *Work and Leisure,* Routledge and Kegan Faul, London, 1961.

Archer, B.H. : *Demand Forecasting in Tourism,* University of Wales Press, Cardiff, 1974.

Archer, B.H. : *The Impact of Domestic Tourism,* University of Wales Press, Cardiff, 1973.

Ashworth, G. J. : *Marketing in the Tourism Industry,* Routledge, London, 1990.

Ashworth, G. : *Recreation and Tourism,* Bell and Hyman, London, 1984.

Beazely, E. : *Designed for Recreation,* Faber, London, 1970.

Bernecker, Paul. . *Methods and Media of Tourist Publicity,* Austrian National Tourist Office, Vienna, 1961.

Bhatia, A. K. : *International Tourism : Fundamentals and Practices,* Sterling, New Delhi, 1991.

Bhatia, A. K. : *Tourism Management and Marketing,* Sterling, New Delhi, 1997.

Bhatia, A. K : *Tourism in India : History and Development,* Sterling, New Delhi, 1978.

Boniface, B. and Cooper, C. : *The Geography of Travel and Tourism* Heinemann, London, 1987.

Brunner, E. : *Holiday Making and the Holiday Trades,* Oxford University Press, London, 1945.

Bryden, John M. : *Tourism and Development,* Cambridge University Press, Cambridge, 1973.

Bull, A. : *The Economics of Travel and Tourism,* Pitman, London, 1991.

Burkart, A.J. and Medlik, S. : *Tourism: Past, Present and Future,* Heinemann, London, 1976.

Burkart, A.J. : *The Management of Tourism,* Heinemann, London, 1975.

Burton, T.L. : *Recreation Research and Planning,* Allen and Unwin, London, 1970.

Calder, N. : *The Environment Game,* Panther, London, 1969.

Cherry, G.E. : *Town Planning and its Social Context,* Hill, London, 1970.

Chuck, Y. Gee. : *The Travel Industry,* Van National Reinhold, New York, 1989.

Clare, Gunn : *Tourism Planning,* Taylor and Francis, New York, 1988.

Clayne, R. Jensen : *Leisure and Recreation-Introduction and Overview,* Lea and Febiger, Philadelphia, 1977.

Cleverdon, Robert : *The Economic and Social Impact of International Tourism on Developing Countries,* The Economic Intelligence Unit Ltd., London, 1979.

Colley, G. : *International Tourism Today,* Lloyds Bank Review, London, 1967.

Cosgrove, Isabel and Jackson; R. : *The Geography of Recreation and Leisure,* Hutchinson, London, 1972.

Crampon, L.T. : *An Analysis of Tourist Markets,* University of Colorado Press, Colorado, 1963.

—— : *The Development of Tourism,* University of Colorado Press, Colorado, 1963.

Dale, E. : *Management Theory and Practice,* McGraw-Hill, New York, 1973.

Davidson, R. : *Business Travel,* Pitman, London, 1994.

—— : *Tourism in Europe,* Pitman, London, 1992.

Davis, H.D. : *Potentials for Tourism of Developing Countries,* Finance and Development, London, 1968.

Donald, E. Hawking : *Tourism Planning and Development Issues,* George Washington University, Washington, 1980.

—— : *Tourism Marketing and Management Issues,* George Washington University, Washington, 1980.

Douglas Pearce : *Tourist Development,* Longman, 1989.

—— : *Tourism Today: A Geographical-Analysis,* Longman, New York, 1987.

Dower, M. : *The Challenge of Leisure,* Civic Trust, London, 1965.

Dumazedier, J. : *Towards a Society of Leisure,* Free Press, New York, 1967.

Ed Gell, D. L. : *International Tourism Policy,* Van Nostrand Reinhold, New York, 1990.

Edmunds : *Environmental Administration,* McGraw-Hill, New York, 1973.

Edward, J. Mayo : *The Psychology of Leisure Travel,* CBI Publishing Company, Boston, 1981.

Edwards, Francis, G. : *How to Focus ? Your Marketing Efforts,* Louis A. Allen Associates, London, 1976.

Engel, James F. : *Market Segmentation: Concepts and Applications,* Holt, Rinehart and Winston, New York, 1962.

Feiffer, M. : *Giving Places,* MacMillan, London, 1985.

Foster, D. : *Travel and Tourism Management,* MacMillan, London, 1985.

Frank, R.E. : *Market Segmentation,* Prentice-Hall, New Jersey, 1972.

Gearing Charles, E. : *Planning or Tourism Development,* Praeger Publishers, New York, 1976.

Gray, H. Peter : *International Travel-International Trade,* Health Lexington Books, Lexington, 1970.

Gunn, C. : *Tourism Planning,* Taylor and Francis, New York, 1988.

Heath, E. : *Marketing Tourism Destinations,* Wiley, New York, 1992.

Hibbert, Christopher : *The Grand Tour,* Weidenfel and Nicolson, London, 1969.

Hodyson, A. : *The Travel and Tourism Industry,* Pergamon, Oxford, 1987.

Hollander, S. : *Passenger Transportation,* Michigan State University, Michigan, 1968.

Holloway, J. C. : *Marketing or Tourism,* Longman, Harlow, 1995.

Howard : *Marketing Made Simple,* W.H. Allen, London, 1972.

Hurdman, L.E. : *Tourism : A Shrinking World,* Viley, New York, 1980.

Inskeep, E. : *Tourism Planning,* Van Nostrand Reinhold, New York, 1991.

Jefferson, A. : *Marketing Tourism-A Practical Guide,* Harlow, Longman, 1991.

Jenkins, J. R. Zif, J.J. : *Planning the Advertising Campaign,* MacMillan, New York, 1973.

John M. Bryden. : *Tourism and Development,* Cambridge University Press, London, 1973.

John, Lea : *Tourism Development in the Third World,* Routledge, New York, 1988.

Kaiser, Charles Jr. and Larry E. Helber : *Tourism Planning and Development,* CBI Publishing Company, Boston, 1978.

Katler, P. : *Introduction to Marketing Management, Analysis, Planning and Control*, Prentice-Hall, London, 1975.

Kerry Godrey and Jackie Clarke : *The Tourism Development Handbook,* Cassell, London, 2000.

Kotler P. : *Principles of Marketing,* Prentice-Hall, New York, 1999.

Lansing, J.B. Blood, D.M. : *The Changing Travel Market,* University of Michigan, Michigan, 1964.

Law, C. : *Urban Tourism: Attracting Visitors to Large Cities,* Mansell, London, 1993.

Laws, E.C. : *Tourist Destination Management: Issues, Analysis and Policies,* Routledge, London, 1995.

Lawson, Malcom : *Teaching Tourism-Education and Training in Western Europe : A Comparative Study,* Tourism International Press, London, 1975.

Leadley, P. : *Leisure Marketing,* Longman, Harlow, 1992.

Lickorish, L.J. and Kershaw, A.G. : *The Travel Trade,* Practical Press, London, 1974.

Lundberg, D.E. : *The Tourist Business,* Van Nostrand Rheinold, New York, 1990.

Lundberg : *International Travel and Tourism,* Institute of Certified Travel Agents, New York, 1970.

Mathieson, A : *Tourism: Economic, Physical and Social Impacts,* Longman, London, 1982.

McIntosh, R.W. : *Tourism Principles, Practices and Philosophies,* Grid, Ohio, 1977.

Medlik, S. : *Economic Importance of Tourism,* University of Surrey, Surrey, 1972.

—— : *Higher Education and Research in Tourism in Western Europe,* University of Surrey, London, 1966.

—— : *Profile of the Hotel and Catering Industry,* Heinemann, London, 1972.

Middleton, V.T.C. : *Marketing in Travel and Tourism,* Heinemann, London, 1988.

Mill, R.C. : *The Tourism Business: an Introductory Text,* Prentice-Hall, London, 1985.

—— : *The Tourism System,* Prentice-Hall International, London, 1985.

—— : *Tourism : The International Business,* Prentice-Hall, New Jersey, 1990.

Morisson, A. M. : *Hospitality and Travel Marketing,* Delmar, New York, 1989.

Murphy, Peter E. : *Tourism : A Community Approach,* Methuen, 1985.

Nicholson, M. : *The Environmental Revolution,* Penguin, London, 1972.

Norval, A.J. : *The Tourist Industry,* Issac Pitman and Sons Ltd., London, 1936.

Ogilvie, F.W. : *The Tourist Movement: An Economic Study,* Staples Press, London, 1933.

Parker, S. : The *Future of Work and Leisure,* Mac Gibbon and Kee, London, 1971.

Patmore, J. A. : *Land and Leisure,* David and Charles, London, 1970.

Peaker, A. : *"Holiday Spending by the British at Home and Abroad",* National Westminster Bank Quarterly Review, 1973.

Pearce, D. : *Tourism Organisations,* Longman, Harlow, 1992.

—— : *Tourism Today,* Longman, Harlow, 1987.

—— : *Tourist Development,* Longman, Harlow, 1989.

Pearce, Sales, J. : *Travel and Tourism Encyclopedia,* Blandford, London, 1959.

Pigram, J. : *Outdoor Recreation and Resource Management,* Croom Helm, London, 1993.

Pudney, John : *The Thomas Cook Story,* Michael Joseph, London, 1953.

Rae, W.F. : *The Business of Travel,* Thomas Cook and Son, London, 1891.

Ram Acharya : *Civil Aviation and Tourism Administration in India,* National Publishing House, New Delhi, 1978.

Raymond, R. : *Ecological Principles for Economic Development,* John Wiley, London, 1978.

Reilly, R. T. : *Travel and Tourism Marketing Techniques,* Delmar, New York, 1988.

Richards, G. : *Tourism and the Economy,* University of Surrey, Surrey, 1972.

Robinson, H. : *A Geography of Tourism,* MacDonald and Evans, London, 1976.

Ross, G. F. : *The Psychology of Tourism,* Hospitality Press, Melbourne, 1994.

Rothfield, Crampon, Wahab : *Tourism Marketing,* Tourism International Press, London, 1975.

Ryan, C. : *Recreational Tourism :A Social Science Perspective,* Routledge, London, 1991.

Schmoll, G.A. : *Tourism Promotion,* Tourism International Press, London, 1977.

Sessa, Alberto : *Tourism in Developing Countries,* UNESCO, Paris, 1970.

Seth, P.N. : *Successful Tourism Planning and Management,* Cross Section Publications, New Delhi, 1978.

Sigaux, G. : *History of Tourism,* Leisure Arts, London, 1966.

Smith, S. : *Tourism Analysis,* Longman, New York, 1989.

—— : *Tourism Analysis,* Longman, Harlow, 1995.

—— : *Recreation Geography,* Longman, Harlow, 1983.

Susan Horner : *Marketing Tourism Hospitality and Leisure in Europe,* International Thomson Business Press, London, 1996.

Tull, D. S. : *Marketing Research: Measurements and Methods,* Prentice-Hall, London, 1993.

Wahab, Crampon Rothfield : *Tourism Marketing,* Tourism International Press, London, 1976.

Wahab, Salah : *Tourism Management,* Tourism International Press, London, 1975.

White, J. : *History of Tourism,* Leisure Art, London, 1967.

Young, George : *Tourism: Blessing or Blight,* Penguin, London, 1973.

Yukic, T.S. : *Fundamentals of Recreation,* Harper Row, London, 1963.

Zeithaml, V.A. : *Services Marketing,* McGraw-Hill, London, 1996.